Web Designing

Web Designing

Jim Harrison

Web Designing
Jim Harrison
ISBN: 978-1-63989-568-7 (Hardback)

© 2022 States Academic Press

Published by States Academic Press,
109 South 5th Street,
Brooklyn, NY 11249, USA

Cataloging-in-Publication Data

Web designing / Jim Harrison.
    p. cm.
Includes bibliographical references and index.
ISBN 978-1-63989-568-7
1. Web sites--Design--Vocational guidance. 2. Web site development--Vocational guidance. I. Harrison, Jim.
TK5105.888 .W43 2022
006.7--dc23

This book contains information obtained from authentic and highly regarded sources. All chapters are published with permission under the Creative Commons Attribution Share Alike License or equivalent. A wide variety of references are listed. Permissions and sources are indicated; for detailed attributions, please refer to the permissions page. Reasonable efforts have been made to publish reliable data and information, but the authors, editors and publisher cannot assume any responsibility for the validity of all materials or the consequences of their use.

Trademark Notice: All trademarks used herein are the property of their respective owners. The use of any trademark in this text does not vest in the author or publisher any trademark ownership rights in such trademarks, nor does the use of such trademarks imply any affiliation with or endorsement of this book by such owners.

For more information regarding States Academic Press and its products, please visit the publisher's website www.statesacademicpress.com

Table of Contents

Preface   **VII**

Chapter 1   Web Design and Development: An Overview   1
- a. Web Design   1
- b. How to Learn Web Design   5
- c. Web Development   11

Chapter 2   Designing Web Pages   15
- a. Web Application Framework   15
- b. How to develop Web Pages   19
- c. How to create a Simple Webpage using Notepad   22
- d. How to create a Simple Web Page with HTML   26
- e. How to make a Web Page using Dreamweaver   31
- f. How to Design a Simple Web Page in Div   34
- g. How to create a Basic Flash Interactive Web Page   36
- h. How to create a Landing Page   39
- i. How to Password Protect a Web Page   42

Chapter 3   Website: Planning, Designing and Creating   48
- a. Website   48
- b. How to choose an Idea for creating Website or Blog   51
- c. How to Plan a Website   56
- d. How to Design a Website   66
- e. How to create your First Website   72
- f. How to Design a Modern Website   76
- g. How to Build a Dynamic Website   80
- h. How to Design a Responsive Website   84
- i. How to make a Free Website   86
- j. How to Learn HTML   93
- k. How to create CSS   102

Chapter 4   Tools and Techniques used in Web Designing   109
- a. How to make a Website with Word   109
- b. How to make a Website using Wordpress   112
- c. How to use Photoshop to Design a Website   113
- d. How to make a Website Fast by using Templates   117
- e. How to make a Website using a Web Editing Program   122
- f. How to Design a Form   126
- g. How to create a Link   129
- h. How to make a Web Browser   131
- i. How to Design a Website Template   137
- j. How to create a Secure Login Script in PHP and MySQL   140
- k. How to set up a Local Testing Server   169

Chapter 5 Search Engine Optimization — 175
    a. How to develop a Commercial Website — 175
    b. Search Engine Optimization — 178
    c. How to Improve Search Engine Optimization — 183
    d. How to Design a Website for SEO — 189
    e. How to create a Quality Website — 193

Chapter 6 Web Designing as a Career — 197
    a. How to become a Professional Web Designer and Programmer — 197
    b. How to develop a Portfolio for Web Design — 200
    c. How to Advertise your Web Design Business — 204
    d. How to become a Successful Web Designer — 208
    e. How to become a Web Developer — 214
    f. How to Outsource your Web Development Project Effectively — 227

Permissions

Index

Preface

The methods and techniques involved in the design, production and maintenance of websites is known as web design. Different areas of web design include web graphic design, interface design, user experience, search engine optimization, authoring code, etc. Graphics editor tools are used to provide the desired user interface and HTML or CSS is used to create the overall layout. SEO writing, graphic design, Internet marketing, and user experience design are some of the occupations related to professional web design. This book unfolds the innovative aspects of web design, which will be crucial for the holistic understanding of the subject matter. It will serve as a valuable source of reference for those interested in this field.

A detailed account of the significant topics covered in this book is provided below:

Chapter 1- The set of techniques and skills that are required to design and maintain websites is known as web design. It requires creative skills and a good understanding of various software. The chapter on web design and development offers an insightful focus, keeping in mind the complex subject matter.

Chapter 2- Web pages have a variety of elements ranging from simple text to multimedia. They are created using programming languages like HTML, JavaScript, CSS, etc. Different web applications and resources are managed using a web application framework. This chapter is an overview of the subject matter incorporating all the major aspects of web page designing.

Chapter 3- Websites are pages on the Internet that are meant to convey and provide information, entertainment, education, social networking platforms, etc. Creating a layout, choosing a language, using content and media are some of the steps that are involved in building a website. The topics discussed in the chapter are of great importance to broaden the existing knowledge on web designing.

Chapter 4- Websites can be created using various packages such as Microsoft Word, Wordpress, Adobe Photoshop, etc. Links, forms, templates, etc. are some of the most basic elements found on websites. Tools and techniques are an important component of this field of study. The following chapter elucidates the various tools and techniques that are related to web designing.

Chapter 5- A commercial website needs to be visible and provide relevant information that users are looking for. Search Engine Optimization (SEO) compliant websites prove to have more views and visitors. Trending keywords direct traffic towards websites where these keywords are available. This chapter will provide an integrated understanding of search engine optimization.

Chapter 6- Professional web design and development is an important industry. Almost all businesses, organizations and companies have a presence on the Internet. Familiarity with various Internet tools, programming languages and multimedia editing is a must for making a career in this field. Professional web designing is best understood in confluence with the major topics listed in the following chapter.

I would like to make a special mention of my publisher who considered me worthy of this opportunity and also supported me throughout the process. I would also like to thank the editing team at the back-end who extended their help whenever required.

Jim Harrison

Web Design and Development: An Overview

The set of techniques and skills that are required to design and maintain websites is known as web design. It requires creative skills and a good understanding of various software. The chapter on web design and development offers an insightful focus, keeping in mind the complex subject matter.

Web Design

Web design encompasses many different skills and disciplines in the production and maintenance of websites. The different areas of web design include web graphic design; interface design; authoring, including standardised code and proprietary software; user experience design; and search engine optimization. Often many individuals will work in teams covering different aspects of the design process, although some designers will cover them all. The term web design is normally used to describe the design process relating to the front-end (client side) design of a website including writing mark up. Web design partially overlaps web engineering in the broader scope of web development. Web designers are expected to have an awareness of usability and if their role involves creating mark up then they are also expected to be up to date with web accessibility guidelines.

Tools and Technologies

Web designers use a variety of different tools depending on what part of the production process they are involved in. These tools are updated over time by newer standards and software but the principles behind them remain the same. Web designers use both vector and raster graphics editors to create web-formatted imagery or design prototypes. Technologies used to create websites include W3C standards like HTML and CSS, which can be hand-coded or generated by WYSIWYG editing software. Other tools web designers might use include mark up validators and other testing tools for usability and accessibility to ensure their websites meet web accessibility guidelines.

Skills and Techniques

Marketing and Communication Design

Marketing and communication design on a website may identify what works for its target market. This can be an age group or particular strand of culture; thus the designer may understand the trends of its audience. Designers may also understand the type of website they are designing, meaning, for example, that (B2B) business-to-business website design considerations might differ greatly from a consumer targeted website such as a retail or entertainment website. Careful consideration might be made to ensure that the aesthetics or overall design of a site do not clash with the clarity and accuracy of the content or the ease of web navigation, especially on a B2B website. Designers may also consider the reputation of the owner or business the site is representing to make sure they are portrayed favourably.

User Experience Design and Interactive Design

User understanding of the content of a website often depends on user understanding of how the website works. This is part of the user experience design. User experience is related to layout, clear instructions and labeling on a website. How well a user understands how they can interact on a site may also depend on the interactive design of the site. If a user perceives the usefulness of the website, they are more likely to continue using it. Users who are skilled and well versed with website use may find a more distinctive, yet less intuitive or less user-friendly website interface useful nonetheless. However, users with less experience are less likely to see the advantages or usefulness of a less intuitive website interface. This drives the trend for a more universal user experience and ease of access to accommodate as many users as possible regardless of user skill. Much of the user experience design and interactive design are considered in the user interface design.

Advanced interactive functions may require plug-ins if not advanced coding language skills. Choosing whether or not to use interactivity that requires plug-ins is a critical decision in user experience design. If the plug-in doesn't come pre-installed with most browsers, there's a risk that the user will have neither the know how or the patience to install a plug-in just to access the content. If the function requires advanced coding language skills, it may be too costly in either time or money to code compared to the amount of enhancement the function will add to the user experience. There's also a risk that advanced interactivity may be incompatible with older browsers or hardware configurations. Publishing a function that doesn't work reliably is potentially worse for the user experience than making no attempt. It depends on the target audience if it's likely to be needed or worth any risks.

Page Layout

Part of the user interface design is affected by the quality of the page layout. For example, a designer may consider whether the site's page layout should remain consistent on different pages when designing the layout. Page pixel width may also be considered vital for aligning objects in the layout design. The most popular fixed-width websites generally have the same set width to match the current most popular browser window, at the current most popular screen resolution, on the current most popular monitor size. Most pages are also center-aligned for concerns of aesthetics on larger screens.

Fluid layouts increased in popularity around 2000 as an alternative to HTML-table-based layouts and grid-based design in both page layout design principle and in coding technique, but were very slow to be adopted. This was due to considerations of screen reading devices and varying windows sizes which designers have no control over. Accordingly, a design may be broken down into units (sidebars, content blocks, embedded advertising areas, navigation areas) that are sent to the browser and which will be fitted into the display window by the browser, as best it can. As the browser does recognize the details of the reader's screen (window size, font size relative to window etc.) the browser can make user-specific layout adjustments to fluid layouts, but not fixed-width layouts. Although such a display may often change the relative position of major content units, sidebars may be displaced below body text rather than to the side of it. This is a more flexible display than a hard-coded grid-based layout that doesn't fit the device window. In particular, the relative position of content blocks may change while leaving the content within the block unaffected. This also minimizes the user's need to horizontally scroll the page.

Responsive Web Design is a newer approach, based on CSS3, and a deeper level of per-device specification within the page's stylesheet through an enhanced use of the CSS @media rule.

Typography

Web designers may choose to limit the variety of website typefaces to only a few which are of a similar style, instead of using a wide range of typefaces or type styles. Most browsers recognize a specific number of safe fonts, which designers mainly use in order to avoid complications.

Font downloading was later included in the CSS3 fonts module and has since been implemented in Safari 3.1, Opera 10 and Mozilla Firefox 3.5. This has subsequently increased interest in web typography, as well as the usage of font downloading.

Most site layouts incorporate negative space to break the text up into paragraphs and also avoid center-aligned text.

Motion Graphics

The page layout and user interface may also be affected by the use of motion graphics. The choice of whether or not to use motion graphics may depend on the target market for the website. Motion graphics may be expected or at least better received with an entertainment-oriented website. However, a website target audience with a more serious or formal interest (such as business, community, or government) might find animations unnecessary and distracting if only for entertainment or decoration purposes. This doesn't mean that more serious content couldn't be enhanced with animated or video presentations that is relevant to the content. In either case, motion graphic design may make the difference between more effective visuals or distracting visuals.

Motion graphics that are not initiated by the site visitor can produce accessibility issues. The World Wide Web consortium accessibility standards require that site visitors be able to disable the animations.

Quality of Code

Website designers may consider it to be good practice to conform to standards. This is usually done via a description specifying what the element is doing. Failure to conform to standards may not make a website unusable or error prone, but standards can relate to the correct layout of pages for readability as well making sure coded elements are closed appropriately. This includes errors in code, more organized layout for code, and making sure IDs and classes are identified properly. Poorly-coded pages are sometimes colloquially called tag soup. Validating via W3C can only be done when a correct DOCTYPE declaration is made, which is used to highlight errors in code. The system identifies the errors and areas that do not conform to web design standards. This information can then be corrected by the user.

Generated Content

There are two ways websites are generated: statically or dynamically.

Static Websites

A static website stores a unique file for every page of a static website. Each time that page is requested, the same content is returned. This content is created once, during the design of the website. It is usually manually authored, although some sites use an automated creation process, similar to a dynamic website, whose results are stored long-term as completed pages. These automatically-created static sites became more popular around 2015, with generators such as Jekyll and Adobe Muse.

The benefits of a static website are that they were simpler to host, as their server only needed to serve static content, not execute server-side scripts. This required less server administration and had less chance of exposing security holes. They could also serve pages more quickly, on low-cost server hardware. These advantage became less important as cheap web hosting expanded to also offer dynamic features, and virtual servers offered high performance for short intervals at low cost.

Almost all websites have some static content, as supporting assets such as images and stylesheets are usually static, even on a website with highly dynamic pages.

Dynamic Websites

Dynamic websites are generated on the fly and use server-side technology to generate webpages. They typically extract their content from one or more back-end databases: some are database queries across a relational database to query a catalogue or to summarise numeric information, others may use a document database such as MongoDB or NoSQL to store larger units of content, such as blog posts.

In the design process, dynamic pages are often mocked-up or wireframed using static pages. The skillset needed to develop dynamic web pages is much broader than for a static pages, involving server-side and database coding as well as client-side interface design. Even medium-sized dynamic projects are thus almost always a team effort.

When dynamic web pages first developed, they were typically coded directly in languages such as Perl, PHP or ASP. Some of these, notably PHP and ASP, used a 'template' approach where a server-side page resembled the structure of the completed client-side page and data was inserted into places defined by 'tags'. This was a quicker means of development than coding in a purely procedural coding language such as Perl.

Both of these approaches have now been supplanted for many websites by higher-level application-focused tools such as content management systems. These build on top of general purpose coding platforms and assume that a website exists to offer content according to one of several well recognised models, such as a time-sequenced blog, a thematic magazine or news site or a user forum. These tools make the implementation of such a site very easy, and a purely organisational and design-based task, without requiring any coding.

Homepage Design

Usability experts, including Jakob Nielsen and Kyle Soucy, have often emphasised homepage design for website success and asserted that the homepage is the most important page on a website.

However practitioners into the 2000s were starting to find that a growing number of website traffic was bypassing the homepage, going directly to internal content pages through search engines, e-newsletters and RSS feeds. Leading many practitioners to argue that homepages are less important than most people think. Jared Spool argued in 2007 that a site's homepage was actually the least important page on a website.

In 2012 and 2013, carousels (also called 'sliders' and 'rotating banners') have become an extremely popular design element on homepages, often used to showcase featured or recent content in a confined space. Many practitioners argue that carousels are an ineffective design element and hurt a website's search engine optimisation and usability.

Occupations

There are two primary jobs involved in creating a website: the web designer and web developer, who often work closely together on a website. The web designers are responsible for the visual aspect, which includes the layout, coloring and typography of a web page. Web designers will also have a working knowledge of markup languages such as HTML and CSS, although the extent of their knowledge will differ from one web designer to another. Particularly in smaller organizations one person will need the necessary skills for designing and programming the full web page, while larger organizations may have a web designer responsible for the visual aspect alone.

Further jobs which may become involved in the creation of a website include:

- Graphic designers to create visuals for the site such as logos, layouts and buttons
- Internet marketing specialists to help maintain web presence through strategic solutions on targeting viewers to the site, by using marketing and promotional techniques on the internet
- SEO writers to research and recommend the correct words to be incorporated into a particular website and make the website more accessible and found on numerous search engines
- Internet copywriter to create the written content of the page to appeal to the targeted viewers of the site
- User experience (UX) designer incorporates aspects of user focused design considerations which include information architecture, user centered design, user testing, interaction design, and occasionally visual design.

How to Learn Web Design

Web design is a very good skill to have, especially in today's Internet-centered world. If you're really good, you can make money from clients, start membership websites, and pursue other money-making projects. If you want to know how to learn web design, you're in the right place.

Part 1
Beginning

1. Note what web designs differs from. Web design is not book design, it is not poster design, it is not illustration, and the highest achievements of those disciplines are not what web design aims for. Although websites can be delivery systems for games and videos, and although those delivery systems can be lovely to look at, such sites are exemplars of game design and video storytelling, not of web design.

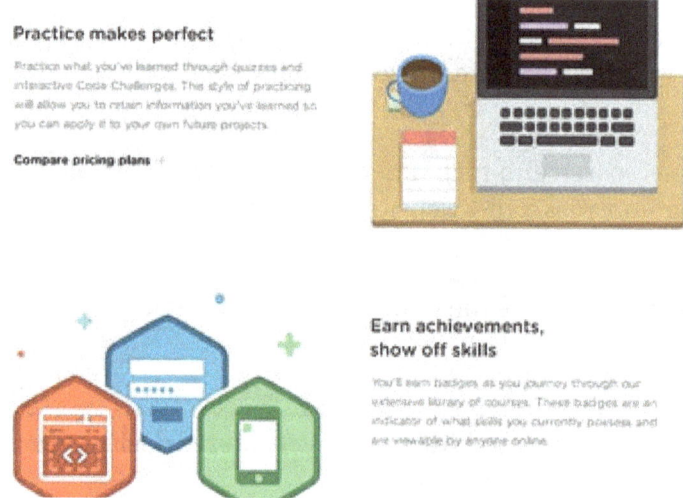

2. Understand what web design involves. Web design is the creation of digital environments that:

- facilitate and encourage human activity;
- reflect or adapt to individual voices and content; and
- change gracefully over time while always retaining their identity.

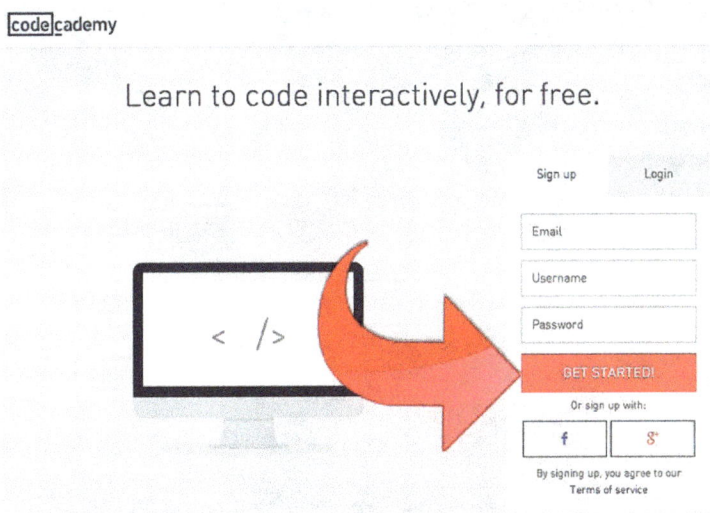

3. Determine what resource you want to use. The main resources are websites, videos, and books. Some popular websites are Codecademy and W3Schools. However, there are many more, so feel free to experiment.

- Sign up for an account if you've chosen a website. You will be able to save your progress this way.

- If you've chosen videos, bookmark all the videos you'll need.

- Go to your local library or bookstore if you've chosen the book route. If you want something cheaper (or even free), download eBooks or PDF files.

- If you're willing to pay, you might be able to get individualized lessons from a professional web designer.

4. Figure out how much time you'll need. You'll need to figure out how to fit this into your day if you're a busy person.

5. Download a web design program if you haven't already. While Notepad will work, it's a good idea to have a program like Adobe Dreamweaver, Microsoft Expression Web, or KompoZer. There are many, many others, so browse around and get what you like.

Part 2

Learning

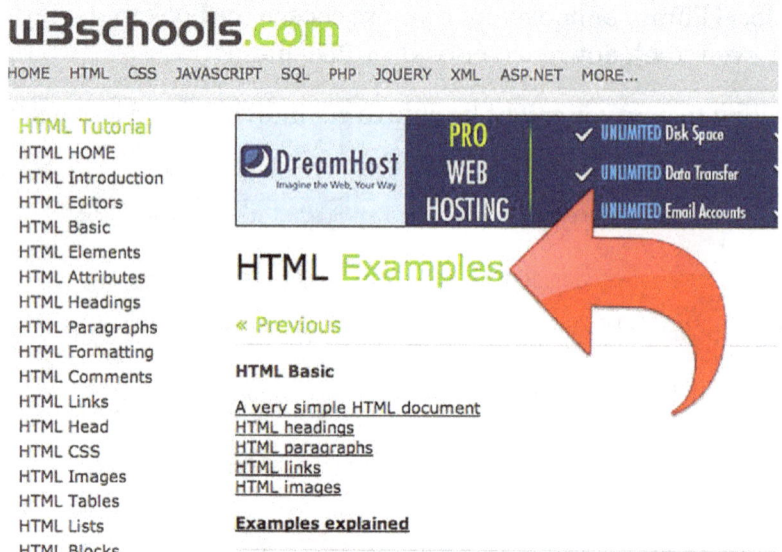

1. Get started with HTML. HTML is an absolute requirement for any web designer. Master the concept of tags, classes, IDs, inputs, etc.

- The newest version of HTML is HTML5. HTML5 incorporates some new technologies, so that is probably the best one to learn.

- XHTML is also an option, but it's a little bit stricter in its rules.

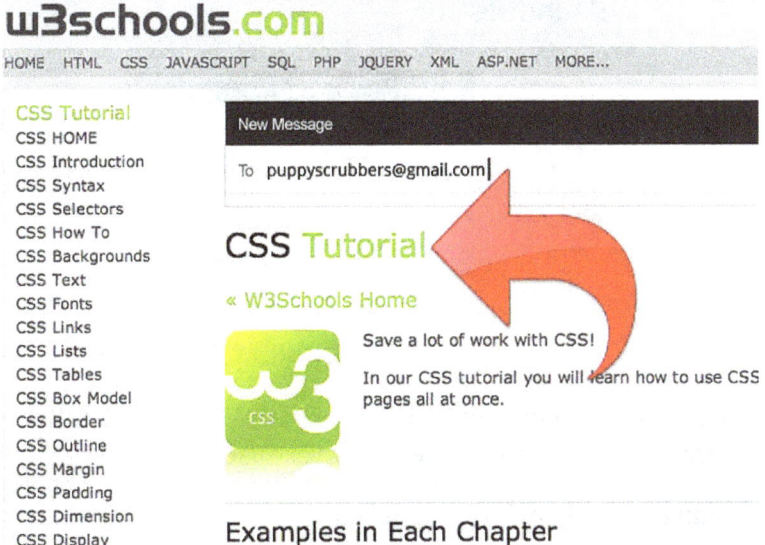

2. Learn CSS. CSS stands for "Cascading Style Sheet". Without CSS, there wouldn't be the pretty designs you see on some websites. HTML is merely the skeleton, but CSS is what makes a website colorful and pretty.

- CSS is a bit stricter in its rules. For instance, if you forgot to put a semicolon at the end of each line, you could be in for some headaches trying to figure out what went wrong.

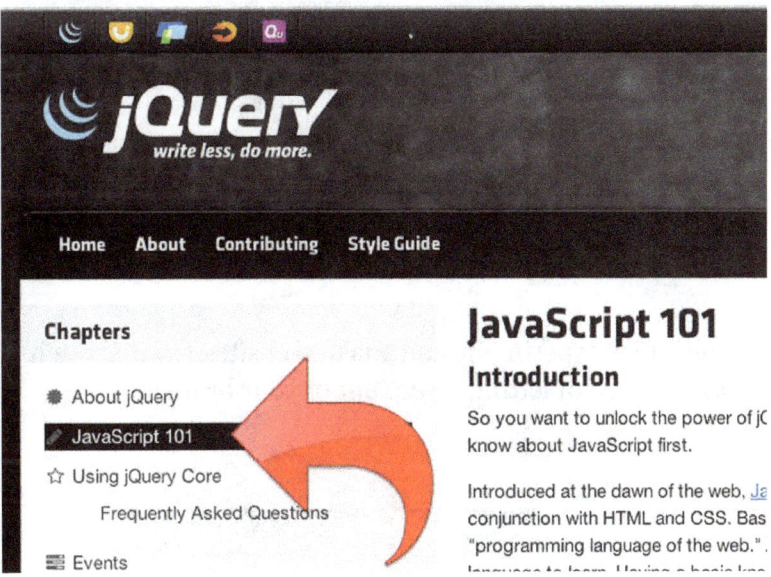

3. Learn JavaScript and jQuery. This is optional for ones that plan to make simple website, but it's essential if you want interactive websites.

- If you're going to use jQuery, you really only need a basic knowledge of JavaScript, because jQuery makes things pretty simple.

- With jQuery, you can insert widgets like an accordion, a calendar, etc. There are different styles of it, too, so you can pick the style you want for your website.

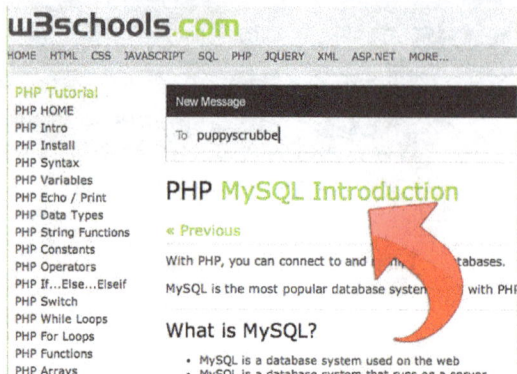

4. Move on to the more advanced languages. There's PHP, MySQL, Perl, Ruby, and some others. Again, this is optional for simple website builders, but very useful for interactive and large websites.

- Some of these languages, like PHP, require a test server, so make sure to have an account with a web hosting company or install server software on your computer.

Part 3
Applying your knowledge

1. Make project websites. Just experiment and make websites from scratch. This helps you put your knowledge to work, instead of letting it rust out in your brain.

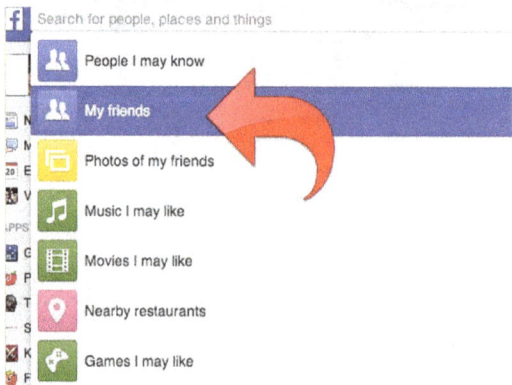

2. Ask friends or family if they want a website. You could do it for free to get some experience.

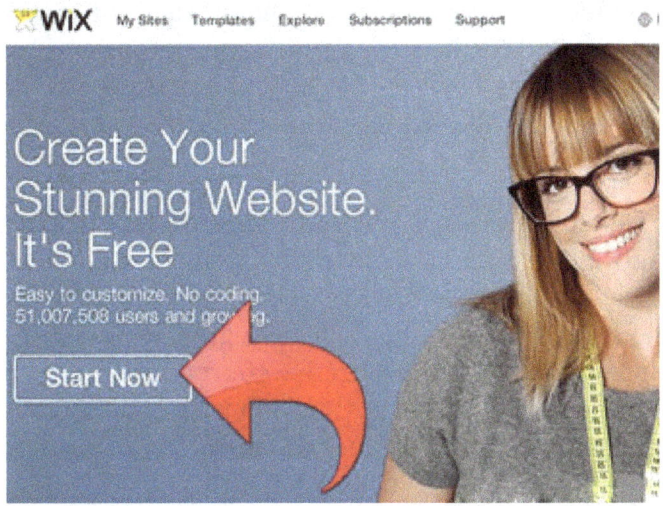

3. Start your own website. It can be about whatever you want, but it gives you an opportunity to show your work to the general public.

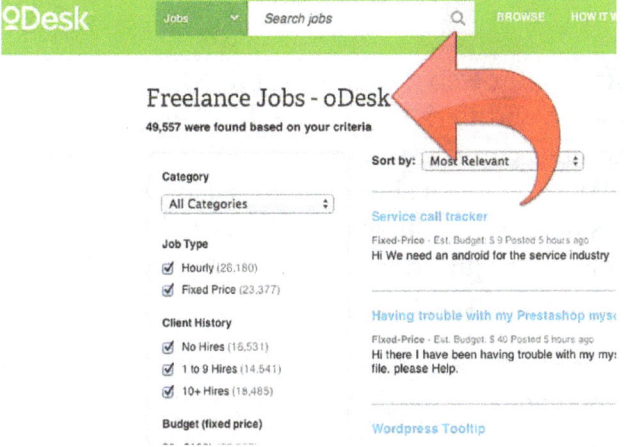

4. Do freelance web design, if you want to. Charge reasonable rates and post a portfolio on your site. Your business may eventually grow into a full-fledged company.

Web Development

Web development is a broad term for the work involved in developing a web site for the Internet (World Wide Web) or an intranet (a private network). Web development can range from developing the simplest static single page of plain text to the most complex web-based internet applications (or just 'web apps') electronic businesses, and social network services. A more comprehensive list of tasks to which web development commonly refers, may include web engineering, web design, web content development, client liaison, client-side/server-side scripting, web server and network security configuration, and e-commerce development. Among web professionals, "web development" usually refers to the main non-design aspects of building web sites: writing markup and coding. Most recently Web development has come to mean the creation of content management systems or CMS. These CMS can be made from scratch, proprietary or open source. In broad terms the CMS acts as middleware between the database and the user through the browser. A principle benefit of a CMS is that it allows non-technical people to make changes to their web site without having technical knowledge.

For larger organizations and businesses, web development teams can consist of hundreds of people (web developers) and follow standard methods like Agile methodologies while developing websites. Smaller organizations may only require a single permanent or contracting developer, or secondary assignment to related job positions such as a graphic designer or information systems technician. Web development may be a collaborative effort between departments rather than the domain of a designated department. There are three kinds of web developer specialization: front-end developer, back-end developer, and full-stack developer.

Web Development as an Industry

Since the commercialization of the web, web development has been a growing industry. The growth of this industry is being driven by businesses wishing to use their website to sell products and services to customers.

There is open source software for web development like BerkeleyDB, GlassFish, LAMP (Linux, Apache, MySQL, PHP) stack and Perl/Plack. This has kept the cost of learning web development to a minimum. Another contributing factor to the growth of the industry has been the rise of easy-to-use WYSIWYG web-development software, such as Adobe Dreamweaver, BlueGriffon and Microsoft Visual Studio. Knowledge of HyperText Markup Language (HTML) or of programming languages is still required to use such software, but the basics can be learned and implemented quickly with the help of help files, technical books, internet tutorials, or face-to-face training.

An ever-growing set of tools and technologies have helped developers build more dynamic and interactive websites. Further, web developers now help to deliver applications as web services which were traditionally only available as applications on a desk-based computer. This has allowed for many opportunities to decentralize information and media distribution. Examples can be seen with the rise of cloud services such as Adobe Creative Cloud, Dropbox and Google Docs. These web services allow users to interact with applications from many locations, instead of being tied to a specific workstation for their application environment.

Examples of dramatic transformation in communication and commerce led by web development include e-commerce. Online auction sites such as eBay have changed the way consumers find and purchase goods and services. Online retailers such as Amazon.com and Buy.com (among many others) have transformed the shopping and bargain-hunting experience for many consumers. Another good example of transformative communication led by web development is the blog. Web applications such as WordPress and Movable Type have created easily implemented blog-environments for individual websites. The popularity of open-source content management systems such as Joomla!, Drupal, XOOPS, and TYPO3 and enterprise content management systems such as Alfresco and eXo Platform have extended web development's impact at online interaction and communication.

Web development has also impacted personal networking and marketing. Websites are no longer simply tools for work or for commerce, but serve more broadly for communication and social networking. Web sites such as Facebook and Twitter provide users with a platform to communicate and organizations with a more personal and interactive way to engage the public.

Practical Web Development

Basic

In practice, many web developers will have basic interdisciplinary skills / roles, including:

- Graphic design / web design
- Information architecture and copywriting/copyediting with web usability, accessibility and search engine optimization in mind
- Mobile responsiveness

The above list is a simple website development hierarchy and can be extended to include all client side and server side aspects. It is still important to remember that web development is generally split up into client side coding, covering aspects such as the layout and design, and server-side coding, which covers the website's functionality and back-end systems.

Testing

Testing is the process of evaluating a system or its component(s) with the intent to find whether it satisfies the specified requirements or not. Testing is executing a system in order to identify any gaps, errors, or missing requirements in contrary to the actual requirements The extent of testing varies greatly between organizations, developers, and individual sites or applications.

Security Considerations

Web development takes into account many security considerations, such as data entry error checking through forms, filtering output, and encryption. Malicious practices such as SQL injection can be executed by users with ill intent yet with only primitive knowledge of web development as a whole. Scripts can be used to exploit websites by granting unauthorized access to malicious users that try to collect information such as email addresses, passwords and protected content like credit card numbers.

Some of this is dependent on the server environment on which the scripting language, such as ASP, JSP, Perl, PHP, Python, Perl or Ruby is running, and therefore is not necessarily down to the web developer themselves to maintain. However, stringent testing of web applications before public release is encouraged to prevent such exploits from occurring. If some contact form is provided in a website it should include a captcha field in it which prevents computer programs from automatically filling forms and also mail spamming.

Keeping a web server safe from intrusion is often called *Server Port Hardening*. Many technologies come into play to keep information on the internet safe when it is transmitted from one location to another. For instance TLS certificates (or "SSL certificates") are issued by certificate authorities to help prevent internet fraud. Many developers often employ different forms of encryption when transmitting and storing sensitive information. A basic understanding of information technology security concerns is often part of a web developer's knowledge.

Because new security holes are found in web applications even after testing and launch, security patch updates are frequent for widely used applications. It is often the job of web developers to keep applications up to date as security patches are released and new security concerns are discovered.

Designing Web Pages

2

Web pages have a variety of elements ranging from simple text to multimedia. They are created using programming languages like HTML, JavaScript, CSS, etc. Different web applications and resources are managed using a web application framework. This chapter is an overview of the subject matter incorporating all the major aspects of web page designing.

Web Application Framework

A web framework (WF) or web application framework (WAF) is a software framework that is designed to support the development of web applications including web services, web resources, and web APIs. Web frameworks provide a standard way to build and deploy web applications. Web frameworks aim to automate the overhead associated with common activities performed in web development. For example, many web frameworks provide libraries for database access, templating frameworks, and session management, and they often promote code reuse. Although they often target development of dynamic web sites, they are also applicable to static websites.

Types of Framework Architectures

Most web frameworks are based on the model–view–controller (MVC) pattern.

Model–View–Controller (MVC)

Many frameworks follow the MVC architectural pattern to separate the data model with business rules from the user interface. This is generally considered a good practice as it modularizes code, promotes code reuse, and allows multiple interfaces to be applied. In web applications, this permits different views to be presented, such as web pages for humans, and web service interfaces for remote applications.

Push-based vs. Pull-based

Most MVC frameworks follow a push-based architecture also called "action-based". These frameworks use actions that do the required processing, and then "push" the data to the view layer to render the results. Django, Ruby on Rails, Symfony, Spring MVC, Stripes, CodeIgniter are good examples of this architecture. An alternative to this is pull-based architecture, sometimes also called "component-based". These frameworks start with the view layer, which can then "pull" results from multiple controllers as needed. In this architecture, multiple controllers can be involved with a single view. Lift, Tapestry, JBoss Seam, JavaServer Faces, (µ)Micro, and Wicket are examples of pull-based architectures. Play, Struts, RIFE, and ZK have support for both push- and pull-based application controller calls.

Three-tier Organization

In three-tier organization, applications are structured around three physical tiers: client, application, and database. The database is normally an RDBMS. The application contains the business logic, running on a server and communicates with the client using HTTP. The client on web applications is a web browser that runs HTML generated by the application layer. The term should not be confused with MVC, where, unlike in three-tier architecture, it is considered a good practice to keep business logic away from the controller, the "middle layer".

Framework Applications

Frameworks are built to support the construction of internet applications based on a single programming language, ranging in focus from general purpose tools such as Zend Framework and Ruby on Rails, which augment the capabilities of a specific language, to native-language programmable packages built around a specific user application, such as Content Management systems, some mobile development tools and some portal tools.

General-purpose Website Frameworks

Web frameworks must function according to the architectural rules of browsers and web protocols such as HTTP, which is stateless. Webpages are served up by a server and can then be modified by the browser using JavaScript. Either approach has its advantages and disadvantages.

Server-side page changes typically require that the page be refreshed, but allow any language to be used and more computing power to be utilized. Client-side changes allow the page to be updated in small chunks which feels like a desktop application, but are limited to JavaScript and run in the user's browser, which may have limited computing power. Some mix of the two is typically used. Applications which make heavy use of JavaScript are called single-page applications and typically make use of a client-side JavaScript web framework to organize the code.

Server-side

- Django
- Zend Framework

Client-side

Examples include Backbone.js, AngularJS, EmberJS, ReactJS and Vue.js.

Organizational Portals

- JBoss Portal
- eXo Platform

Content Management Systems (CMS)

In web application frameworks, content management is the way of organizing, categorizing, and structuring the information resources like text, images, documents, audio and video files so that they can be stored, published, and edited with ease and flexibility.

A content management system (CMS) is used to collect, manage, and publish content, storing it either as components or whole documents, while maintaining dynamic links between components.

Some projects that have historically been termed content management systems have begun to take on the roles of higher-layer web application frameworks. For instance, Drupal's structure provides a minimal *core* whose function is extended through *modules* that provide functions generally associated with web application frameworks. The Joomla platform provides a set of APIs to build web and command-line applications. However, it is debatable whether "management of content" is the primary value of such systems, especially when some, like SilverStripe, provide an object-oriented MVC framework. Add-on *modules* now enable these systems to function as full-fledged applications beyond the scope of content management. They may provide functional APIs, functional frameworks, coding standards, and many of the functions traditionally associated with *Web application frameworks*.

Features

Frameworks typically set the control flow of a program and allow the user of the framework to "hook into" that flow by exposing various events. This "inversion of control" design pattern is considered to be a defining principle of a framework, and benefits the code by enforcing a common flow for a team which everyone can customize in similar ways. For example, some popular "microframeworks" such as Ruby's Sinatra (which inspired Express.js) allow for "middleware" hooks prior to and after HTTP requests. These middleware functions can be anything, and allow the user to define logging, authentication and session management, and redirecting.

Caching

Web caching is the caching of web documents in order to reduce bandwidth usage, server load, and perceived "lag". A web cache stores copies of documents passing through it; subsequent requests may be satisfied from the cache if certain conditions are met. Some application frameworks provide mechanisms for caching documents and bypassing various stages of the page's preparation, such as database access or template interpretation.

Security

Some web frameworks come with authentication and authorization frameworks, that enable the web server to identify the users of the application, and restrict access to functions based on some defined criteria. Drupal is one example that provides role-based access to pages, and provides a web-based interface for creating users and assigning them roles.

Database Access, Mapping and Configuration

Many web frameworks create a unified API to a database backend, enabling web applications to work with a variety of databases with no code changes, and allowing programmers to work with higher-level concepts. Additionally, some object-oriented frameworks contain mapping tools to provide object-relational mapping, which maps objects to tuples.

Some frameworks minimize web application configuration through the use of introspection and/or following well-known conventions. For example, many Java frameworks use Hibernate as a persistence layer, which can generate a database schema at runtime capable of persisting the necessary information. This allows the application designer to design business objects without needing to explicitly define a database schema. Frameworks such as Ruby on Rails can also work in reverse, that is, define properties of model objects at runtime based on a database schema.

Other features web frameworks may provide include transactional support and database migration tools.

URL mapping

A framework's URL mapping or routing facility is the mechanism by which the framework interprets URLs. Some frameworks, such as Drupal and Django, match the provided URL against pre-determined patterns using regular expressions, while some others use rewriting techniques to translate the provided URL into one that the underlying engine will recognize. Another technique is that of graph traversal such as used by Zope, where a URL is decomposed in steps that traverse an object graph (of models and views).

A URL mapping system that uses pattern matching or rewriting to route and handle requests allows for shorter more "friendly URLs" to be used, increasing the simplicity of the site and allowing for better indexing by search engines. For example, a URL that ends with "/page.cgi?cat=science&topic=physics" could be changed to simply "/page/science/physics". This makes the URL easier for people to remember, read and write, and provides search engines with better information about the structural layout of the site. A graph traversal approach also tends to result in the creation of friendly URLs. A shorter URL such as "/page/science" tends to exist by default as that is simply a shorter form of the longer traversal to "/page/science/physics".

Ajax

Ajax, shorthand for *"Asynchronous JavaScript and XML"*, is a web development technique for creating web applications. The intent is to make web pages feel more responsive by exchanging small amounts of data with the server behind the scenes, so that the entire web page does not have to be reloaded each time the user requests a change. This is intended to increase a web page's interactivity, speed, and usability.

Due to the complexity of Ajax programming in JavaScript, there are numerous Ajax frameworks that exclusively deal with Ajax support. Some Ajax frameworks are even embedded as a part of larger frameworks. For example, the jQuery JavaScript library is included in Ruby on Rails.

With the increased interest in developing "Web 2.0" rich media applications, the complexity of programming directly in Ajax and JavaScript has become so apparent that compiler technology has stepped in, to allow developers to code in high-level languages such as Java, Python and Ruby. The first of these compilers was Morfik followed by Google Web Toolkit, with ports to Python and Ruby in the form of Pyjs and RubyJS following some time after. These compilers and their associated widget set libraries make the development of rich media Ajax applications much more akin to that of developing desktop applications.

Web Services

Some frameworks provide tools for creating and providing web services. These utilities may offer similar tools as the rest of the web application.

Web Resources

A number of newer Web 2.0 RESTful frameworks are now providing resource-oriented architecture (ROA) infrastructure for building collections of resources in a sort of Semantic Web ontology, based on concepts from Resource Description Framework (RDF).

How to develop Web Pages

Here's a topic to get you started with developing web pages.

Steps

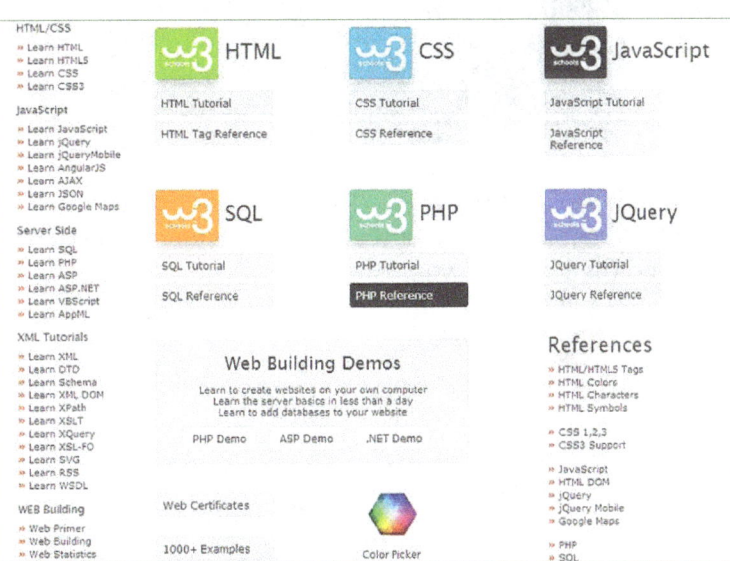

1. Learn web technologies and languages. The basic ones you'll need to know to code your own websites are HTML, XHTML, CSS and JavaScript. After that you can go on with learning others like XML, ASP, PHP, plenty of examples and an editor so you can try out what you've learned and see results on spot.

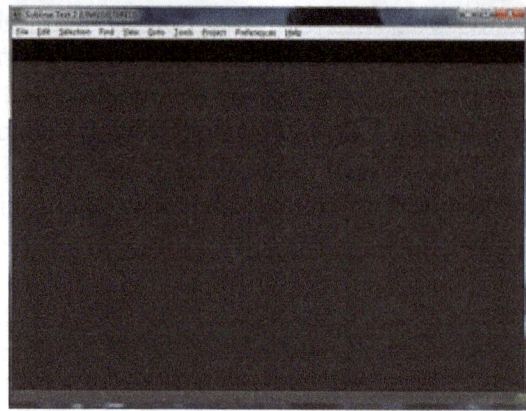

2. You'll need an editor. Web page code files are basically text files so you can create a web page using only notepad. But it might get hard to read through creating big and complex pages, in which case you might need an editor with more advanced features such as color-coding, tag completion. Some of this include notepad++, Microsoft Visual Web Developer Express, BBEdit (for Mac) which are free and some of them need to be bought like Adobe Dreamweaver or MS Visual Web Developer (the non-free versions).

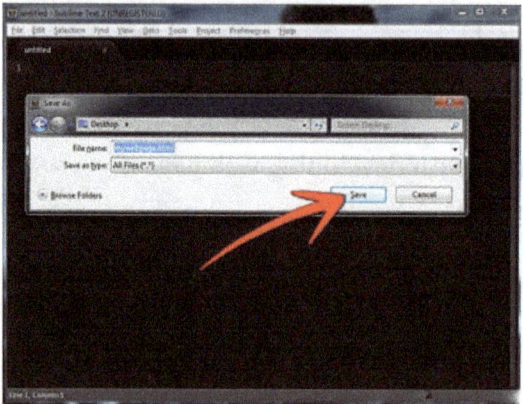

3. Creating a web page could be as simple as creating a text file ex: page.txt and renaming the extension to .html i.e page.html, open it using notepad or your preferred editor, write the (X)HTML code of the page, save it and the load it in your browser.

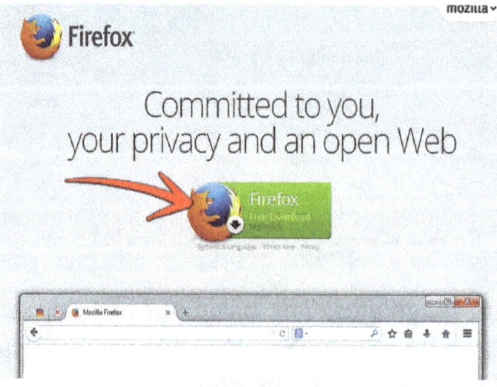

4. To make sure your website is consistent, download all the major browsers like Internet Explorer,

Firefox, Safari, Chrome, Opera (they're all free) and test your pages in each of the browser cause different people use different browsers and you'd want your pages to look the same everywhere.

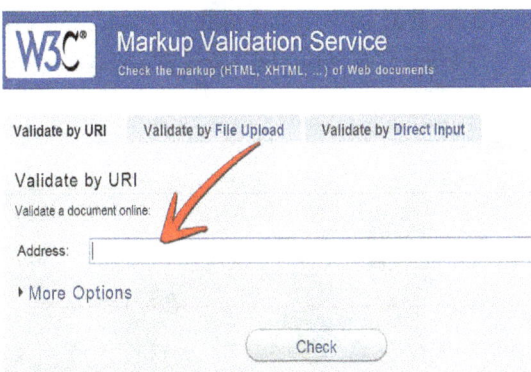

5. You should also make sure your page is valid and it conforms to the standards and recommendations, you can validate your page using the validator which will tell you if your site is okay or contains errors.

6. Once you've mastered creating pages, plan and create your website; which is just a group of related pages.

7. Visit your favorite sites and, study them and get some ideas. You can even see the page source by right-clicking on an empty area in your browser and selecting view source (the method can vary with different browsers).

How to create a Simple Webpage using Notepad

Webpages. We use them every day. But how hard is it to make a webpage? In this topic, you will find out how to create a simple HTML webpage using Notepad.

Creating your own Webpage

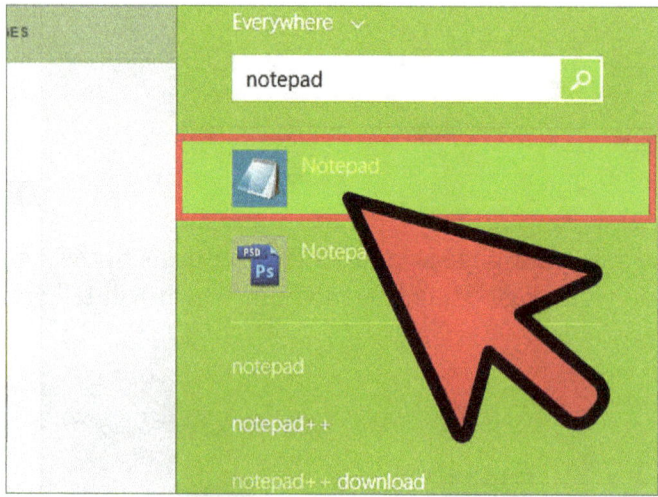

1. Open Notepad. Notepad is automatically installed on all Windows computers. You can find it in the Start Menu. Once you are in Notepad, click "File" and then click "Save As" in the dropdown menu. Choose "All Files" in the file type menu. Save your file as an HTML file. Usually, the main page of a website is known as "index.html" in order to be able to access everything on the website from that single page.

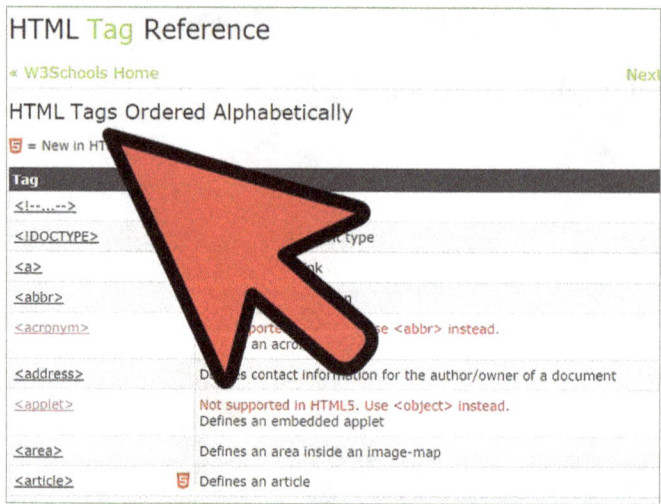

2. HTML (Hypertext Markup Language) uses tags. Tags are basically some text inside of `<angle brackets>`. You will use a variety of tags to create your webpage. There are also "end tags" which end a line of code. An example is of an end tag is:`</text>`. These end things like a bold font or a paragraph.

Designing Web Pages | 23

3. The first tag of a webpage is usually: `<html>`. You can put this at the top of your Notepad file.

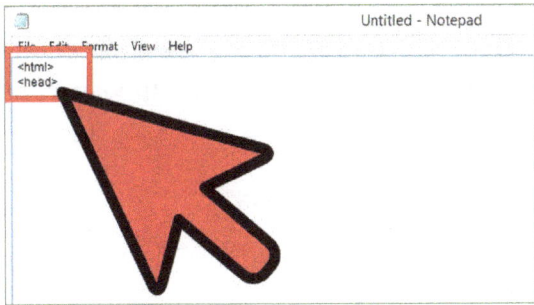

4. The next tag is `<head>`

The next tag, `<title>`, tells the browser what to put at the top of the window, and the optional *meta tags*, tells search engines like Google what the site is about.

5. On the next line after your head tag, put a title: `<title>How HTML</title>`

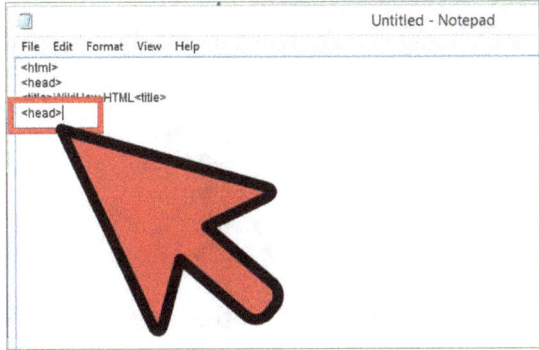

6. Now end your head by typing `</head>`

7. Next in our website comes the `<body>` tag. Please note that not all colors are supported on all browsers. (for instance, dark grey probably wouldn't be supported on most browsers).

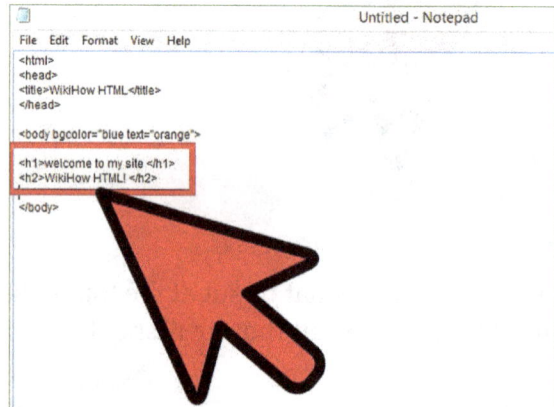

8. Between the two body tags goes the content of your webpage, what the user sees. Let's start with a header. A header a a section of large text, and is specified in HTML with `<h1>` through `<h6>`, with `<h1>` being the largest. So at the top of your webpage, after the body tag, might be something like `<h1>Welcome to my site!</h1>` Make sure you remember the end tag, or your whole webpage will be in giant.

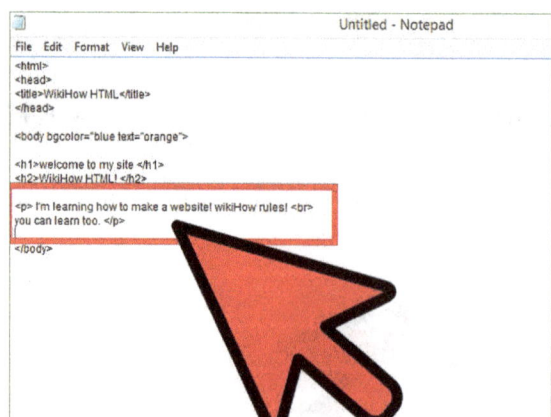

9. Another tag that can go in the webpage body is the `<p>` tag, or paragraph tag. So after your header, you might have `<p>`. I'm learning how to make a website! How rules! If you want a new line in your site, use the `<br>` tag, or break tag.

Designing Web Pages | 25

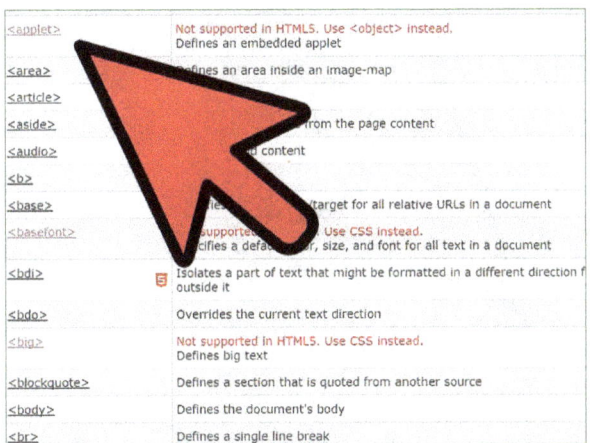

10. You probably don't want a webpage that's all plain text. So let's put in some formatting. `<b>` for bold text, `<i>` for italics, and `<u>` for underlining. Remember your end tags.

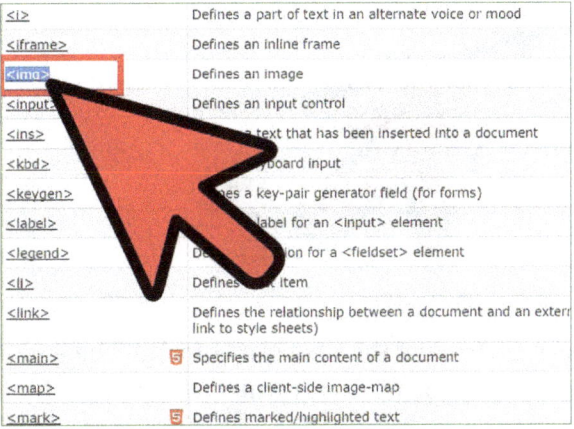

11. What really makes a website interesting is pictures. Even with formatting, who wants to look at endless words? Use the `<img>` tag to do this. But, like the body tag, it needs some extra information. An img tag might look like this: `<img alt=dog src="dog.jpg" width=200 height=200>`. The src (source) is what the picture is called. The width and height are the width and height of the picture in pixels.

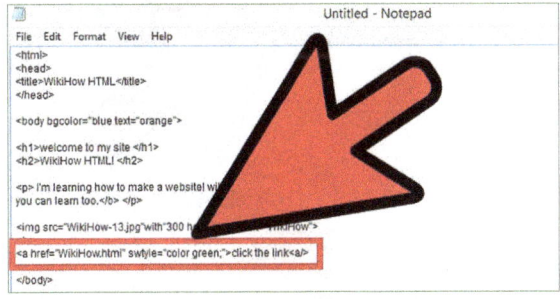

12. Almost done! You want your visitors to be able to see more than just one page. To create links, use: `<a href="otherpage.html">Another page</a>`. The text in between the tags is what the user clicks on to get to the next page, and the href part is where their click takes them. Using a tags you can let your users move effortlessly around your website.

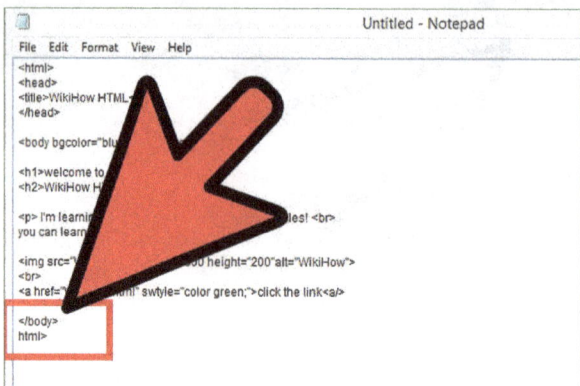

13. To finish up, you need to end your body with `</body>`, and entire webpage with `</html>`

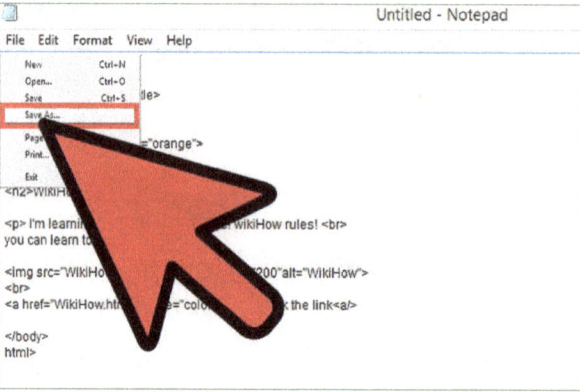

14. Save your work, making sure to save the file with '.html' at the end. Open the .html file in your favourite web browser to see how it looks. Congratulations! You just made a webpage.

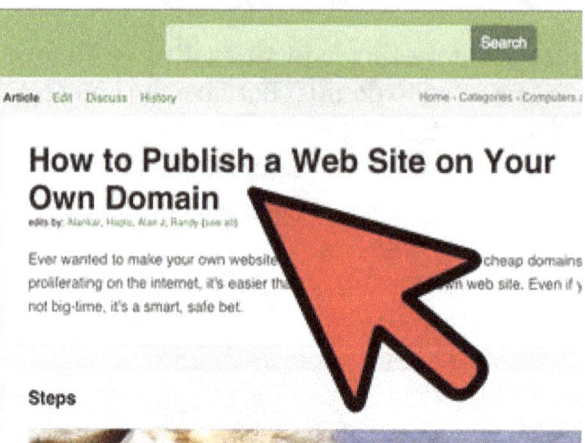

How to create a Simple Web Page with HTML

Although you can make a webpage without knowing HTML, you will have inevitable problems no matter what webpage editor you're using and you will need to know HTML to fix it. There are many good websites where you can learn HTML, but this topic shows you the basics of creating a website by using HTML. With this basic introduction, you'll soon be able to make a webpage from scratch.

Using HTML

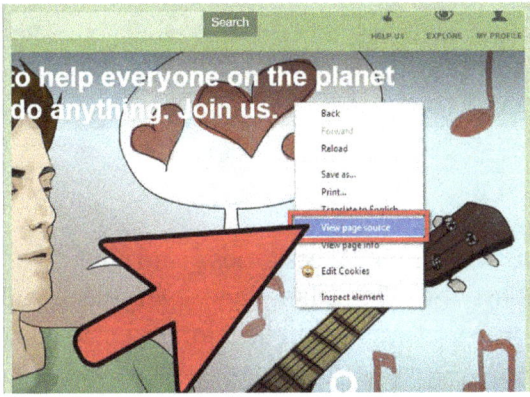

1. Understand what HTML is. HTML (Hyper Text Markup Language) is the coding language that makes web-pages, it is the skeleton of every web-page that exists. To see what it looks like, go into Internet Explorer, navigate to any website and right-click on the web-page selecting "View Source". You will see a page of code, and that is HTML. That code is what your browser sees and interprets into a human friendly web-page.

- In Google Chrome press F12.
- In Mozilla Firefox, press Ctrl + U to view the page's source code.
- In Safari, select View→View Source (or Option + Command + U).
- In Internet Explorer, the VIEW menu option is "source".

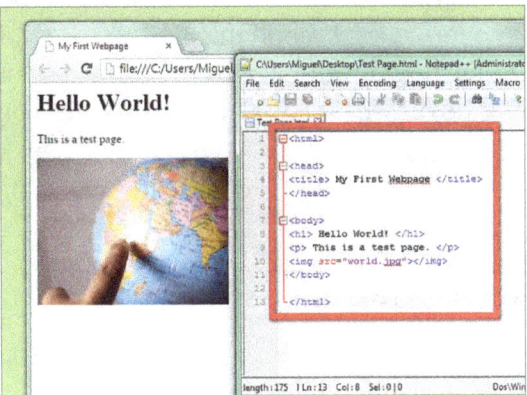

2. Make your initial web page as simple as possible. If you don't, you'll likely get overwhelmed by the syntax and the script languages.

- It's important to remember that you'll be writing your information between an opening HTML tag and a closing HTML tag. An opening tag looks like this: <___> . A closing tag looks like this: </___> . Eventually, the ___ is replaced with a code.

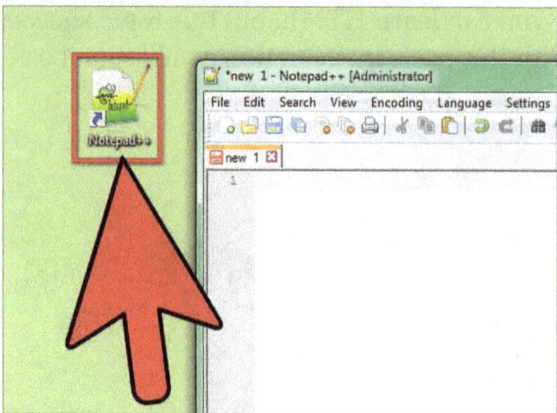

3. Go to Start, then "Programs" and then "Accessories." and click "Notepad." It is a lot easier if you use Notepad++ once you choose the HTML language, everything you write will be automatically connected with different colors - that way it will be a lot easier to correct possible mistakes.

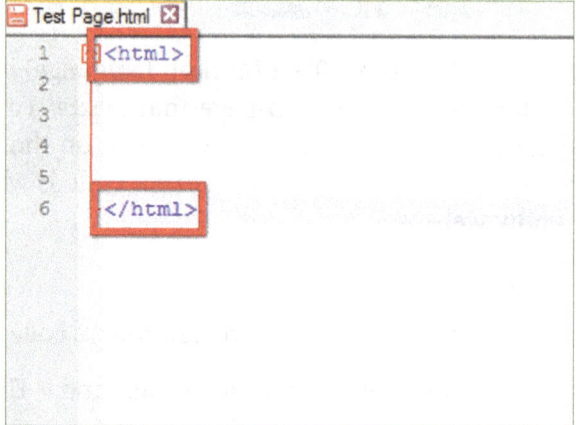

4. Tell the browser what language you are using. On the first line, type `<!DOCTYPE>`, this should always be the first tag in your code. On the second line add `<html>`. It is the second tag you write that tells the computer you're starting a web-page. It will also be closed last, so at the end of the document, close it off by typing this: `</html>`. This ends the web page.

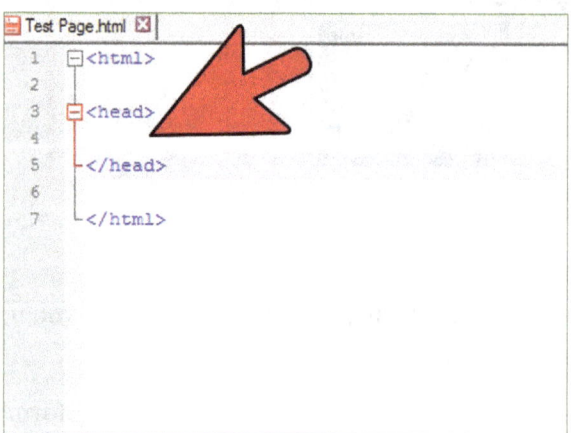

5. Add the heading of the page as shown.

```
Test Page.html
1    <html>
2
3    <head>
4    <title> My First Webpage </title>
5    </head>
6
7    </html>
```

6. Give your page a title. A title is important because it gives your users an idea on what the page is all about. Also, when users bookmark your site, that title is all they will see in their bookmark list. The title for HTML code is `<title>`. Close it off at the end of your title by writing `</title>` The title is going to show on the tab, don't expect it to be the title of the actual website.

```
Test Page.html
1    <html>
2
3    <head>
4    <title> My First Webpage </title>
5    </head>
6
7    <body>
8
9
10   </body>
11
12   </html>
```

7. Work on the body of the page. Type `<body>` to open the body tag. Then close the body tag by typing `</body>`. The bulk of the information for your web-page goes between `<body>` and `</body>`.

- To give your web-page a background color, you can add a style to the body. To add a background color, add this tag `<body style="background-color:silver">`. You can try a different color or even a hex code. The words in the quotation marks are known as "attributes." They must be surrounded by quotation marks.

```
Test Page.html
1    <html>
2
3    <head>
4    <title> My First Webpage </title>
5    </head>
6
7    <body>
8    <h1> Hello World! </h1>
9    <p> This is a test page. </p>
10
11   </body>
12
13   </html>
```

8. Write some text between the body tags.

- To make the text go to the next line (like pressing "Enter" on your keyboard), write `<br><br>`
- Want to add a marquee, otherwise known as a word that moves across a screen? Simply type `<marquee>TEXT GOES HERE</marquee>`.

```
Test Page.html
1   <html>
2
3   <head>
4     <title> My First Webpage </title>
5   </head>
6
7   <body>
8     <h1> Hello World! </h1>
9     <p> This is a test page. </p>
10    <img src="world.jpg"></img>
11  </body>
12
13  </html>
```

9. Add some pictures. If you want to put a picture from the Internet onto your web page, the HTML code for pictures is `<img src="URL">` . The closing tag is: However, the closing tag is optional.

```
Test Page.html
1   <html>
2
3   <head>
4     <title> My First Webpage </title>
5   </head>
6
7   <body>
8     <h1> Hello World! </h1>
9     <p> This is a test page. </p>
10    <img src="world.jpg"></img>
11  </body>
12
13  </html>
```

10. Check to make sure all of your tags are closed. Your webpage should look something like this:

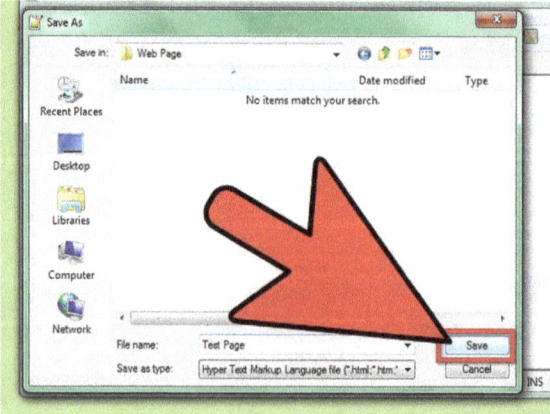

11. Save your work. Go to "save as", put a filename with an .html extension (such as "testfile.html") and choose "all files" or "text" under file type. It won't work if both are not done. Go find the page

wherever you saved it, double click it, and your default web browser should open up your very own web-page.

How to make a Web Page using Dreamweaver

Adobe Dreamweaver is a very useful program -- if you know how it works. To expedite the process of using this program to make a webpage, you'll need to know a few tricks. And then you'll be armed and ready to start creating.

Steps

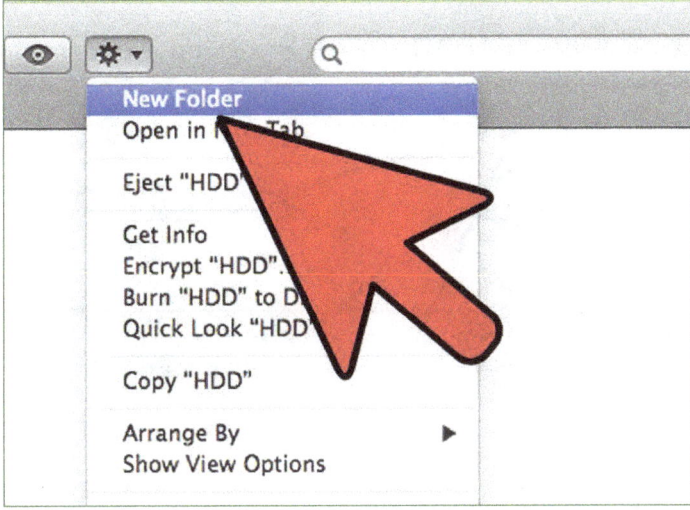

1. Create a folder in the hard drive (not in Dreamweaver) and name it whatever you want. This is your root folder.

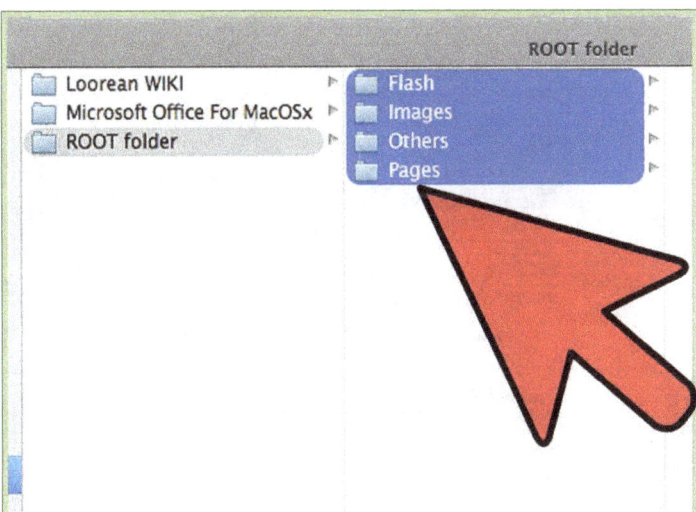

2. Inside this folder create 4 sub-folders and name them: Images, Flash, Pages, and Other.

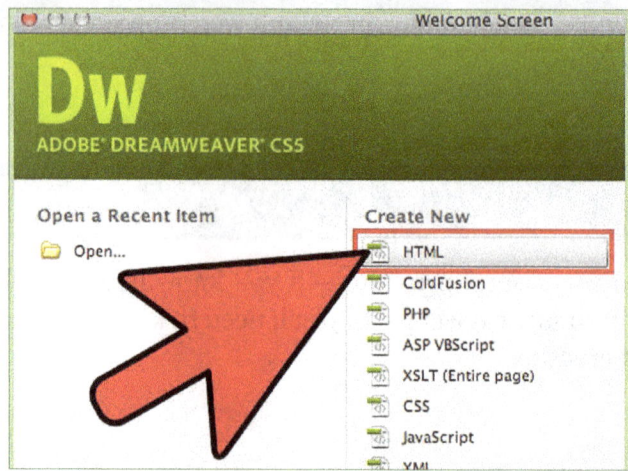

3. Go into Dreamweaver and click on HTML. Save this page into your root folder as Home Page.

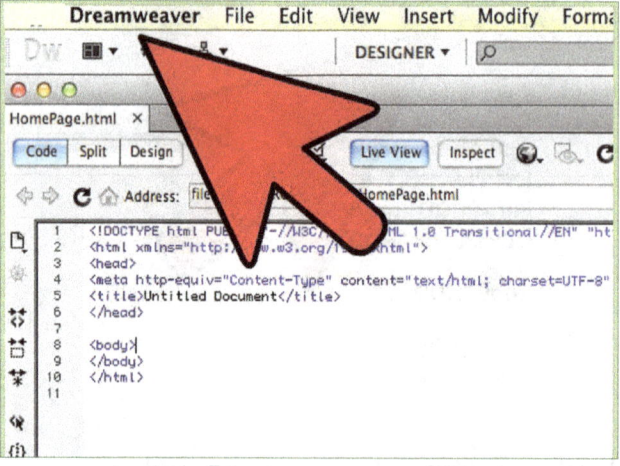

4. Get Started.

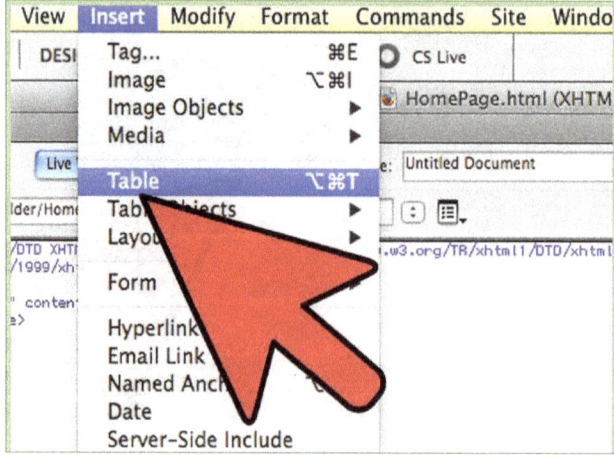

5. Dreamweaver is a little bit screwy so to put images, buttons, etc where you want them you have to add in tables. Go to insert, new table. You can set it to as many cubes as you want. It's a little tricky to get it where you want but a little playing with it works.

Designing Web Pages | 33

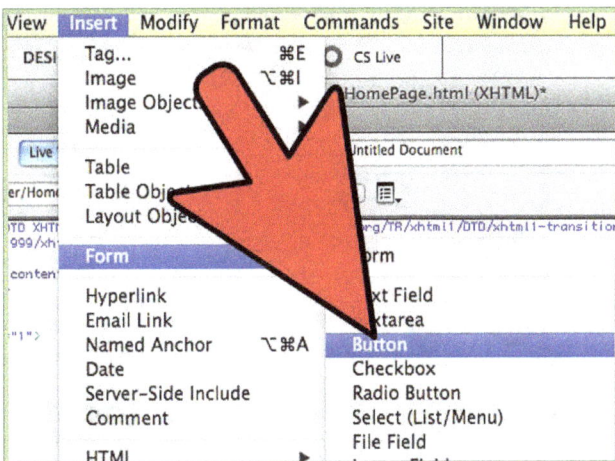

6. If you want to, you can insert buttons by going to insert, form, button. Once you get it, you can right click on it and look for the page you want to connect it to or type in the url of the site.

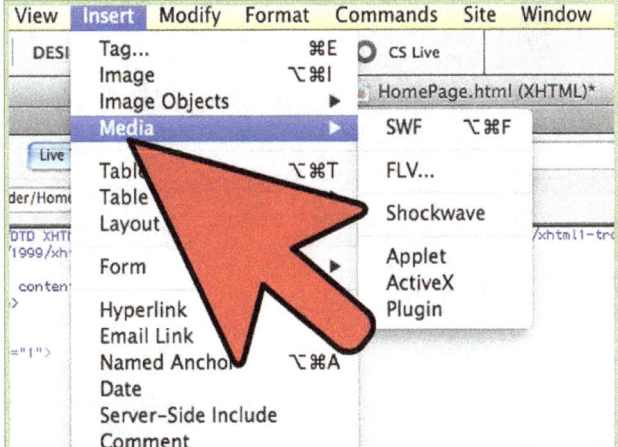

7. You can also use flash text and you can add in pictures.

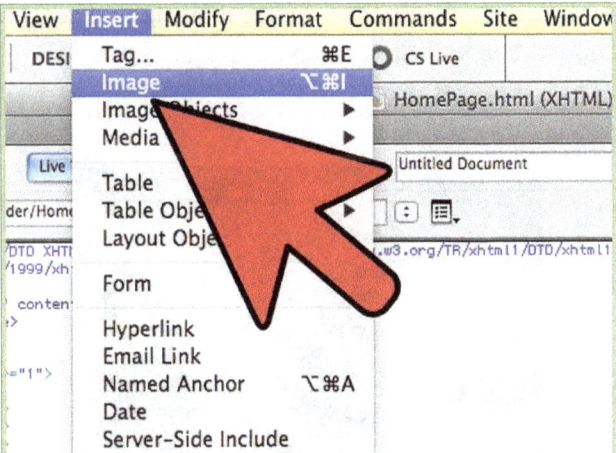

8. When adding a picture, do not copy/paste it. Go to insert, image and then search for the pic you want. Again, Dreamweaver is a little screwy.

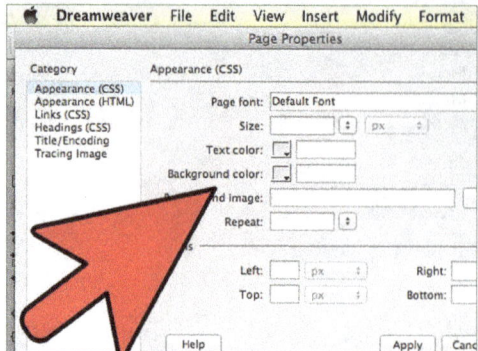

9. To change the background color and font go to modify, page properties, and it's self explanatory from there.

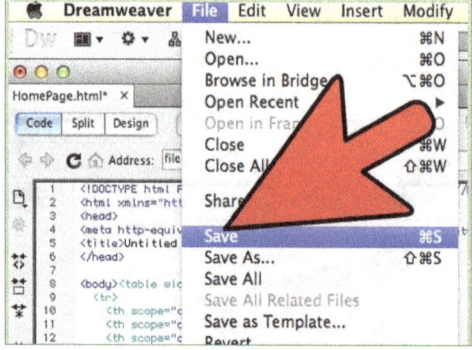

10. That should get you on the right track.

How to Design a Simple Web Page in Div

If you have a site, then exploring its design by using CSS and div tags can take you and your website business one step ahead. Easy maintenance, faster loading and search engine friendly features shall give you benefits of better marketing strategy.

Steps

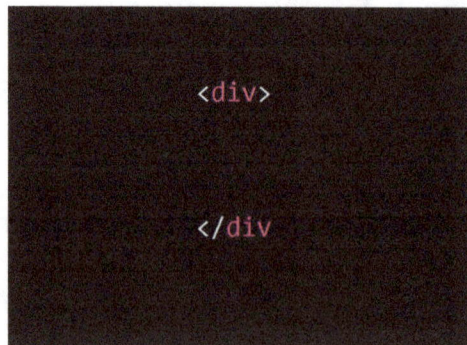

1. Know that the 'div' tag is basically utilized to establish separate areas or divisions of the website

page. This is amongst the extremely powerful elements in "XHTML", since it is necessary for placing the design of web page using "CSS".

```
<div id="container">
    <div id="head">
        <div id="logo"><img src = "images/BANNER.png"><div id="logo1">
            <img src = "images/pakra4.gif"><br></div></div>
        <div id="navigation">
            <ul>
                <li><a href="" ><b>Home</b>  </a></li>
                <li><a href="" ><b>About Us</b> </a> </li>
                <li><a href="" ><b>Services</b> </a> </li>
                <li><a href="" ><b>Location</b> </a> </li>
                <li><a href="" ><b>Contact</b> </a> </li>
            </ul>
        </div>
    </div>
</div>
```

2. Consider redesigning an existing website with 'div' tags. In simple words, this process means implementing sites devoid of making use of tables for layout and positioning. 'Div' tags use style sheets which are commonly referred to as "Cascading style sheets" or "CSS" which allow the web design of the site to be independent of data. Designing backgrounds with colors and fonts, width, height, layout and positioning of rows or columns can all be inserted into style sheets leaving only div code and information on actual pages.

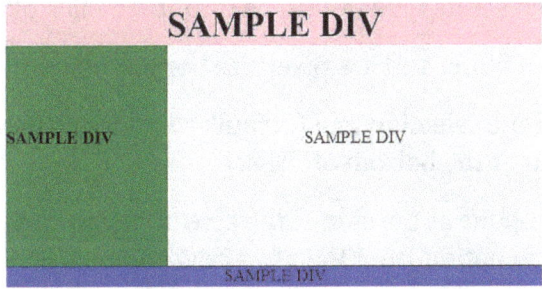

3. Understand the benefits of making use of div tags or table-less:

- Loading of sites become faster. Websites that are based on 'div' tags render browsers to run much faster as they come in a very light weight. 'Div' is controlled through Cascading style sheets and therefore, needs less coding that helps in keeping the file size to the minimal.

- 'Div' is friendly to all search engines – CSS based websites are search engine optimization friendly as these enable the web designer to keep main articles on top allowing search engines to find main contents more easily.

- A 'div' tag based website saves bandwidth. A table-less website has smaller file size, which means that it saves your bandwidth. If you have a huge traffic site, where each page is browsed by the site visitors, you shall save on the bandwidth size by not having tables. This saved bandwidth amount could be useful over a time period or at the end of the month.

- Cleaner Code – The websites using 'div' tags and CSS generates cleaner code. This cleaner code permits crawlers of search engines to read the actual content.

How to create a Basic Flash Interactive Web Page

With this information, you too can build your own website. Many large companies have excellent flash websites, yet so many small businesses seem incapable of designing a smooth and clean website. In this tutorial, we will create a Tropics-themed website. NOTE: This tutorial assumes you know how to use Flash 8 or MX.

Steps

1. Open your Macromedia Flash application, and select "New Flash Document".

2. On the "Properties" bar at the bottom of the screen (if you cannot see this, go to Window -> Property -> click on Property , click the button that says "Size" next to it.

3. A window called "Document Properties" should pop up, in the two blanks next to "Dimensions", fill in 625 for width and 750 for length.

4. On the same "Properties" bar, change the background color to a soft green, #BAE29E (use the text box at the top of the color picker) is a good shade to use, and click ok.

5. Create a symbol by pressing CTRL + F8.

6. Name it "banner_mc", and set its type to "Movie Clip" then click ok.

7. Create a rectangle, with no filling and a 2-pixel size border, using the rectangle tool on the left.

8. Select the rectangle using the selection tool (default - 'V') and set its width to 750, and its Height to 172 using the property bar at the bottom of the screen.

9. On the "Color Mixer" side-pane at the side of the screen (if you cannot see this go to Window -> Color Mixer, select the Radial option from the drop-down box.

10. On the far left of the radial color bar, select a leaf color (by double clicking on the slider). #66CC00 should work nicely.

11. 3/4's of the way along the bar, place a solid white by just clicking and double-clicking on it and selecting white.

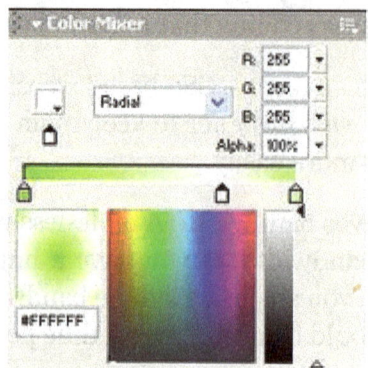

12. All the way to the right side end of the bar, place a tropical kiwi color. #99FF66 is a good choice here.

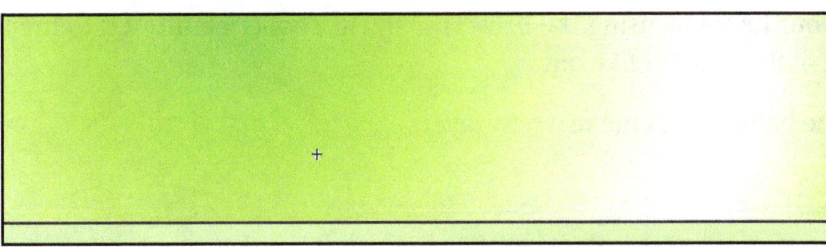

13. Now, using the Paint Bucket tool (default - 'K'), fill in your banner with the radial. Where you click to fill will represent the center of your circle-type design. Placing the center of the circle at the top of the bar, about 3/4's of the way to the left end.

14. Look up to your layers bar, and call this layer "Base".

15. Create a layer by using the New Layer button (at the bottom of the bar) - call this "Text".

16. Select the text tool (Default - 'T') on the left, and make sure the text is set to the "Static Text" option on the bottom of the property bar.

17. Set the color of the text to black.

18. Select a font to use. Some of the fonts listed are custom-made fonts, and the brackets next to them contain the website to download them from.

- Scriptina (Abstract Fonts)
- WirWenzlaw (Abstract Fonts)
- Viner Hand ITC
- Sylfaen
- Monotype Corsiva
- HandScript
- Lucida Blackletter
- Papyrus

19. Type your name of your website into the textfield and find a proper size.

20. Place the text to the left side. Leave enough room to paste an image.

21. Go onto the internet, to Google Images, and type in "Palm tree".

22. Select a photo of a palm tree.

23. Save this photo, and import it into your flash document using File -> Import.

24. Name it in the Library as "palm tree_bmp"

25. Create a symbol (Ctrl + F8), name it palm tree_gr, and select the Graphic radio button.

26. Resize it to your liking by using the Free Transform Tool (Default - Q) to the left of the screen and cut any part of it you don't like out.

27. Go back to the banner, and make a new layer.

28. Call it "Picture".

29. Put your palm tree_gr, and scale it so it fits in the left hand corner.

30. Now place your banner_mc on Scene 1.

31. Create a new symbol (Ctrl + F8), call it navigation_mc, and make it a movie clip.

32. Create a thin, long rectangle to house your links.

33. Name the layer "Base"

34. Make it have a 2-Pixel size boundary

35. Fill the rectangle with #66CC00.

36. Create a second (button) symbol (Ctrl + F8), call it "home_bt".

37. Look back at the list of fonts I provided, and choose a DIFFERENT font than your banner, one that looks good with the other. Make sure all of your buttons are using the same font and size.

38. Write "Home",

39. Break it apart using CTRL + B.

40. Copy Frame "Up", and paste it to the other frames.

41. Name this layer "text".

42. Create another layer, call it "Hidden".

43. Make a rectangle roughly covering your text.

44. Give the rectangle no border, and set its Alpha to 0%.

45. Copy the rectangle frame and paste it onto the other frames of that layer.

46. Go back to the navigation_mc and make a new layer.

47. Call it "buttons".

48. Put your button there.

49. Repeat steps 43-54 for as many buttons you need.

50. Put a 1-Pixel line between your buttons on navigation_mc, on the "base" layer.

51. Go back to scene 1 and name the layer with your banner "Banner".

52. Create a second layer, and call it Navigation.

53. Place your navigation on this.

54. Create as many frames as you have buttons on your menu.

55. Make them all keyframes (by right clicking on the frame and selecting "Insert Key Frame", or press F6).

56. Click onto your navigation_mc.

57. Click your home button, and open the actionscript by clicking the action panel at the bottom of the screen or the shortcut i use most often F9.

58. Using "expert Mode" type in the following: on (release) {gotoAndStop(1);} This will make it so whenever the mouse is clicked and released it will go to the frame '1' and stop.

59. On your next button, do the same, except in the "gotoAndStop" bracket, write the next number (in sequence).

60. Go back to scene 1.

61. Open the actions for frame 1 (F9).

62. Type in: stop();

63. Make a new layer on Scene 1, and call it "Text".

64. Convert all frames on that layer to keyframes, and make as many as you need to have a keyframes to match your other layers.

65. Make a textfield by using the Text Tool (T), and write whatever you want on each page.

66. Test the webpage, and let whoever you want test it.

67. Go to File -> Publish Settings, make sure .html is selected and press publish. This will publish the flash website you created into a html file for you to wherever you have saved it to. If this did not work make sure you have saved then repeat this step.

68. Double click on the file you published (.html) and you're done.

How to create a Landing Page

In web design, the page known as a landing page is an important and common part of many web projects, particularly those associated with sales or the advertisement or promotion of services. Two types of landing pages do 2 different things. A reference landing page presents data to a user, where a transactional landing page seeks to get web surfers to fill out a form or application, or do some other task. If you are trying to find ways to create a landing page, take advantage of these basic steps to build a page that works and makes sense for your business or enterprise.

Steps

1. Set up web hosting. In order to create a landing page, you'll need to have a web hosting service, a server that will keep all your data available and let your pages be accessible to the Internet. Web hosting services abound, and you can easily make a simple contract with one of these companies to get your own online space for presenting landing pages and other aspects of your site.

2. Acquire a domain name. The domain name is also an important part of a web project. The domain name is the name of your URL or web address, and choosing the right ones is important. Find the right web real estate to give your project visibility.

- Check with nationally recognized domain name sellers. An elite group of organizations is involved with selling the rights to different domain names. Find out what is available and what will fit your business needs.

3. Use web design tools to create basic page design. Start building your page, adding text, images and whatever else you need to make your landing page work.

- Use graphic design to create a visually compelling web page. You may want to rely on graphic design professionals, or put much of your own work into the visual appeal of the landing page. Using high-contrast color graphics and text, as well as stylized fonts or borders, can help make your page more appealing and draw in more visitors.

- Optimize your web content. The text that you put on your landing page matters a great deal to the success of your web project. You may want to optimize your SEO, or search engine optimization, with certain keywords, but be sure that your text is reader-friendly and sounds natural to get the best chances of success.

- Build in elements according to your type of landing page. For a reference landing page, work on elegant graphics and slogans. For example, if you have a landscaping business with an existing color logo and a slogan related to your craft, try to make sure that both of these can be reproduced on the reference landing page in the same way that they are printed on a business card or other promotional materials. This will make your reference landing page a more effective way to increase your brand visibility.

4. For a transactional landing page, make sure that you have included code modules that present a usable form or application for visitors to complete. The code modules on your functional transactional page should be pieces of computer code that allow users to do the things that you want them to do on your page. They need to be written flawlessly in order to work well.

- Build in functionality to your landing page with an auto-responder. The auto-responder can send out email messages based on who visits your site. This is a way to use information compiled from your web visitors to your advantage.

- Add pay per click (PPC) items or other monetizing functions. In a pay per click scenario, a web page owner places advertisements from other companies on their site. These outside or "affiliate" advertisers pay the web page owner when the ad is clicked into by a user. Some web builders can use these kinds of programs to get more money out of their web project. Take a look at PPC or other helpful elements of site design.

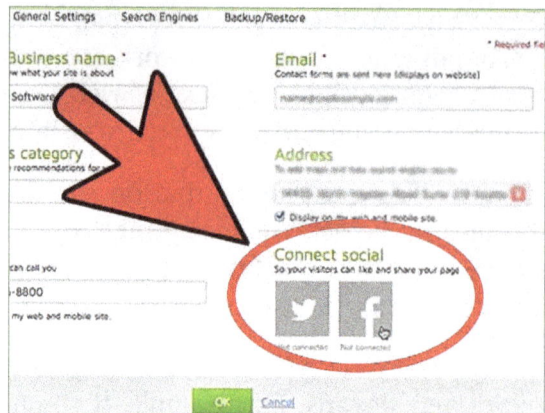

5. Think about using social media links in your landing page. One of the best ways to reach out to a diverse modern audience is through today's social media sites, which many web users look to for a variety of their daily searches and online tasks.

- Evaluate Facebook markup language (FBML). This new markup language allows webpage designers to link their pages to Facebook, a social media platform that gives visibility to all sorts of businesses, public events and more.

How to Password Protect a Web Page

There are many reasons to password protect a web page you control: sensitive personal information, snooping co-workers, or content not intended for children. Learning about basic password protection can also be a nice way to expand your understanding of coding. Please note: web data security is an ever-evolving field and attackers are extremely sophisticated. In order to protect very important data (credit card numbers, financial passwords, etc.) you should always consult an expert.

Method 1

Adding the HTML Code yourself

```
<SCRIPT>
function passWord() {
var testV = 1;
var pass1 = prompt('Please Enter Your Password',' ');
while (testV < 3) {
if (!pass1)
history.go(-1);
if (pass1.toLowerCase() == "letmein") {
alert('You Got it Right!');
window.open('www.wikihow.com');
break;
}
testV+=1;
var pass1 =
prompt('Access Denied - Password Incorrect, Please Try Again.','Password')
}
if (pass1.toLowerCase()!="password" & testV ==3)
history.go(-1);
return " ";
}
</SCRIPT>
<CENTER>
<FORM>
<input type="button" value="Enter Protected Area" onClick="passWord()">
</FORM>
</CENTER>
```

1. Create or copy the basic code. This method is best if you are hosting your own page or are simply

trying to learn more about password protection coding. There are many different variations on code for basic password protection (we've reprinted one), and we will explain how to set your own password and customize the code in a later step.

```
<SCRIPT>
function passWord() {
var testV = 1;
var pass1 = prompt('Please Enter Your Password',' ');
while (testV < 3) {
if (!pass1)
history.go(-1);
if (pass1.toLowerCase() == "letmein") {
alert('You Got it Right!');
window.open('www.xyz.com');
break;
}
testV+=1;
var pass1 =
prompt('Access Denied - Password Incorrect, Please Try Again.','Pass-
word');
}
if (pass1.toLowerCase()!="password" & testV ==3)
history.go(-1);
return " ";
}
</SCRIPT>
<CENTER>
<FORM>
<input type="button" value="Enter Protected Area" onClick="passWord()">
</FORM>
</CENTER>
```

44 | Web Designing

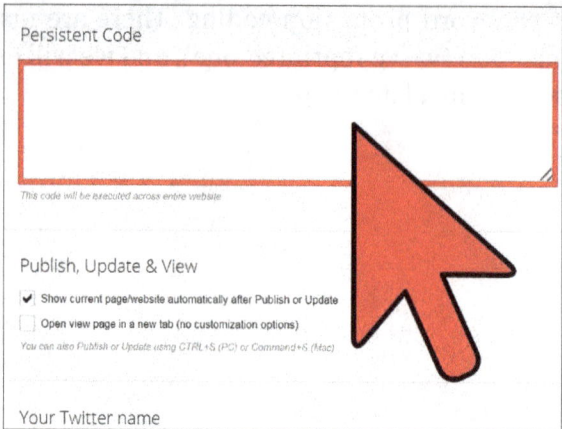

2. Add it to your page's code. In order to implement this code you will need editing access to your web page's underlying code. Once in the editor, add the protection template code within the body section of the page (after `<body>` tag).

3. Add your own password. This password protection code requires you to add in your own password (in the code template it is set as "letmein"). Replace the text between the quotation marks with your own case-sensitive password.

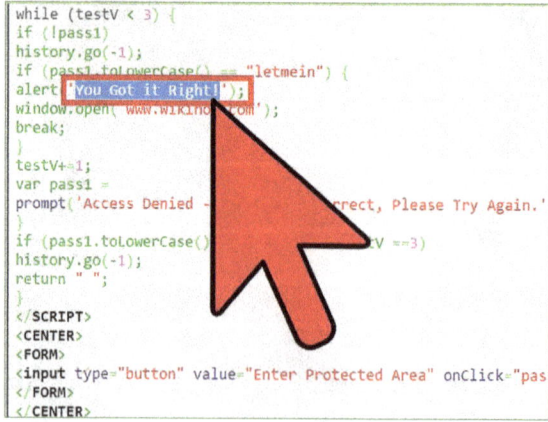

4. Customize the code. Now write display messages for users entering either the correct password ("You Got it Right!") or incorrect answers ("Password Incorrect, Please Try Again."). You must

also specify the web page URL where the user will be directed if they get the password correct. This should be replaced your own password protected URL.

- An incorrect password leads back to the password prompt in this code. In other code templates you can choose to redirect these users to a different page altogether.

5. Test it out. Now that you've protected your page with a password it's time to test it out. Open the page in your browser and try entering an incorrect password, then the correct one. Double check both the password accuracy and the display messages you've coded in.

- If you're struggling with the HTML coding aspect of this method, have a closer look at Create a Simple Web Page With HTML for a bit more guidance.

Method 2

Protection Through your Hosting Company

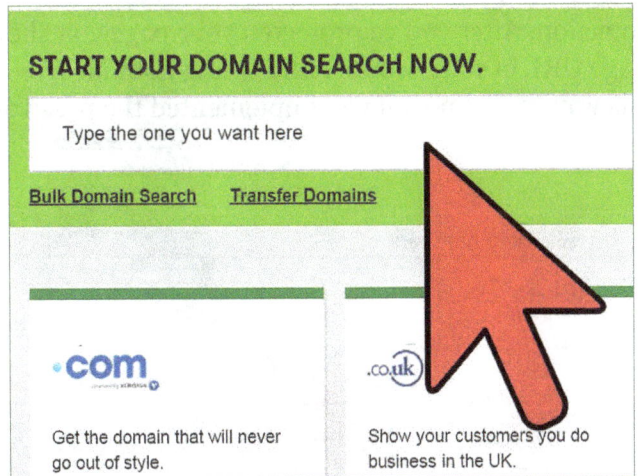

1. Research your current web hosting plan features. Login to your web hosting account and search for password protection as part of your hosting subscription package. Many hosts offer the ability to password protect a page you control with a simple-to-use widget from your account dashboard.

- Different web hosts offer different feature sets, so consider this when choosing your next web host.

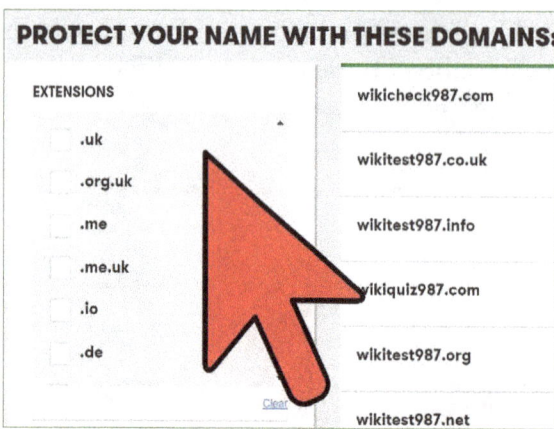

2. Follow the instructions. If your host offers password protection as a built-in feature, implementation should be as simple as filling out a form.

3. Test the password protection. After you've protected your page you should always test it out by opening the protected page URL in your browser and trying both incorrect and correct passwords to see what happens. This way you'll know if you implemented the password protection correctly.

4. Contact your web host directly. If you're unsure of whether this feature is available to you or of

how best to implement it, try emailing your web host for assistance. Most web hosts are run by experienced webmasters and will be more than willing to help. They will also know all the details about your hosting setup and can advise you on best practices for the specific data you'd like protected.

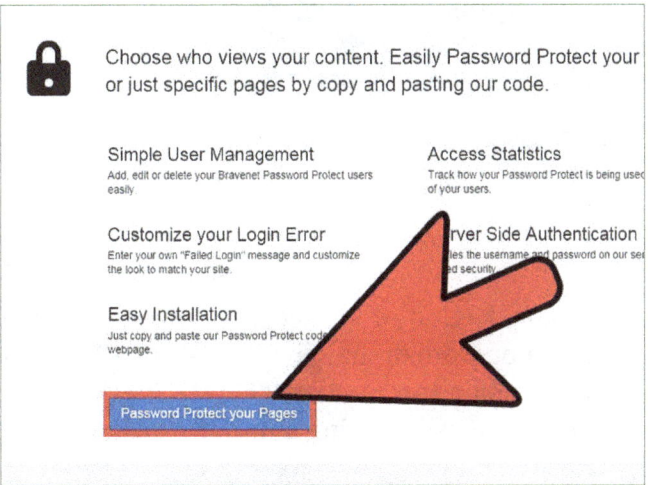

5. Look into 3rd party protection. Although your web host will offer the best advice on how to proceed, know that there are many 3rd party password protection options for you to consider implementing for your webpage.

- 3rd party protection can be useful in a variety of ways - by generating difficult to crack passwords or by setting up a fully-automated web login.

Website: Planning, Designing and Creating

3

Websites are pages on the Internet that are meant to convey and provide information, entertainment, education, social networking platforms, etc. Creating a layout, choosing a language, using content and media are some of the steps that are involved in building a website. The topics discussed in the chapter are of great importance to broaden the existing knowledge on web designing.

Website

A website, or simply site, is a collection of related web pages, including multimedia content, typically identified with a common domain name, and published on at least one web server. A website may be accessible via a public Internet Protocol (IP) network, such as the Internet, or a private local area network (LAN), by referencing a uniform resource locator (URL) that identifies the site.

A NASA.gov homepage

Websites have many functions and can be used in various fashions; a website can be a personal website, a commercial website for a company, a government website or a non-profit organization website. Websites are typically dedicated to a particular topic or purpose, ranging from entertainment and social networking to providing news and education. All publicly accessible websites collectively constitute the World Wide Web, while private websites, such as a company's website for its employees, are typically a part of an intranet.

Web pages, which are the building blocks of websites, are documents, typically composed in plain text interspersed with formatting instructions of Hypertext Markup Language (HTML, XHTML). They may incorporate elements from other websites with suitable markup anchors. Web pages are accessed and transported with the Hypertext Transfer Protocol (HTTP), which may optionally employ encryption (HTTP Secure, HTTPS) to provide security and privacy for the user. The user's application, often a web browser, renders the page content according to its HTML markup instructions onto a display terminal.

Hyperlinking between web pages conveys to the reader the site structure and guides the navigation of the site, which often starts with a home page containing a directory of the site web content. Some websites require user registration or subscription to access content. Examples of subscription websites include many business sites, news websites, academic journal websites, gaming websites, file-sharing websites, message boards, web-based email, social networking websites, websites providing real-time stock market data, as well as sites providing various other services. As of 2016 end users can access websites on a range of devices, including desktop and laptop computers, tablet computers, smartphones and smart TVs.

Static Website

A static website is one that has web pages stored on the server in the format that is sent to a client web browser. It is primarily coded in Hypertext Markup Language (HTML); Cascading Style Sheets (CSS) are used to control appearance beyond basic HTML. Images are commonly used to effect the desired appearance and as part of the main content. Audio or video might also be considered "static" content if it plays automatically or is generally non-interactive. This type of website usually displays the same information to all visitors. Similar to handing out a printed brochure to customers or clients, a static website will generally provide consistent, standard information for an extended period of time. Although the website owner may make updates periodically, it is a manual process to edit the text, photos and other content and may require basic website design skills and software. Simple forms or marketing examples of websites, such as *classic website*, a *five-page website* or a *brochure website* are often static websites, because they present pre-defined, static information to the user. This may include information about a company and its products and services through text, photos, animations, audio/video, and navigation menus.

Static websites can be edited using four broad categories of software:

- Text editors, such as Notepad or TextEdit, where content and HTML markup are manipulated directly within the editor program.

- WYSIWYG offline editors, such as Microsoft FrontPage and Adobe Dreamweaver (previously Macromedia Dreamweaver), with which the site is edited using a GUI and the final HTML markup is generated automatically by the editor software.

- WYSIWYG online editors which create media rich online presentation like web pages, widgets, intro, blogs, and other documents.

- Template-based editors such as iWeb allow users to create and upload web pages to a web server without detailed HTML knowledge, as they pick a suitable template from a palette and add pictures and text to it in a desktop publishing fashion without direct manipulation of HTML code.

Static websites may still use server side includes (SSI) as an editing convenience, such as sharing a common menu bar across many pages. As the site's behaviour *to the reader* is still static, this is not considered a dynamic site.

Dynamic Website

Server-side programming languages repartition.

A dynamic website is one that changes or customizes itself frequently and automatically. Server-side dynamic pages are generated "on the fly" by computer code that produces the HTML (CSS are responsible for appearance and thus, are static files). There are a wide range of software systems, such as CGI, Java Servlets and Java Server Pages (JSP), Active Server Pages and ColdFusion (CFML) that are available to generate dynamic web systems and dynamic sites. Various web application frameworks and web template systems are available for general-use programming languages like Perl, PHP, Python and Ruby to make it faster and easier to create complex dynamic websites.

A site can display the current state of a dialogue between users, monitor a changing situation, or provide information in some way personalized to the requirements of the individual user. For example, when the front page of a news site is requested, the code running on the web server might combine stored HTML fragments with news stories retrieved from a database or another website via RSS to produce a page that includes the latest information. Dynamic sites can be interactive by using HTML forms, storing and reading back browser cookies, or by creating a series of pages that reflect the previous history of clicks. Another example of dynamic content is when a retail website with a database of media products allows a user to input a search request, e.g. for the keyword Beatles. In response, the content of the web page will spontaneously change the way it looked before, and will then display a list of Beatles products like CDs, DVDs and books. Dynamic HTML uses JavaScript code to instruct the web browser how to interactively modify the page contents. One way to simulate a certain type of dynamic website while avoiding the performance loss of initiating the dynamic engine on a per-user or per-connection basis, is to periodically automatically regenerate a large series of static pages.

Multimedia and Interactive Content

Early websites had only text, and soon after, images. Web browser plug ins were then used to add audio, video, and interactivity (such as for a rich Internet application that mirrors the complexity of a desktop application like a word processor). Examples of such plug-ins are Microsoft Silverlight, Adobe Flash, Adobe Shockwave, and applets written in Java. HTML 5 includes provisions for audio and video without plugins. JavaScript is also built into most modern web browsers, and allows for website creators to send code to the web browser that instructs it how to interactively modify page content and communicate with the web server if needed. The browser's internal representation of the content is known as the Document Object Model (DOM) and the technique is known as Dynamic HTML. A 2010-era trend in websites called "responsive design" has given the best of viewing experience as it provides with a device based layout for users. These websites change their layout according to the device or mobile platform thus giving a rich user experience.

Website: Planning, Designing and Creating | 51

Spelling

While "web site" was the original spelling sometimes capitalized "Web site", since "Web" is a proper noun when referring to the World Wide Web), this variant has become rarely used, and "website" has become the standard spelling. All major style guides, such as *The Chicago Manual of Style* and the *AP Stylebook*, have reflected this change.

Types

Websites can be divided into two broad categories—static and interactive. Interactive sites are part of the Web 2.0 community of sites, and allow for interactivity between the site owner and site visitors or users. Static sites serve or capture information but do not allow engagement with the audience or users directly. Some websites are informational or produced by enthusiasts or for personal use or entertainment. Many websites do aim to make money, using one or more business models, including:

- Posting interesting content and selling contextual advertising either through direct sales or through an advertising network.
- E-commerce: products or services are purchased directly through the website
- Advertising products or services available at a brick and mortar business
- Freemium: basic content is available for free but premium content requires a payment

How to choose an Idea for creating Website or Blog

Stumped on a good idea? Don't let yourself get stuck before you even get started! There are an unfathomable number of different ideas for starting your own website or blog. You just have to open your mind and your horizons.

Steps

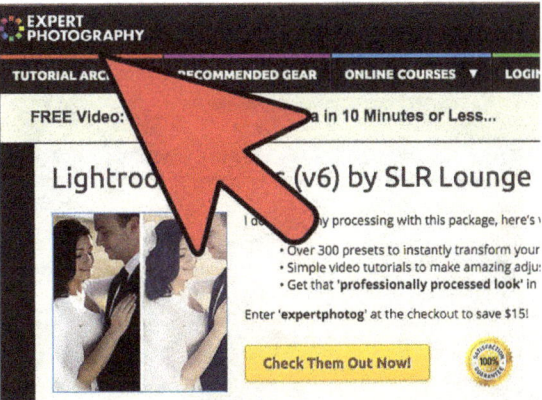

1. Assess the potential of your passion. What are you passionate about? What is exciting to you? What topics or activities turns you into a completely focused whirlwind? Passion and a love of something (or anything) is one of the perfect springboards for starting a website or blog.

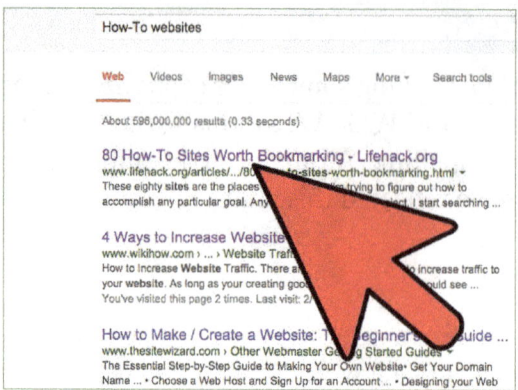

2. "How-To" websites have a tremendous valuable potential. Provide step-by-step instruction and education on choosing the right business clothes, hair care, cook, baby care, household maintenance, holiday decorations, win a college scholarship, train a puppy, landscaping. Ask yourself what do you know how to do well. There is an entire world of people out there who want to learn how to do just about anything.

3. Consider other questions such as Why? Who? What? When? Where? What do you wonder about? What do you search for on the internet? Do you find the information you want quickly and easily? Does it answer your question and provide the information that you were interested in learning? If not, consider starting a comprehensive website or blog that does provide extensive information on that topic.

4. Self-help sites and blogs are a great resource to help people through just about any problem or

issue you can think of such as dieting, exercise, divorce, child rearing, budgeting, organizing, relationships, caring for aging parents.

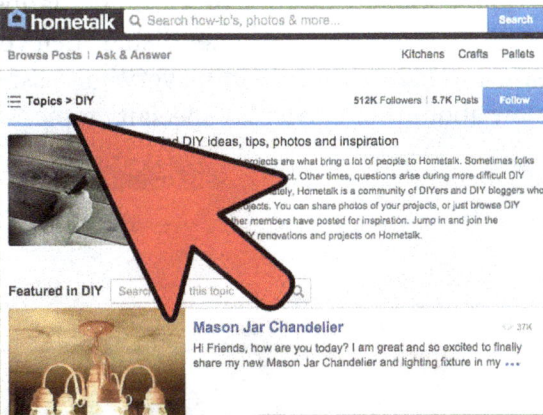

5. Do-It-Yourself topics are always great topics. Do you have a hobby or skill that you are good at? Crafts, automobiles, construction, gardening, writing, gaming, real estate, computers, sewing, animals, collecting the sky's the limit for interesting DIY instructional websites or blogs.

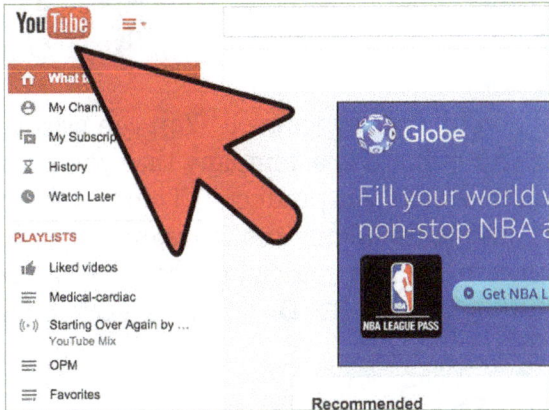

6. Humor is always popular! Explore your own hidden inner comic and build a fun site around a collection of the funniest YouTube videos, the health benefits of laughing, great comedies on DVD, comic books.

7. Adventure, sports, fashion, leisure activities, retirement, education, news, recreation are all

topics that lend themselves to a million different specialty website "niches". For example, if you love camping then a specialty niche might be a website on perfect tent camping camp grounds in the USA or what to bring on a hiking camping trip. Or if you happen to love to cook and your specialty is homemade pie, grilling, or shrimp appetizer dishes then you have found a great niche! Finding a good niche to create a website around can be very successful because your visitors will all be people who want to know about that particular specialty topic.

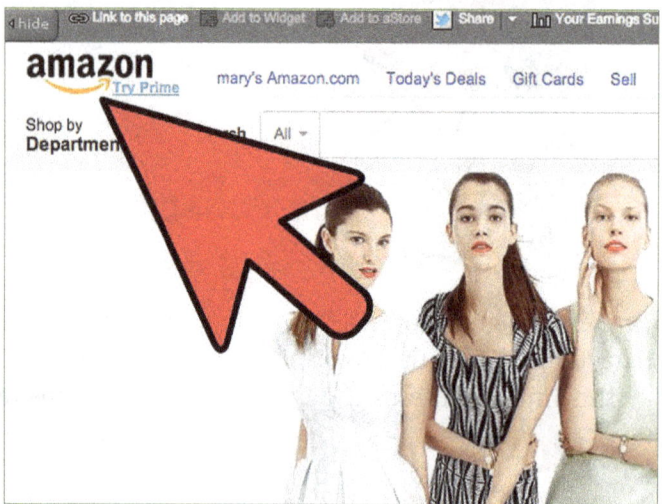

8. Sell products even if you don't have any yourself! You can create entire stores by becoming an affiliate with companies. (An affiliate is a company that you partner with who will pay you commission on the sales you make of their products.) Think of the range of products that Amazon.com has. They are just one choice among the thousands of affiliate companies available to partner with. As an Amazon.com affiliate you can choose any category of products they stock and market them yourself through a website. Do you love electronics, cosmetics, books, music, gourmet food items?

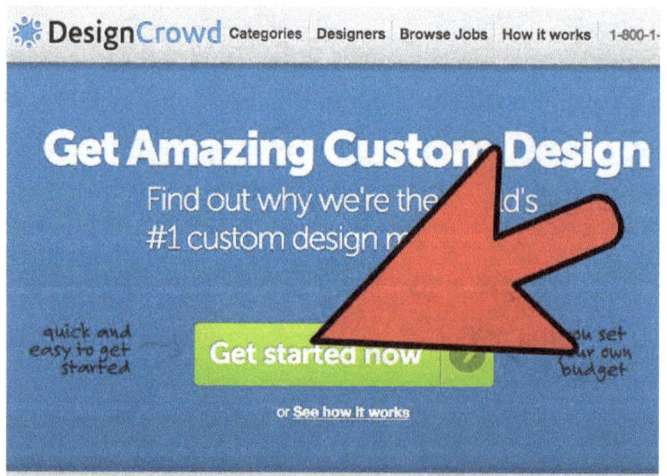

9. Do you have an expertise that you can sell as a service to others? Graphic design, legal, writing, book reviews, editing, website design, financial advise, real estate consulting, home decorating... Begin your own consulting services by promoting them through a website.

10. Do you have information that you would like to share? Start a "best tips" website such as the best laptops, best cat breeds, best annual flowers to plant, best motorcycles, benefits of green tea, best hot tubs, wine and beer tips.

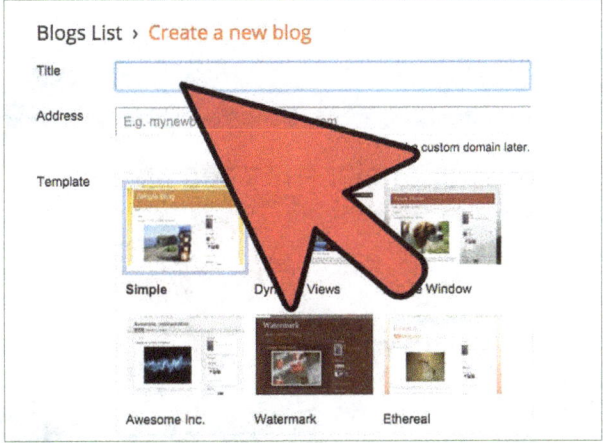

11. Do you like to discuss politics, world peace, meditation, travel or organic gardening? Start your own blog share your views with the world.

12. Are you interested in what other peoples opinions are or want to know what others think about

topics such as global warming, beauty or pro sports teams? Start an interactive forum site on a topic you enjoy.

13. Are you an eBay fanatic? Start a specialty auction website.

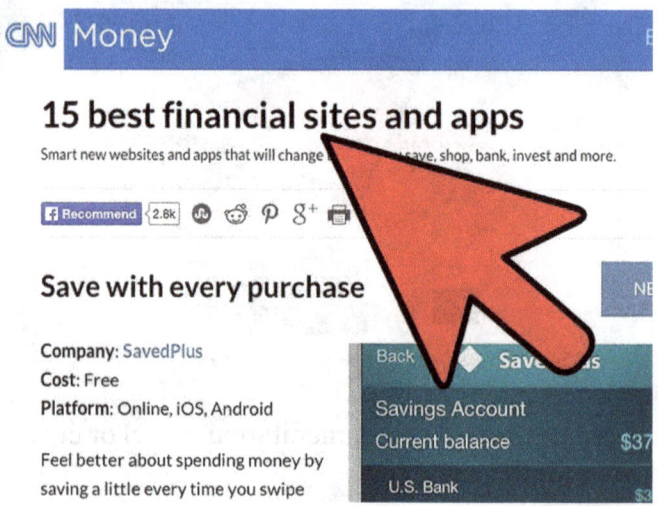

14. Do you want to make extra income? Research what topics or products generate money. Financial websites, real estate websites, consulting, sites that sell "big ticket" items such as computers, cars, vacations... can all offer generous income potential if presented well.

How to Plan a Website

If you want to design and create a website, you'll find it much easier if you spend some time planning it out. The planning phase allows the developer and the client to work together until they find a format and layout that matches their needs. The planning process influences the style choices of the site and is arguably the most important aspect of web design, especially for businesses.

Part 1
Creating the Underlying Structure

1. Determine the site's functionality. If you're making the site for yourself, you probably already know the answer to this. If you're making the site for another person, company, or organization, you'll need to find out what they expect from the site and its functionality. Everything you decide here will have an impact on the final website.

- Does it need a storefront? Do you need user comments? Will users need to create accounts? Is it article-oriented? Image-oriented? All of these questions and more will help inform the design and structure of the site.

- This can be a drawn-out process, especially for larger companies with lots of people involved in the project.

2. Create a site map diagram. A site map diagram is like a flow chart and shows how users move from one page to the next. You don't even need pages at this point, just a general flow of concepts. You can use a computer program to create a diagram, or sketch it out yourself on a piece of paper. Use the site map diagram to show how you envision the web page hierarchy and connectivity.

3. Try some card sorting. A popular method for a group is to use a stack fo cards to figure out everyone's ideal approach. Take a stack of note cards and write the basic content of a single page on each one. Have your team organize the cards in the way that they deem most useful. This is best for situations when you are collaborating with others to create a site.

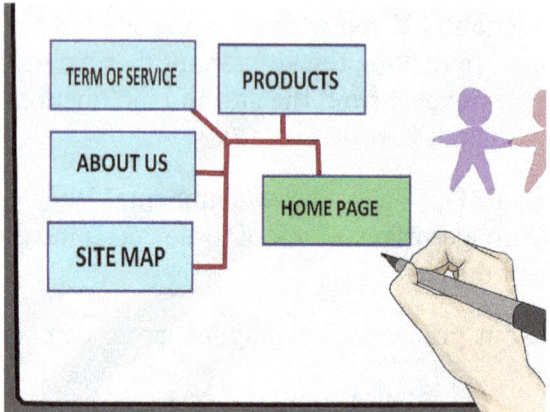

4. Use paper and a bulletin board, or a whiteboard. This is the original low-budget planning method, and allows you to quickly erase or move content and reroute it. Draw the design on pieces of paper and connect them with string, or draw the outline on a whiteboard. Great for brainstorming sessions.

5. Take a Content Inventory. This is more geared towards redesigns than new sites. Enter each of

your pieces of content or existing pages into a spreadsheet. Make notes as to the purpose of each one and use this list to determine what goes and what stays. This will help cut the fat and simplify the redesign process.

Part 2

Making an HTML Wireframe

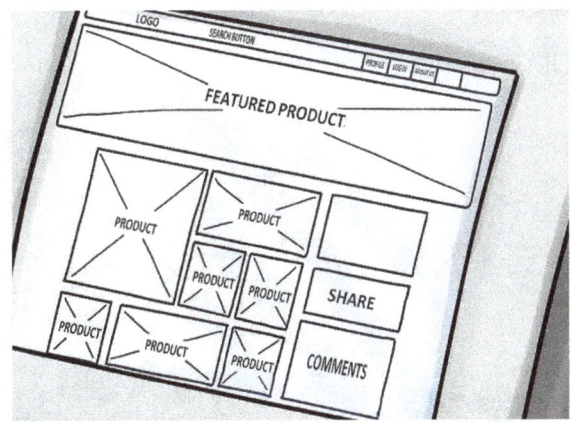

1. Make a wireframe to help solidify the hierarchy. An HTML wireframe is a skeleton of your future site, using only the most basic tags and blocks to represent content. It answers the question, "What goes on the screen and where?" Formatting and style are completely ignored in a wireframe.

- The wireframe allows you to see content structure and flow before committing to style choices.

- HTML wireframes aren't static like PDFs or images, and allow you to quickly move content blocks around to create a new structure.

- A wireframe is interactive, which is beneficial to both the developer and the client. Since the wireframe is written in simple HTML, you can still navigate through it and get a feel for how moving between the pages works. This is something that can't be expressed through a PDF concept.

2. Try the Gray Box method. Block out the content of your page in gray boxes, with the most

important content at the top. The blocks are arranged in a single column, with the most important piece of content on the page at the top. For example, if the page is the company's About page, the company details might go on the top, followed by a staff list, followed by contact information, etc.

- This doesn't include the header and footer. The gray boxes are simply a visual representation of the content that will be found on the page.

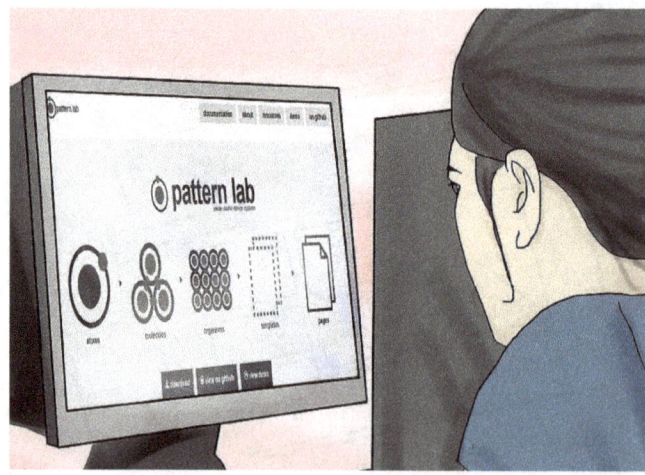

3. Try a wire framing program. There are several programs that can help you with the wireframing process. The amount of coding knowledge required varies from program to program. Some of the more popular programs include:

- Pattern Lab. This site specializes in "atomic design," where each piece of content is thought of as a "molecule" that makes up the larger page.

- Jumpcharts. This is a website planning and wire-framing service. It requires paid subscription but allows you to quickly build wireframes without worrying too much about coding.

- Wirefy. Wirefy is another "atomic design" system. The tools are available for free fro the developers.

4. Use simple HTML markup. A good wireframe can easily be converted into the actual site later.

Don't worry at all about style during the wireframing process. Instead, use markup that can be easily understood and swapped around with little effort.

- Less is more with a wireframe. The goal is to simply build the structure. Visuals can be adjusted later with CSS and advanced markup.

5. Make a wireframe for every page on your site. It may be tempting to make a single wireframe and say "Cool, I can apply that to every page and I'm good." In reality, this will lead to a generic and boring site. Take the time to wireframe each page, and you'll soon find that every page has its own organizational needs.

Part 3
Creating Content

1. Have some content ready before you start building the website. It will be much easier to see how you website style looks if you have your actual content instead of placeholders. You don't need too much content, but it will look much better in mockups if you have some copy and original images.

- You don't necessarily need the body of an article, but you should at least have actual headlines.

2. Remember that good content is more than text. The internet is much more than simple text websites. In order to stand out in your niche, you'll need a variety of different content types to attract and retain visitors. Some possible content to keep in mind:

- Pictures.
- Audio
- Video
- Streams (Twitter)
- Facebook integration
- RSS
- Content feeds

3. Commission a professional photographer. If you are including photos on your site, your initial impressions will be much better with professional photography. A single good photo is worth more than twenty bad ones.

- Look for recent art photography grads for cheaper solutions than long-time professionals.

4. Write quality articles. The written content on your page will determine the vast amount of your web traffic. While you don't need to worry too much about content creation at this point of the design process, it doesn't hurt to start thinking about it, since you'll need content on a regular basis once the site goes live.

- Beyond article content, there are written items that you will most likely during the website construction process. This could include contact information, company names, or anything else that will be used in multiple places on the site.

Part 4

Turning the Concept into a Site

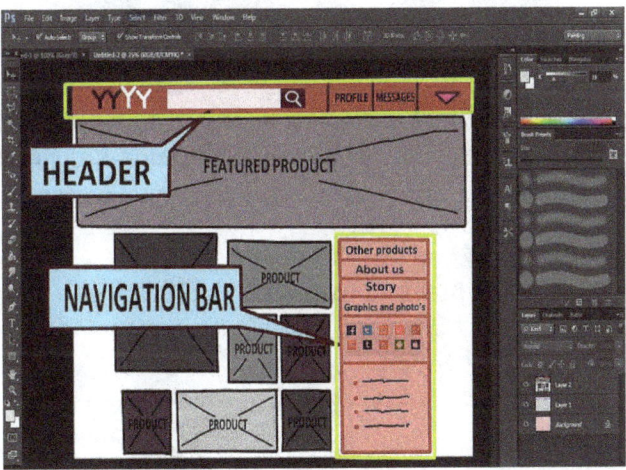

1. Style global elements. These are the things that are seen on every page on your site, such as the header, footer, and navigation menu. Create a very basic style so you can see how all of your pages will look with them in place. This will be very useful as you move into the layout process.

- Don't worry too much about the details, but do try to get it somewhat close to how the headers will eventually look.

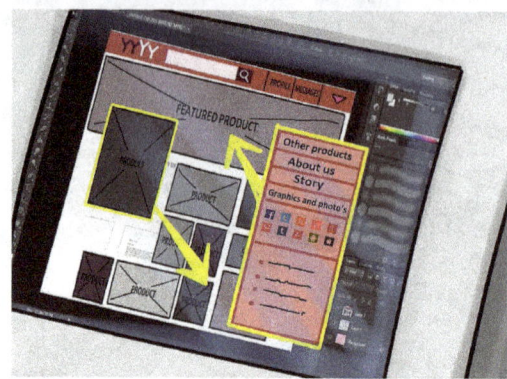

2. Create a basic layout. Start moving the clocks of your wireframe out of the single column and into their general locations on the page. For example, you might move the navigation block to the left side of the page, and a list of headline to the right.

- Keep experimenting with the layouts for a few pages before moving on. Let others test them to see if they feel organic.

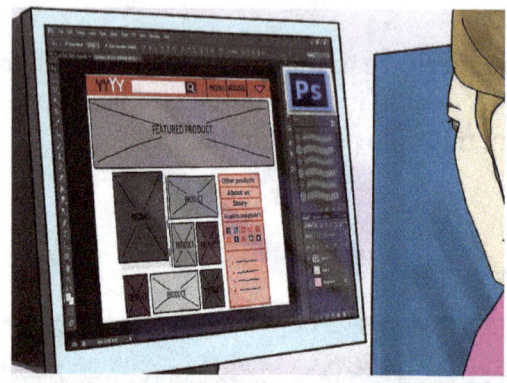

3. Create a mockup. Use a program like Photoshop to create a mockup of a few pages of your site. Use the layout you've settled on as a guide. You can work much quicker in an image editing program and get everything just how you want it. This will allow you to use these images as references when it comes time to actually code.

- Include actual content in the mockup to ensure that everything looks good together.

4. Replace your blocks with content. Start adding your content and elements to the page. Don't

worry about style yet, just get everything in the correct location. This will help you tell if your style changes are going to work.

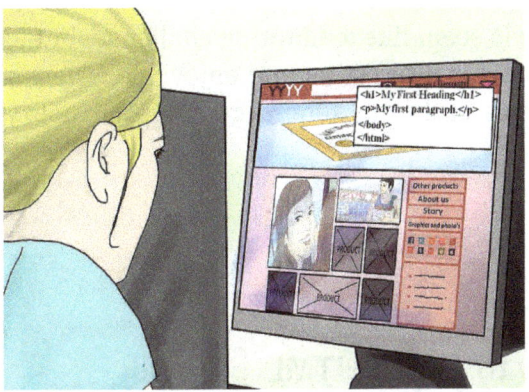

5. Create a style guide. This is essential for maintaining a cohesive style, especially for larger sites. If the site is for a business that already has visual branding, this should be incorporated into the site design. Things to potentially consider in a style guide:

- Navigation
- Headers (<h1>, <h2>, etc.)
- Paragraphs
- Italics
- Bolding
- Links (active, inactive, hovering)
- Image use
- Icons
- Buttons
- Lists

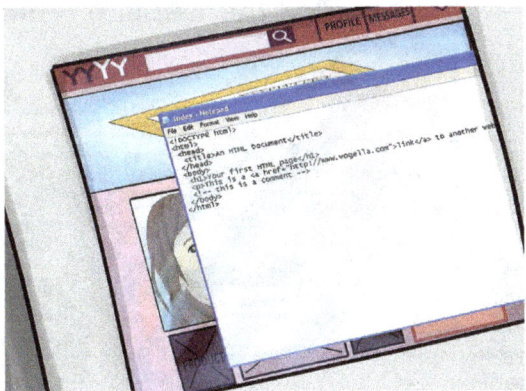

6. Apply your style. Once you've decided on a style and design for the site, it's time to start implementing it. CSS is one of the easiest ways to implement style across a page or the entire site.

How to Design a Website

Designing a great website may seem like a daunting challenge, but as long as you keep the basics in mind, you will find the process interesting and enjoyable. There's more to it than just looking good! We'll show you the basics, and some general guidelines to help you design websites that keep people coming back.

Part 1

Finding your Design

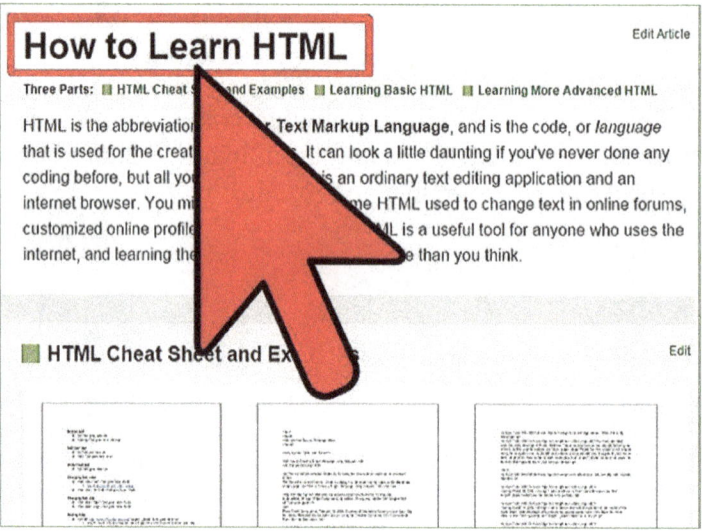

1. Design your own website. if you're new to web coding and design but you really want to build a website yourself, there are many options open to you. You can build a simple site by teaching yourself basic html and CSS coding. Just be sure that you can also make it look nice and professional.

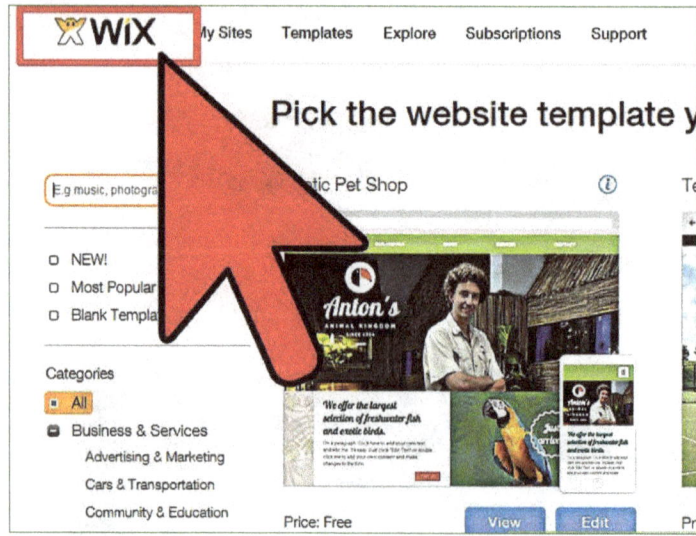

2. Use a pre-made website template. You can purchase or find free pre-made websites very easily

on the internet. These are pre-made codes which you simply use and alter to your own needs. There are many reputable providers of templates, but a good one is Wix.

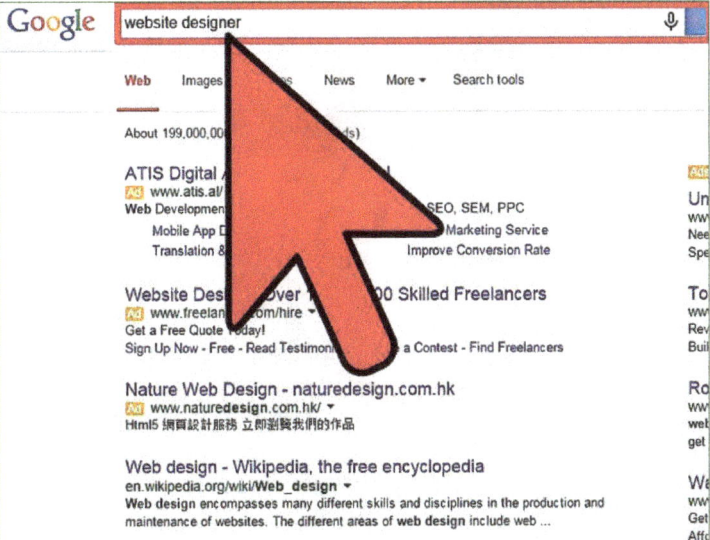

3. Hire a website designer. If you want something tailored to your needs that looks professional and runs great, it's probably a good idea to hire a website designer. While this will definitely cost you money, it won't be as expensive as it sounds. You can get a designer on the cheap by advertising at a local technical college or university. Their experience will help guide you to a more successful, more professional website.

Part 2

Making Basic Design Considerations

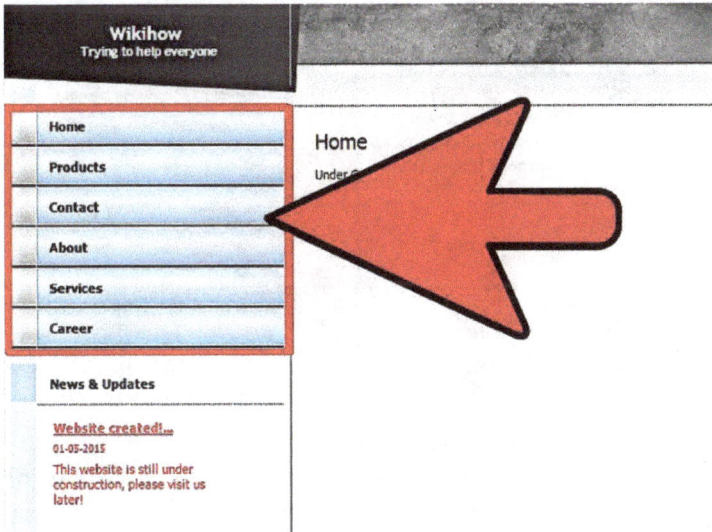

1. Streamline your webpage. You want everything to be as fast and easy to use as possible. Minimize the number of choices that someone has to make, make navigation extremely self-explanatory, and help them get to what they're looking for as quickly as possible.

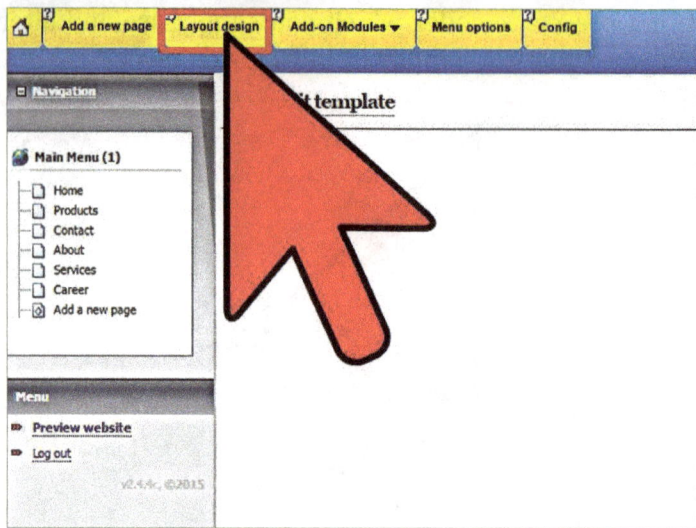

2. Practice good user interface design. Positioning the various elements of the website, such as the title, sidebars, logos, graphics, and text, in the same places on every page will make your site navigable and intuitive.

- Keep the same header at the top of every page. Whether or not your site content lends itself to many repeating elements, making sure that the top of every page is identical is a must.

- Use logic in your design. The elements on a single page should be ordered logically by importance or by topic; the various pages in the site should do the same.

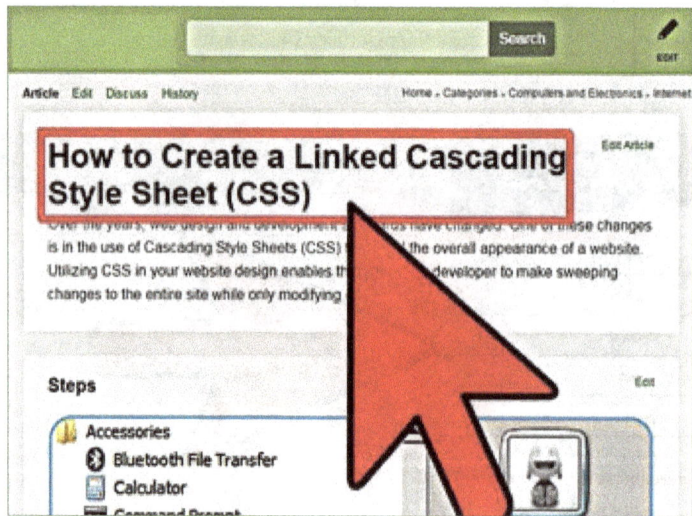

3. Create a consistent style. While the layout should give your site structural consistency, the style should give it thematic harmony. Stick with two or three main colors and make sure they harmonize well. Avoid using too many font styles or sizes; if you do plan to alternate between a few, make sure you use them the same way on every page.

- Use Cascading Style Sheets (CSS) to manage uniform style, and to make it easier to change elements across an entire website without having to go to every individual page.

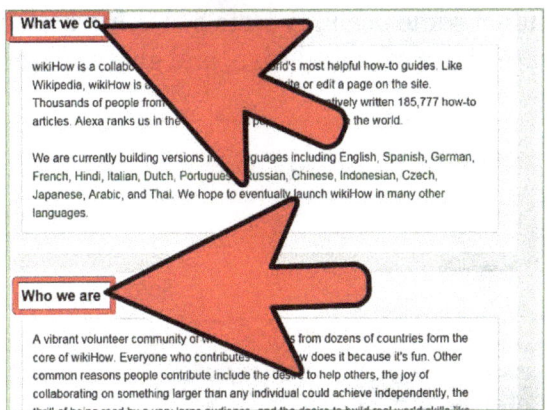

4. Maximize readability. To make your text easier to read, break it into smaller sections. Use subheadings and appropriate spacing to separate each of the sections. Use bold or different-sized fonts to show the hierarchy and importance of the topics.

- Pay attention to text handling. Don't make the font too small, and widen the line spacing to make large blocks of text more readable. Large blocks of text will be harder to read; break these up into smaller paragraphs instead.

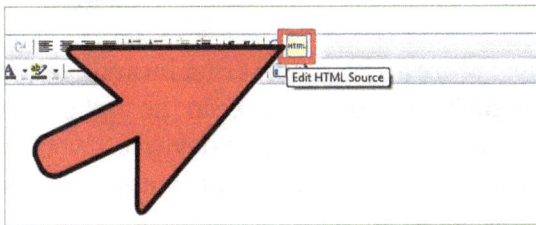

5. Make your website universally readable. Use standard HTML and avoid tags, features, and plug-ins that are only available to one brand or version of a browser.

- Although most modern browsers and computers can handle complex images, everything will be a little snappier if your keep your images smaller in size and optimized for the web. Balance the desire for quality against the need for speed.

6. Test your website. Make sure that every link works as you expect, and that images appear correctly.

- You may want to conduct some usability tests by having members of your target audience test the clarity and ease of use of your design, and give you feedback on your website.

Part 3
Designing for Devices

1. Account for mobile browsing. More and more internet browsing is being done on mobile devices these days. If you want your website to attract and keep the highest number of people, you'll need to design your website to be highly usable on mobile devices. The best thing you can do to ensure this is to have a separate website for mobile users but there are other options as well.

- Look for examples of mobile sites. Often, sticking an "m." in the "www" place in a web address for major websites will bring up the mobile version of the site. You'll need to do something similar.

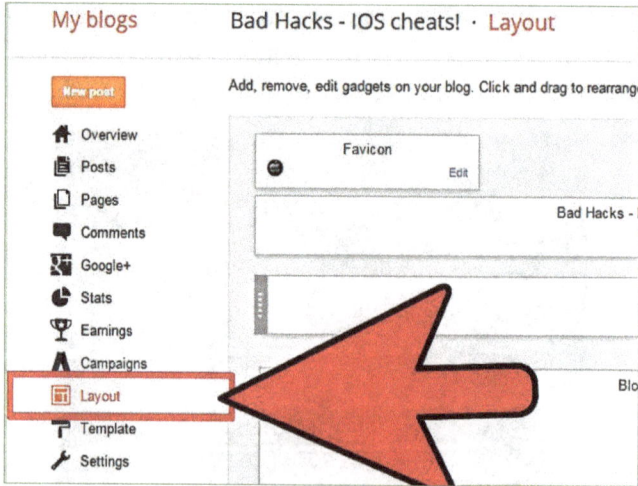

2. Keep your website simple. In general, your design should be simple and to-the-point. Long gone are the days of complex tables and flashing graphics. All users will want something easy to use. This means simple design, minimal columns, and minimal text entry necessary to navigate the site.

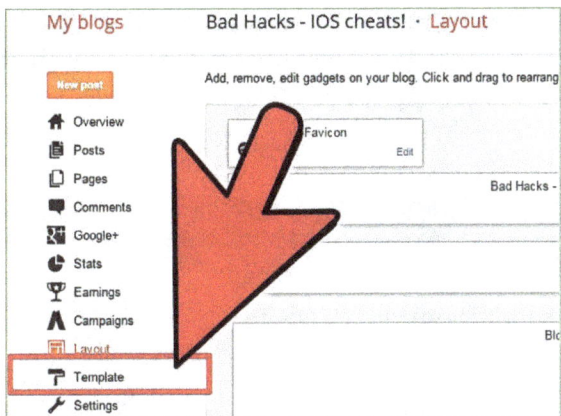

3. Use responsive design. Responsive design is a way of coding your website so that instead of fitting to a few particular sizes of screen, it will adjust to fit any size screen. This is most easily accomplished by setting the column widths to percentages rather than pixels, but more elegant methods also exist.

4. Avoid design features not supported by mobile devices. Many mobile devices can't display things like pop-ups, Flash, Java, or frames. This goes back, again, to wanting to keep your design as simple as possible.

5. Consider making an app. Under certain circumstances it may be easier for you to simply make

an app instead of having a mobile version of your site. You don't have to have amazing programming skills to do this, however! Much like there are providers of website templates, there are also companies which will design a basic app for you. Conduit Mobile is a good service to use.

How to create your First Website

Learn how to design and promote your own website.

Steps

1. Choose a domain name. There are various tools you can use to pick a name if that gets difficult for you. Check out Nameboy.com, makewords.com, and eBay also has some. You can determine if the domain name is available by using sites which can also help you find out if a similar site name has not been registered.

2. Determine what kind of hosting package you will need. Many web hosting companies offer

different packages, some of which are free, which will usually fit almost any web hosting needs. Some popular web hosting companies with low-cost starting packages are:

- GoDaddy.com
- 1&1 Internet Hosting
- HostGator.com
- Hostmonster.com
- BlueHost.com
- DreamHost.com
- and countless other

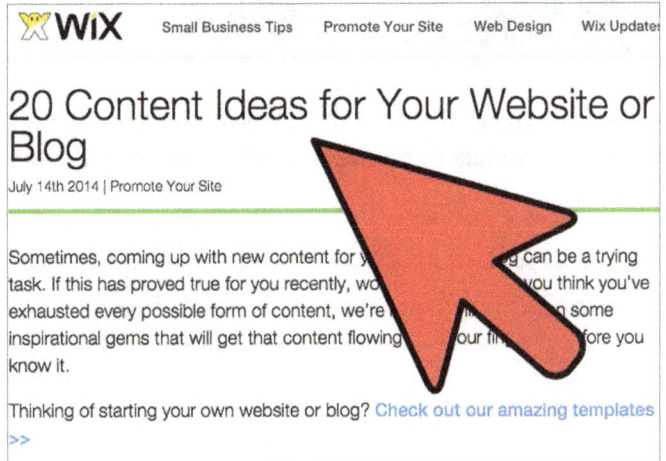

3. Website navigation/ Website content - Make sure your idea for your website is clear. Get a notebook and sketch out what you want the pages to look like and write out as much of the content as you can.

4. You might also want to use a web template to make it easier for you as well if you don't have

time to do it yourself. Some of these are really good and very cheap. Freewebtemplates.com and templatesbox.com.

5. Design your website - Decide what software you're going to use to design your website. Some of the software platforms that you can use to create and edit your websites are:

- Frontpage
- Dreamweaver
- NVU
- Bluefish
- Amaya
- Notepad and Notepad++

6. Text/Graphics and Web buttons - Use Adobe Photoshop to generate a page header for your website. There are websites that can help if you're not a pro at Photoshop. You can use these sites

to generate banner ads, buttons and everything else you need. Check out freebuttons.com, free-buttons.org, buttongenerator.com and flashbuttons.com - You can always use these sites to create advertisement banners for your website.

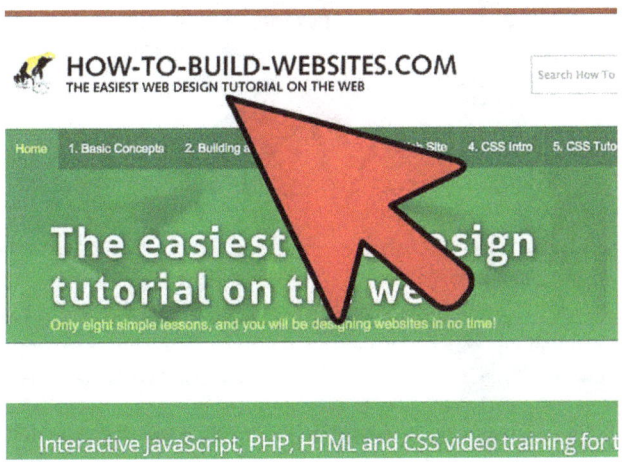

7. Website design and development tools - There are many sites available for learning how to design and develop websites:

- W3Schools Online
- PHPForms.net tutorials
- www.entheosweb.com
- How-to-build-websites.com
- Web Design Tutorials
- About.com
- HTML Help Central Forum

8. Search engine submission - Don't forget try to get it on all the big guys, Google, Yahoo!, MSN, AOL, and Ask.com

9. Their pages will walk you through the submission progress, from adding your sitemap and including your child pages as well. Don't forget to submit to DMOZ and Searchit.com too.

10. Last but not least advertise, you can always use Yahoo or Google Adwords and maintain your own budget.

How to Design a Modern Website

Having a website that executes a strategy in sync with that of your business, has become a vital part of business promotion today. But the focus is no longer solely on putting across the products and services a business offers, but also on their presentation style. The business needs to maintain its rapport on both online and offline platforms.

If you are working on building your business website, it would be a wise call to make it fit for 2014. Designing trends have been changing just as often as the marketing trends. So here are a few tips on how to design a website that is fit for 2014:

Steps

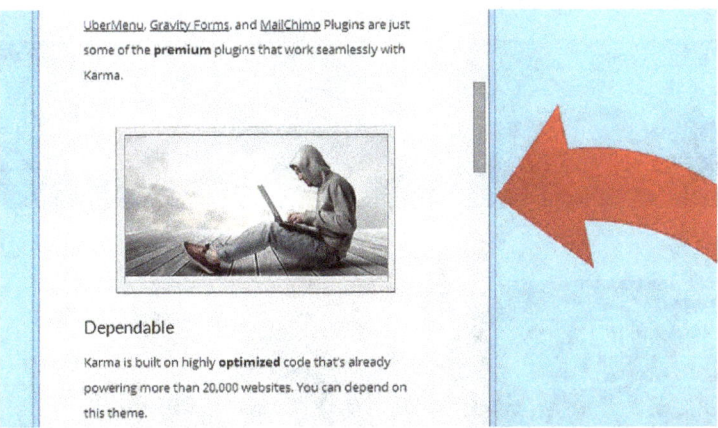

1. Make It Responsive. With an audience that is always on the go, the chances of a website being viewed on a conventional desktop are very less. A website that is solely designed for desktops becomes a pain to access on the mobile devices. A responsive design ensures that when your website is accessed on a mobile device, it delivers the same functionalities in as efficient a manner as it does while being viewed on the desktop.

- With over 20% of web browsing done on mobile devices, you don't want to be missing out on your audience and potential customers just because your business website didn't offer the right call to action functionalities to its viewers.

- Another factor that you need to be taking care of while choosing a theme or a template for your website is its 'retina readiness'. It should be able to support high resolution images that are suited for these.

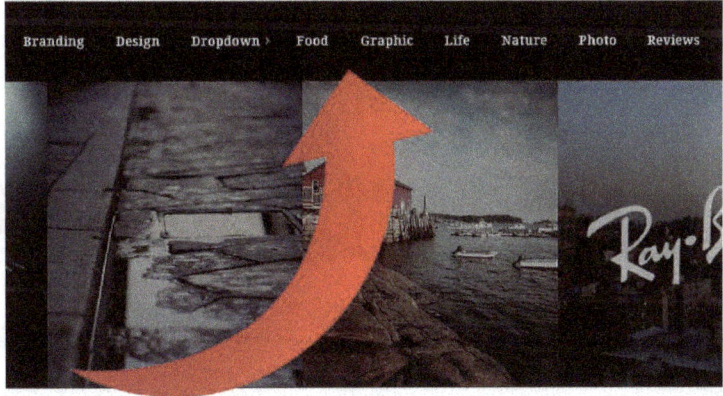

2. Remember, Content Is KING. If you haven't been keeping a tab on what's trending in the digital market, here's what you've missed: Content is the new black; it really is the KING. Your website's performance not just depends on the web design but also on the content in it. A good website keeps the viewer hooked on til all the tabs are explored, but great content makes sure that the viewer keeps coming back for more.

- A constant flow of content is vital to establish a prominent online presence. It ensures constant user engagement thereby guaranteeing more social sharing and higher rankings on the various search engines.

3. Make It Socially Shareable. The growing popularity of social media platforms like Facebook, Twitter etc is stranger to none. The amount of audience that can be driven to your website through these platforms is surprisingly high.

- So while creating your website, take social sharing features into consideration. Most CMSs offer plugins to enable social sharing; all you need to do is activate them and place them at a visible location on your website.

- To make sure your audience stays hooked onto your website, update your social profiles regularly; this ensures a prominent online presence as well.

4. Use Large Images, But Optimize It All! Incorporate a lot of images relevant to your business (and trending in your circles) - they are the most shared post type these days. That's great, but the one thing that most business websites ignore is optimizing these images.

- Make sure all your web content - text, images, audio, video etc - are optimized at all times to ensure a decent load time on all the devices it is viewed on. A load time that exceeds three seconds usually results in greater number of bounce offs.

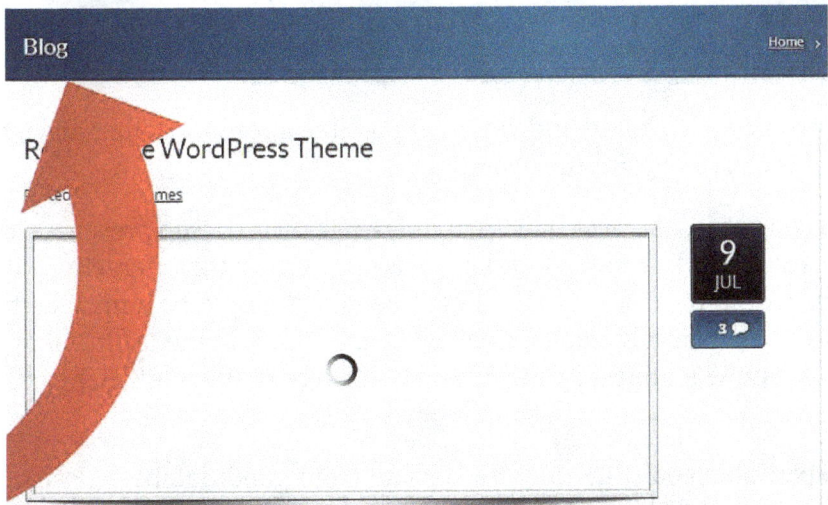

5. Integrate Your Blog. The best way to engage audience on a business website, is to offer them read-worthy content. Adding a blog is a great way to ensure content flow and every article that you add to it gives Google another reason to crawl and index your website better.

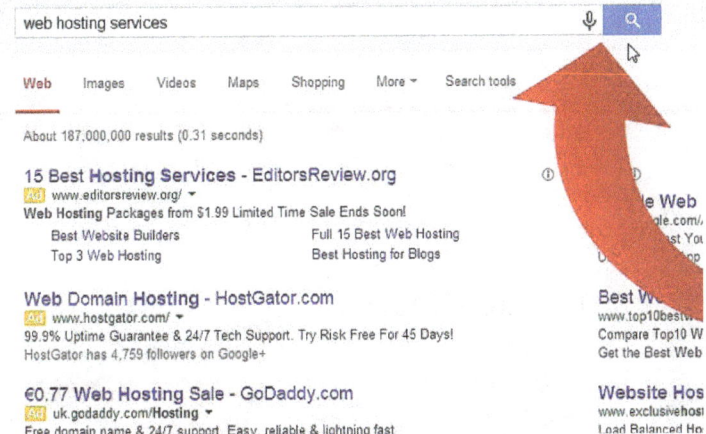

6. Get Your Website Hosted. Once you have all your web content in place, you want it to be easily accessible to all your users at all times. To ensure that, get your website hosted. A webhosting service provider offers web space on its server for you to store all your web content and logs. The server basically serves up your website to the World Wide Web via the Internet in the most efficient manner possible. Depending upon the resources your website needs to run efficiently, you can basically choose from the following hosting plans:

- Shared Hosting
- Dedicated Hosting
- VPS Hosting
- Reseller Hosting
- Cloud Hosting

How to Build a Dynamic Website

The issues of this topic are so broad and varied in possible approaches that any realistic answer to inevitable questions can only point the overall way.

Many people today want and hope to build dynamic (data driven) web presences, the architectures of which readily accommodate new material, revision, and visitor interaction. While the goal of quality projects is within the reach of all diligent people, it would be a mistake to underestimate what in the end is a substantially challenging task, particularly in the technical objects of any prospective project. Even the simplest dynamic web presences require sufficient skills in a variety of disciplines.

In meeting indispensable goals, no one can deviate from good database design. Preparing ourselves in this discipline alone is a substantial (but not a preclusive) body of work. Once we have a summary of project objectives, we must envision sound means of achieving them. Then we have programming languages or tools to choose, based on a vision for ideal project architecture.

Seeing the whole picture from the very beginning then, is the most vital skill of all.

Steps

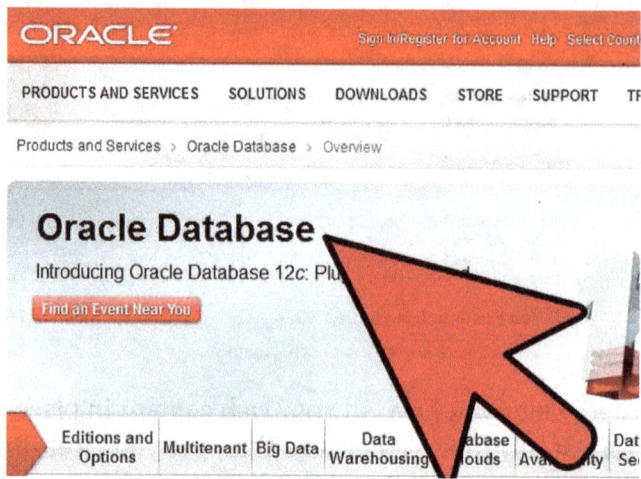

1. Get your brain around what kinds of tools and processes will accomplish your goals. Because the very central core of any dynamic web presence is its database and processing of data, our first vital goal is to make a far-reaching decision on a database engine. It is not a good idea to hope to casually make such a decision in just some seeming, most reasonable initial manner.

   - The vital object of this first decision is to plan our project in a manner (with tools and database engines) which will support your needs all the way down a road through a future, in which, because you made the right initial decisions, you will build effectively upon your initial foundation, efficiently and without eventual obstruction. This means that ideally for instance, the database engine you choose isn't just the easy, or seemingly simple one to deploy today; from the beginning it must be an engine which will support your downstream processing demands.

- Sometimes commercial considerations further affect such choices. What engines are attendance intensive (and costly)? What engines are virtually attendance free in implementations sustaining the processing goals your eventual project must sustain? Generally, the pattern to follow is to select your engine based on one of two possible dispositions.

- To do so, you must first chart out your basic table needs. A professional won't even need to build this map (regardless even if hundreds or thousands of tables are involved), because they will usually immediately see whether the architecture and future needs you will need to support are either read or write intensive. You will then choose an appropriate database, based on this overall disposition, and perhaps further based on personal taste and experience, as working with respective software development tools may predicate. MySQL is the usual choice for read intensive implementations. Many developers look to databases such as PostgreSQL for reliable write intensive implementations. We develop our dispositions toward such vital tools by careful research, and by drawing on the pool of experience of the general software development industry. Expense can generally be avoided, because free deployments of very good tools are available. What we're looking for is performance in either read or write intensive environments, reliability, ease and minimization of administration, and ready integration with prospective software development tools.

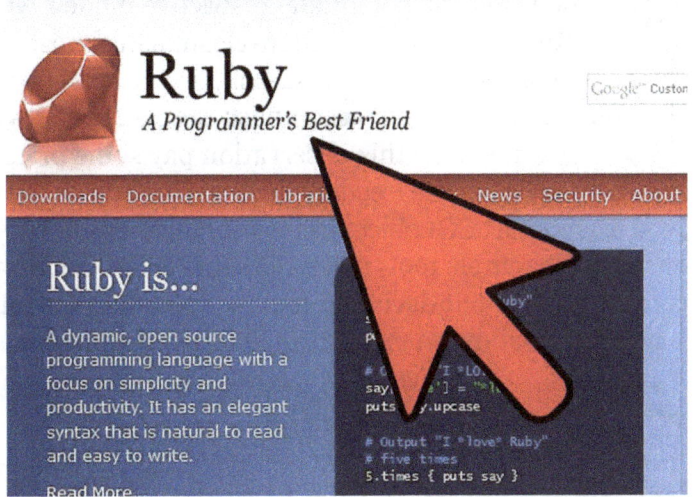

2. Choose your software development tools. There are two patterns to consider in choosing software development tools. Purportedly "easy" tools are rarely in fact easy, when a project inevitably breaks the cast of the development and functionality patterns "easy" tools are generally limited to. Should you want to do something beyond the "easy" tools such as incorporate a language or translation parameter in dynamically generated URLS, it may be so much more difficult to accomplish in the "easy" tools that it may take extremely sophisticated programming skills to as much as trick the easy pattern into doing more complex things. We must master our tools to build good projects. This does not make easy tools the best choice, or the most sophisticated tools a difficult proposition. The trap of "easy" development generally comprises limitations which become very costly to overcome in the inevitable evolution of projects. A huge variety of such tools generally arises, ostensibly meeting such needs. But the pattern of the tools' persistence betrays an ostensible fact of having accomplished this goal; and so, generally we find that the most sophisticated and powerful tools, following good patterns (or availability of objects and libraries), not only alleviate practically

inevitable obstructions to easy tools, but likewise then make "getting there" a far more straightforward process. When we examine the scope of available tools, generally less comprehensive models are presented in initial development concepts, and better concepts are offered by later arising tools (or they wouldn't have a chance to survive in markets which have already been won). If we choose a purportedly easy tool then, what we're looking for is a development pattern which is both wieldy and without eventual obstruction. The paradox for the neophyte then is the difficulty of seeing so far down the road that we can perceive programming obstructions to a given tool set. Some people believe the best tools are the most powerful and the least restrictive in terms of project approach. Freedom to develop what you want and need often means breaking the general model of ostensibly simple tools then, the challenges of which can practically break the brain of the most seasoned and sophisticated software engineer, because succeeding in such an object means making the "simple" model do something it may have no native capacity for supporting. Is "Ruby" for instance really an easier tool than fundamental C++ or C#? No. Not really, especially if you have to break the simple model of Ruby to deliver vital functionality. Like Ruby, GCC is free for Linux and OSX. Ruby also comes on OSX — you just have to discover it on your system. Of the purportedly easier tools, my personal choice is Ruby. Of the truly sophisticated tools, C++ and C# will reign supreme long into the future; and the truth is, these are the only vehicles for development without obstruction. So sit up straight and brace for serious study, because regardless the road you choose, you are going to have to master not only your tools, but the potentially restrictive models which those tools might eventually encumber you with. Ruby is probably far more clean than almost all its "easy" peers. C++ is the tool of unencumbered excellence; and in fact, seasoned gurus will turn out peerless projects probably with far less difficulty than they might accomplish the same goals with a purportedly easy tool. In the end, developers who stray from this observation pay some price: either pick the most conducive "easy" tool, or worry less over the freedom from encumbrance in the most sophisticated tool. In the latter case, you master Fast CGI objects, take the ball and run. Huge concepts are implemented often with little code. Yes, simple tools make the same claim, but by abstracting ostensible difficulty away from us in such ways that deviating from their usually singular pattern poses very difficult engineering challenges, in addition to performance handicaps which C++ resolves.

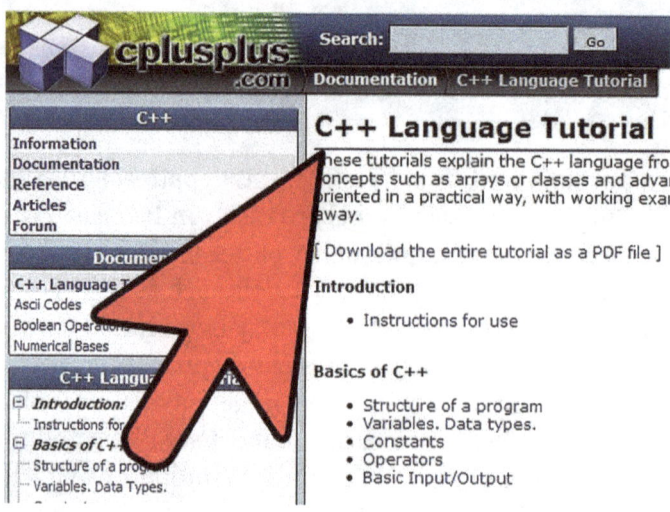

3. In the course of resolving these questions, we inevitably have to examine the basic models or patterns of developing projects of the nature we desire to turn out. This means grabbing the best literature for tools we want to compare, and at least giving our concept some form in which it might

take in a given set of tools, as compared to others. Before you choose Ruby for instance, you might pick up vital books such as "The Ruby Programming Language," and "Agile Web Development with Rails." Your initial study must not only sufficiently master the tools, it must envision how you can get there — how you can provide desired functionality with the tool you might choose. This is a daunting task for the initiate. If you are going to compare a purportedly easy development environment to the best of the best, you're going to have to evaluate the best C tools as well. If you're really going to be a seasoned engineer, you're going to pick C for its freedom from limitation. Is C really more difficult? No. Syntax is syntax. In the end, you have to master expressing the same functionality; and in truth, the C family of languages is excellent. The difficult thing about excelling right out the gate in C++ is putting your hands on the models you might need to build upon. An excellent start from practically 15 years ago was the original FastCGI components which were available in Borland's CPPBuilder — probably still the best C++ for Windows. Even C initiates can go far with such object oriented approaches, because the general model of sustaining functionality is built into the very things you work with. Your work is far more free-flowing than it can be in Ruby for instance, whenever you might break or exceed the Ruby model in your approach. On the other hand, Rails scaffolding techniques expedite much work for the neophyte, if and only if the project fits the general mold of Ruby and Rails. Introduce rudimentary security provisions for instance, recognized in all your Ruby interfaces however, and the next thing you know, you're re-writing a thousand lines of auto-generated Ruby code for every table your application negotiates. Is that easy? Well, I do it with a Windows editor called NoteTab Pro, operating on Ruby projects residing on an OSX system; and sophisticated macros make my revisions in perhaps a second, customizing a thousand lines of code into almost twice that. Still, this relates to relatively simple, basic functionality, which a project is restricted to. The fact is, in C++ we can write our own objects which handle these tasks truly universally — you'd never even have to replicate this process. So these are the trade-offs. In the end, object oriented C is the most powerful and efficient. Which means it's the least work as well.

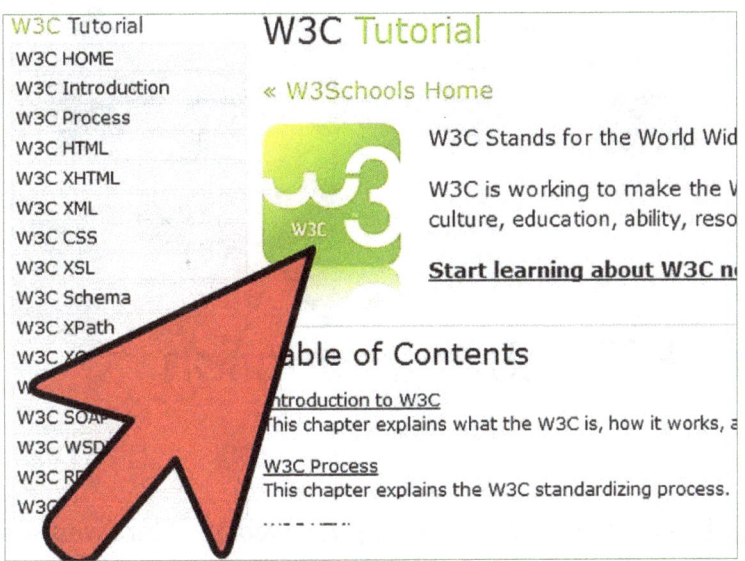

4. No matter your choice of programming tools, there is no way to avoid dependence upon a reasonable mastery of HTML and CSS. Generally, seasoned developers rely on W3C.org for vital material.

How to Design a Responsive Website

Responsive web design is an approach for making websites that can accommodate different screen sizes and resolutions various kinds of devices, in order to provide optimal viewing experience for all users. This topic shows a few of the many available techniques for building a responsive website.

Steps

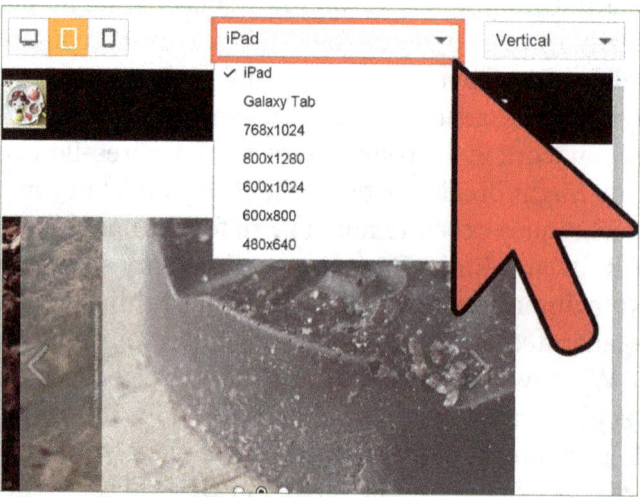

1. Research your website's target audience. Although you could try to make your website respond to all devices in all conditions, this is probably a waste of time and money.

2. Enhance the mobile aspects first when making the website. Start with a design approach for mobile devices. To achieve this, use simple HTML and CSS with less of Javascript, since there are many mobile devices which don't support Javascript.

- Add viewport meta tag using the code as shown: <meta name="viewport" content="width=device-width, initial-scale=1.0"/>

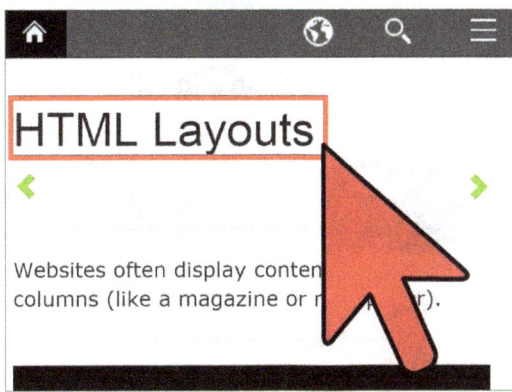

3. Use progressive enhancement. Progressive enhancement uses web technologies in a layered fashion enabling everyone to access the basic content and functionality of a web page, using any browser or Internet connection, while also providing an enhanced version of the page to those with more advanced browser software or greater bandwidth. Now you have a basic website that will work fine for all devices.

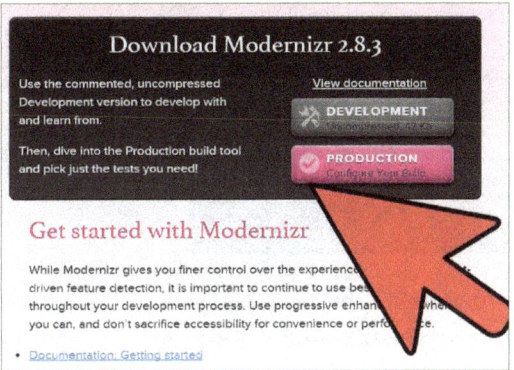

4. Enhance the website's features.

- Use frameworks: Javascript Frameworks: Modernizr, jQuery Mobile, Polyfills.
- Use mobile validators or emulators for validating and checking your website design.

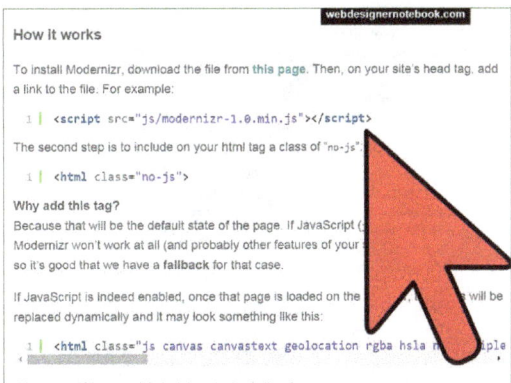

5. Check for cross browser compatibility. With so many browsers available, it is very important to make a website that loads evenly on all the browsers.

- Use Modernizr and Polyfill for identical rendering on different web-browsers.
- Modernizr is a feature detecting JS .We can add fallbacks for features unavailable.The image show code snippet for detecting canvas support .

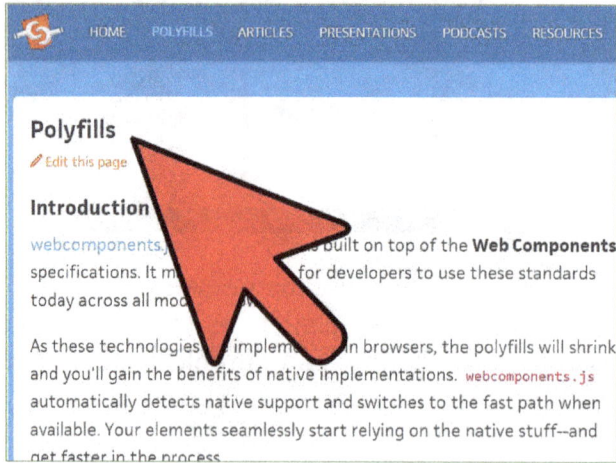

6. Use Polyfills to add feature to the browser if it's not present. As IE versions below IE8 do not recognize new HTML5 elements, use HTML5SHIV.js which includes all the new elements.

How to make a Free Website

Plenty of people have their own website. So how can you join in on the fun, and maybe even make some money while doing it? A free website-making service will allow you to create a website quickly and have it live on the web in just a few minutes.

Part 1
Finding a Service

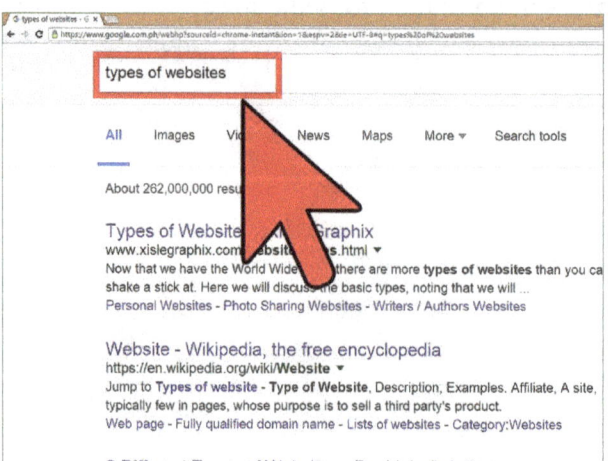

1. Ask yourself what kind of website you want to have. The needs of your website will dictate what

kind of hosting service you should be looking for. If you intend to do business through your website, you'll need to make sure that the host supports online stores. If you want to create a website, there are a variety of free website hosts that specialize in creating and maintaining websites. If you want a blog, blogging sites can get you set up in just a few minutes.

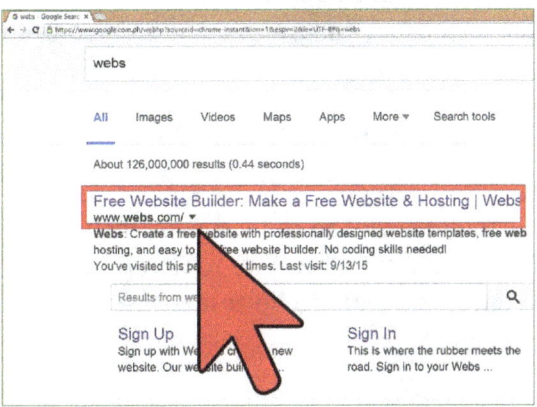

2. Find a free online website-building service. There are a lot of options out there; some great, some poor, some cheap, some expensive; so it's worth spending some time comparing features. Most offer limited services for free sites and typically place advertisements on your site. Your website will most likely also be a subdomain of the host site instead of its own site (e.g. yoursite.host.com instead of yoursite.com). Some of the more popular free hosting sites include:

- Wordpress; great for blogs, small to medium-sized websites of all kinds
- Drupal; great for medium to large-sized websites
- Webs
- Angelfire
- Google Sites
- Webnode
- Wix

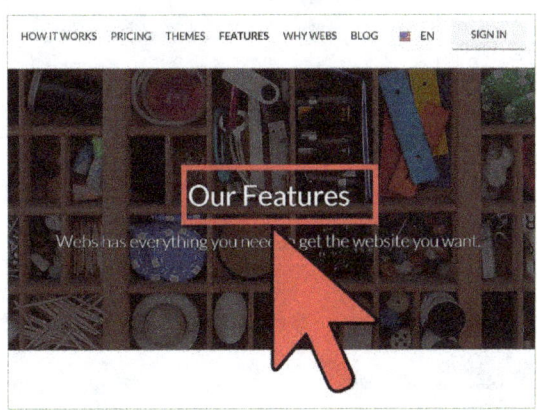

3. Compare service features. Each host will offer different services at the free level. Most hosts have

a limit on how much data you can upload for your webpage, and this is typically very limited. This means that if you intend to have a media-rich site with images and video, you may not be able to effectively use a free site.

- Different free hosts have different policies regarding creating online stores. If you intend to create an e-commerce website, ensure that the service you pick can adequately support your goals.

- Most free hosts have low bandwidth limits as well. This means they don't work very well as file hosts, as downloading files can quickly max your data allowance.

- Check to see if the host allows you to upload your own websites. Most free services have web page creation tools and don't allow you to upload your own custom code. This works for most basic needs, but if you want to be able to create your own site, make sure that the host allows it.

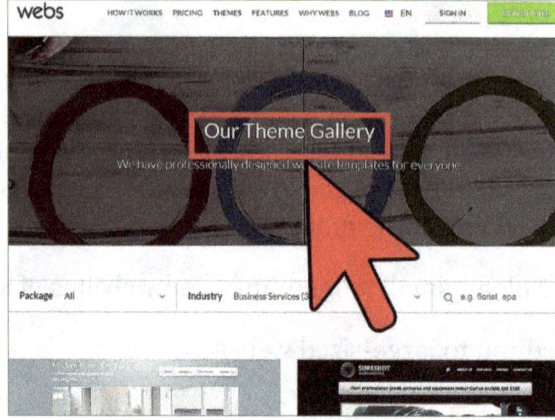

4. Choose a theme that suits you or your business. Browse through the available pre-made themes (sometimes called 'templates' or 'styles'); you can use the software's own available themes, as well as browse theme-selling marketplace websites like Theme Forrest.

- Many hosts have specialized designs for their sites that help maintain a brand identity with that host. Find the design that fits your website's needs the most.

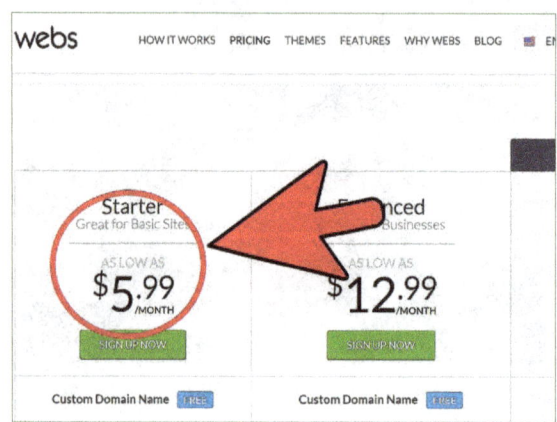

5. Consider how much it will cost you. Even if the service is for free, the business has to make

money to provide it to you; it might use adverts, or it might try to entice you to upgrade to get more features, which might come at a significant monthly cost. Whichever one you choose, make sure you know how much it might cost in the future if you decide to upgrade to get more features.

Part 2
Creating a Site

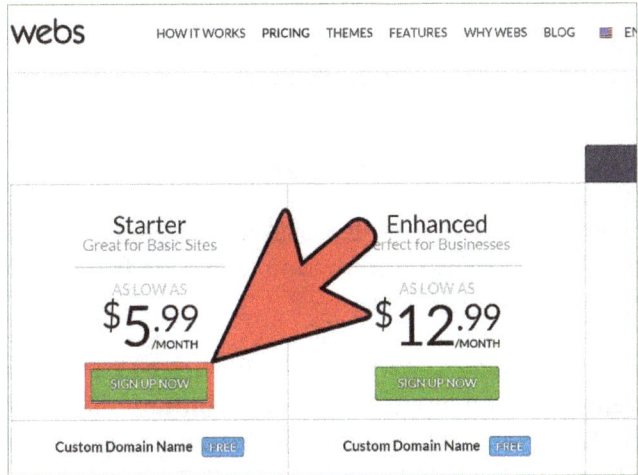

1. Sign up for an account. All free website hosts will require that you create an account. Depending on the service, you may not need to add any billing information unless you plan on upgrading to a paid account.

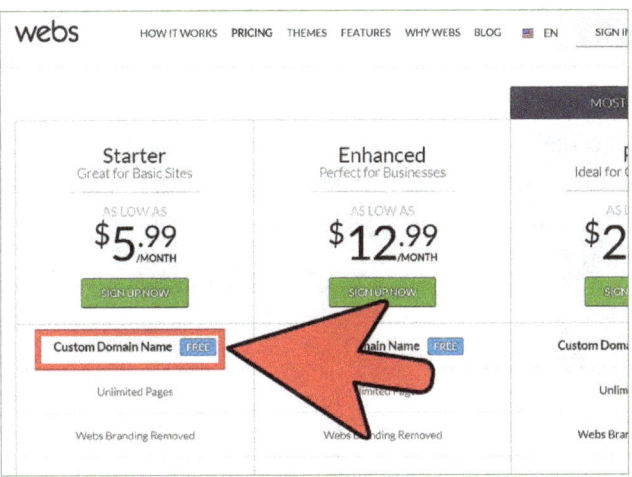

2. Choose and purchase a suitable available domain name. Free websites typically allow you to create a subdomain on the host's domain for free, and offer regular domains for a fee. Some free hosts allow you to connect a domain you already own to their free host.

- You can buy top-level domain names (www.yoursitename.com) for yearly fees, and then connect that domain name to your free site. Be sure to check that your service allows this. Domain registration companies include GoDaddy, Register.com, Domain.com, Dyn.com, and many more.

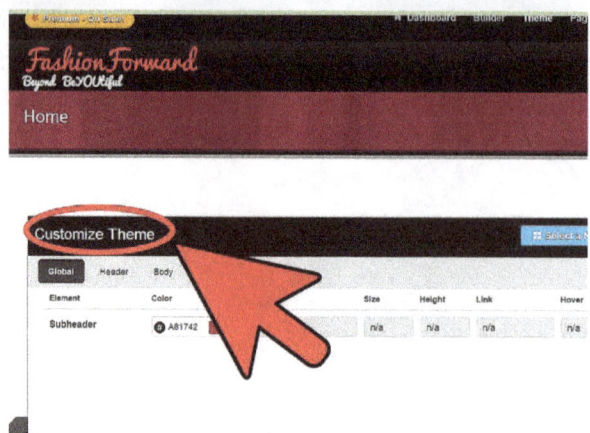

3. Design your website. Almost all free website hosts have web site construction programs available through their website. These programs allow you to choose from pre-made themes, and some allow you to customize elements such as CSS.

- Web page construction programs allow you to add your text and images with minimal fuss and have a functioning website up in a very short amount of time. Many let you simply drag and drop images into the site. Most require little to no coding experience.

- Most free websites provide the tools to create your website online, without the need to download any editing programs. Since you are creating the site through their service, you won't need to worry about using FTP programs and cPanel to upload content to your site.

- Most services offer a variety of tutorials to help get your site up and running as quickly as possible.

- If your web host allow it, you can upload your own HTML files to truly create your own custom website. To learn more about HTML coding, check out this guide. If you want to upload your own site, you will need to use an FTP program in order to access the server.

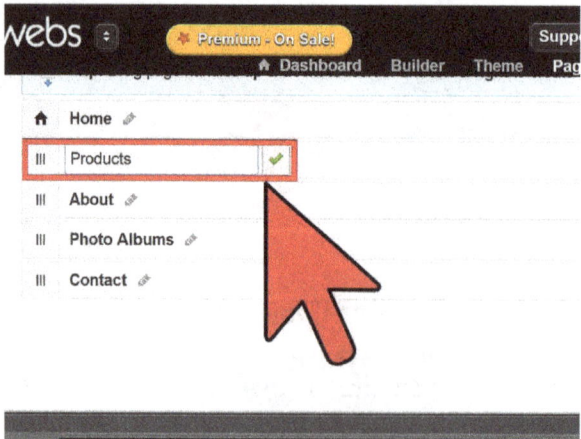

4. Add valuable content. You might need to tell your audience what you do or sell, why you do it (the story behind the business), how to contact you, and so on. Also plan ahead for fresh new content you'd like to add in the future.

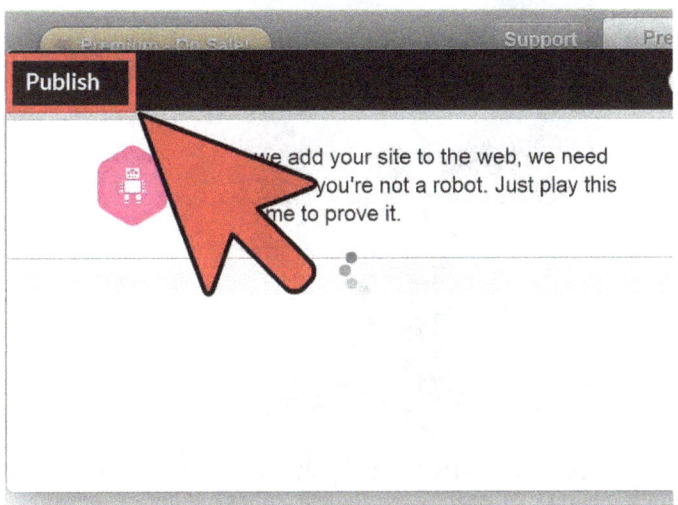

5. Publish your site. Once you are happy with the layout and content of your site, it's time to open up for business! If you have a blog or announcement area, it's a good idea to create a welcome/introduction post, explaining the purpose of the site and introducing yourself. This will help make readers feel more welcome when they visit the site, and give them a quick breakdown of what the site is for.

Part 3

Growing your Site

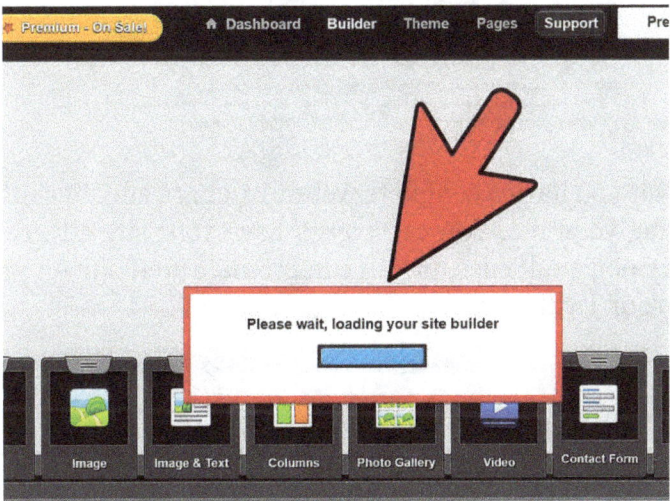

1. Continue to create content. Websites that consistently put out new and useful content will get visited much more often than sites that stagnate. Do your best to produce engaging content that brings the reader back for more. Stick to an update schedule so readers can get used to when new content will be available.

- The number one way to increase traffic to your site is to consistently create good, engaging, original content. This will drive more viewers your way, and help to retain the viewers you already have.

2. To generate a passive income, place advertising on your site. Check with your host to see if this is allowed, because many free hosts do not support ad revenue going to you when you are using free services. Placing ads on your site can help you monetize it, but may also deter people from reading your content if the ads are too intrusive.

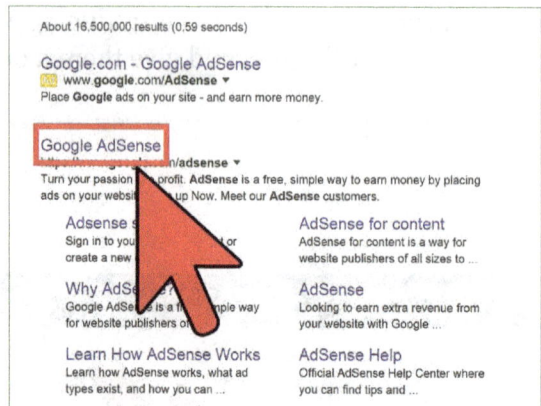

3. Market your site. Once you have a complete website and are adding content on a regular basis, you can start advertising your site. You can pay to have your site advertised on other websites through programs like Google AdSense, or you can promote your site on your own through social media such as Facebook or Twitter.

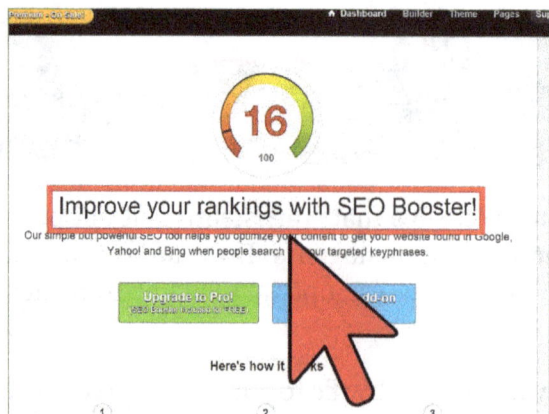

4. Search engine-optimise (SEO) your website. You can start by submitting your site to search

engines. Search engines crawl the web, matching content on websites with users' searches. To really start attracting large numbers of people to your site, you'll want to submit it to all the major search engines. The process varies depending on the search engine, but almost all will require you to create a sitemap of your website first.

- For Google, you can choose to just submit your site's URL, or you can submit the entire sitemap for more optimized searches.

- For Yahoo! Bing, you can submit just the URL, or submit your sitemap in a variety of different ways. Sitemaps should be in the XML format.

How to Learn HTML

HTML is the abbreviation for Hyper Text Markup Language, and is the code, or *language* that is used for the creation of basic website layouts. It can look a little daunting if you've never done any coding before, but all you need to try it out is an ordinary text editing application and an internet browser. You might even recognize some HTML used to change text in online forums, customized online profiles. HTML is a useful tool for anyone who uses the internet, and learning the basics may take you less time than you think.

Part 1

Learning Basic HTML

1. Open an HTML document. Most text editing programs, including Notepad or Notepad++ for Windows, TextEdit for Mac, and gedit for GNU/Linux can be used to write HTML documents. Open a new document and use File → Save As in the top menu to save it as a "Web Page," or to change the file extension to ".html" instead of ".doc," ".rtf," or any other extension.

- You may see a warning that your document will be changed to "plain text" instead of "rich text," or that special formatting and images won't be saved properly. This is fine; HTML documents do not use those options.

94 | Web Designing

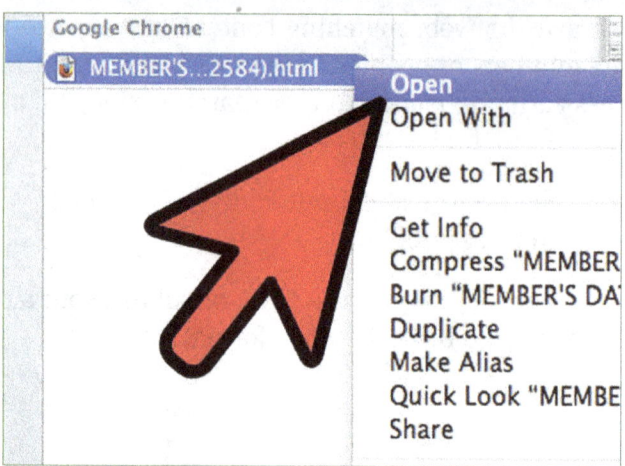

2. View your document with an internet browser. Save your blank document, then find the document icon in your computer and double click to open it. It should open as a blank web page in your browser. If it doesn't, drag the file icon to the URL (address) bar of your browser. As you edit your HTML document in this tutorial, you can keep checking back and seeing how your web page changes.

- Note that this does not actually create a website online. It will not be accessible by other people, and you do not need an internet connection to test out. This just uses a browser to "read" your HTML document as though it were a website.

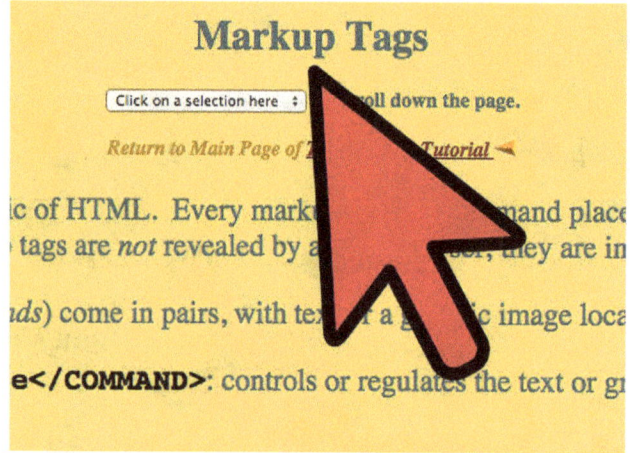

3. Understand markup tags. Markup tags do not show up on a web page like normal text. Instead, they tell your web browser how to display the page and its content. The "start tag" contains instructions. For example, it might tell the browser to display text as bold. You also need an "end tag" to let the browser know where the instructions apply: in this example, all text between the start tag and the end tag will be bold. Write end tags inside angle brackets as well, but start with a slash after the first bracket.

- Write start tags in between angle brackets: <start tag goes here>
- Write end tags in between angle brackets, but put a slash after the first bracket: </end tag goes here>)

- Keep reading to learn how to write functional markup tags. For this step, all you need to remember is the basic format they are written in: < > and </ >
- If you are using other HTML tutorials as well, you might see them refer to the tags as "elements" and the text in between start and end tags as "element content."

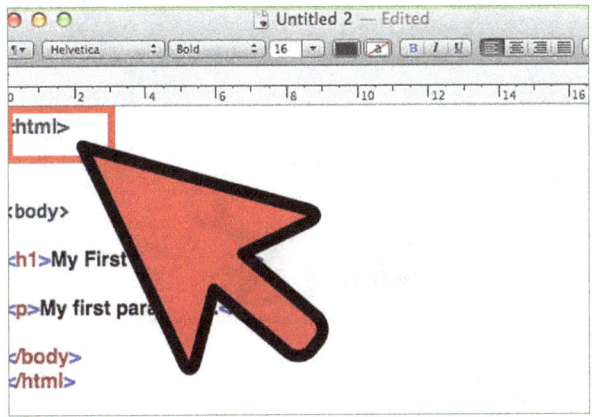

4. Write your first <html> tag. Every html document starts with a <html> tag and ends with a </html> tag. This tells the browser that everything between these tags is in HTML. Add these tags to your document:

- Often, HTML files are started with a <!DOCTYPE html> line that indicates that the file as a whole should be read as a HTML file by browsers. It isn't needed, but may help resolve compatibility issues.
- Write <html> at the top of your document.
- Hit enter or return several times to give yourself some space, then write **</html>**
- Remember to write *everything* else in this tutorial in between these two tags.

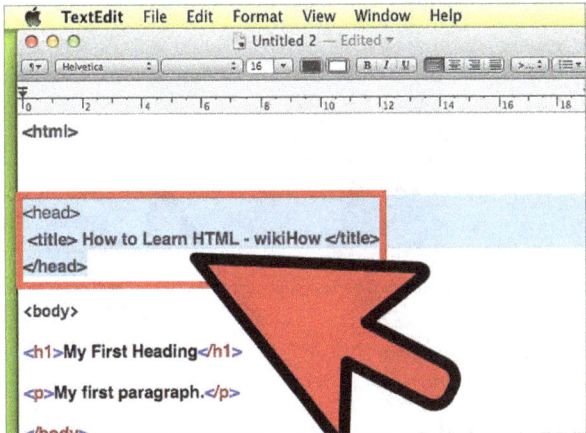

5. Fill out the <head> portion of your document. In between the <html> and </html> tags, write a <head> start tag and a </head> end tag. Give yourself space to write between them. Everything in between these head tags won't actually be displayed on the page itself. Try the following and see where it shows up instead:

- In between the <head> and </head> tags, write <title> and </title>
- In between the <title> and </title> tags, write How to Learn HTML
- Save the document and open it in a browser (or save the document, then refresh the browser page if it's already open.) Do you see what you wrote at the top of the browser, above the address bar?

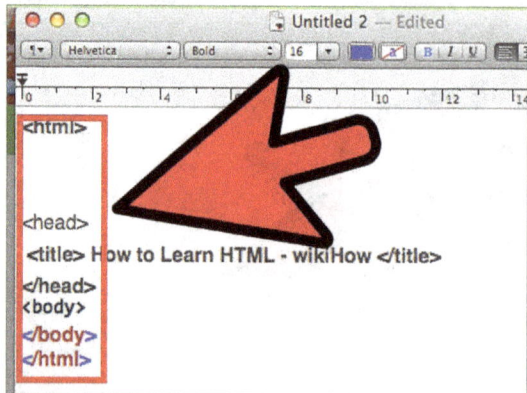

6. Create a <body> section. Everything else in this beginner document will go in a body section, which actually gets displayed on the web page. *After* the </head> end tag, but *before* the </html> tag, write <body> and </body>. For the rest of this tutorial, everything you write will go in between these body tags. You should now have a document that looks like this (ignoring the bullet points):

- <html>
- <head>
- <title>How to Learn HTML
- </head>
- <body>
- </body>
- </html>

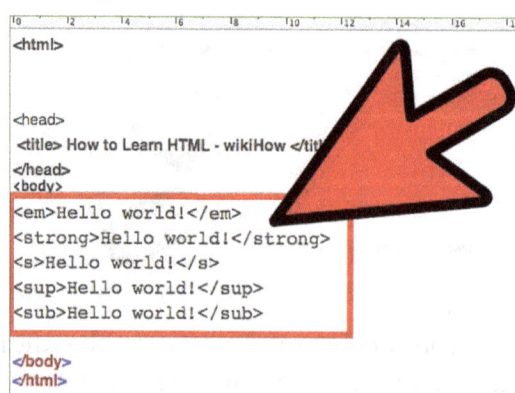

7. Add text in various styles. Now it's time to write something you can actually see in your browser.

Anything you write within the body tags will show up in your browser after you save the HTML document and refresh the browser page. *Don't* write anything with the < or > symbols, however, since your browser will try to interpret it as an HTML instruction instead of normal text. Try writing Hello world! (or anything else you like), then add these new tags around it and see what happens each time:

- `<em>Hello world!</em>` will show up as "emphasized text:" *Hello world*.
- `<strong>Hello world!</strong>` will show up as "strong text:" Hello world.
- `<s>Hello world!</s>` will show up with a strikethrough: Hello world.
- `<sup>Hello world!</sup>` will show up as superscript: Hello world.
- `<sub>Hello world!</sub>` will show up as subscript: Hello world.
- **Try combinations of these:** `What does <em><strong>Hello world!</strong></em> look like?`

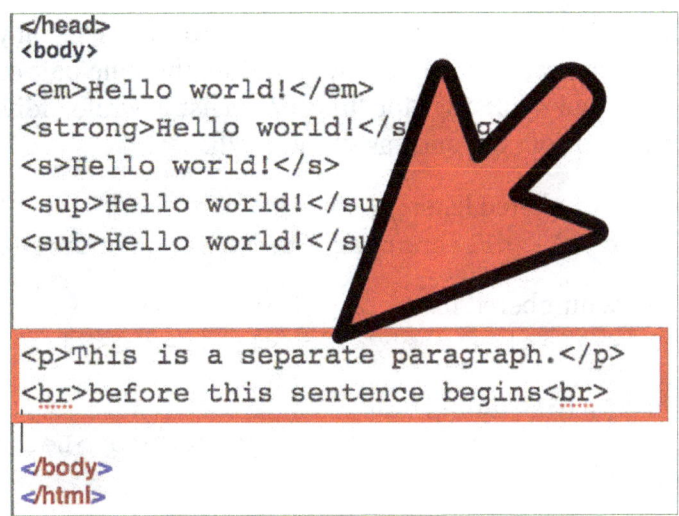

8. Divide your text into paragraphs. If you try to write several lines of text in your HTML document, you might notice that the line breaks don't show up in your browser. You have to code these in yourself:

- `<p>This is a separate paragraph.</p>`
- `This sentence is followed by a line break.<br>before this sentence begins.`

    This is the first tag you've seen that doesn't need an end tag! These are called "empty tags."

- Make headings to display the names of sections:

    `<h1>header text</h1>`: the largest header

    `<h2>header text</h2>` (the 2nd level header)

    `<h3>header text</h3>` (the 3rd level header)

```
<h4>header text</h4> (the 4th level header)

<h5>header text</h5> (the smallest header)
```

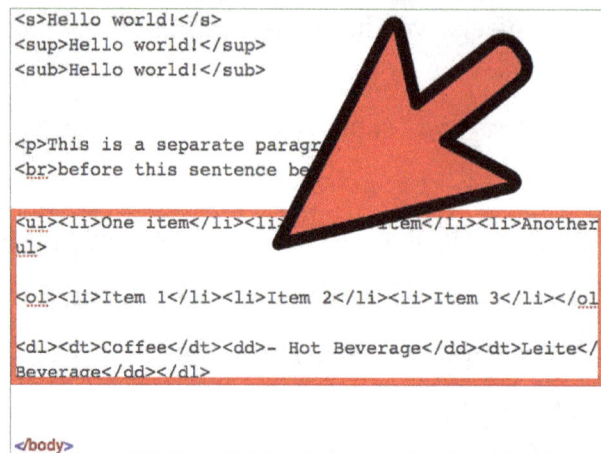

9. Learn how to make lists. There are several different ways to write lists on your webpage. Try out the following types of code and see which one you like. Note that one pair of tags goes around the whole list (such as the <ul> and </ul> tags for "unordered list"), while individual items on the list are surrounded by another pair of tags, such as <li>and</li>.

- Use this code to make bulleted lists:
  ```
  <ul><li>One item</li><li>Another item</li><li>Another item</li></ul>
  ```

- Or this code to make numbered lists:
  ```
  <ol><li>Item 1</li><li>Item 2</li><li>Item 3</li></ol>
  ```

- Or this code to make a list defining terms:
  ```
  <dl><dt>Coffee</dt><dd>- Hot Beverage</dd><dt>Leite</dt><dd>- Cold Beverage</dd></dl>
  ```

10. Spruce up your page with line breaks, horizontal lines, and images. Now it's time to try adding things besides text to your page. Try out the following tags, or click the links for more information. You'll need to use an online image hosting service so you have a URL to link to in the image tag:

- Insert a Line in HTML: `<br>` or `<hr>`
- Add images: `<img src="your_image_url">`

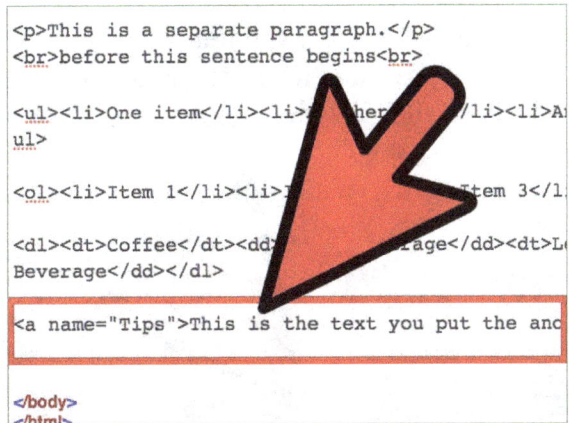

11. Link to other places on the page. You can also use this code to link to other pages and websites, but for now, since you may not have a web site yet, we'll focus on "anchors," or specific places on the page that you can link to:

- First make an anchor with the `<a>` tag at the point on the page that you want to link to. Name it something descriptive and easy to remember.:
  `<a name="Tips">This is the text you put the anchor around.</a>`
- Use the `<href>` to link to those anchors or to another webpage:
  `<a href="url of webpage, or name of anchor within this page">Write the text or image that will be displayed as a link here.</a>`
- To link to an anchor on a different web page, add the # sign after the URL, followed by the name of the anchor.

Part 2

Learning more Advanced HTML

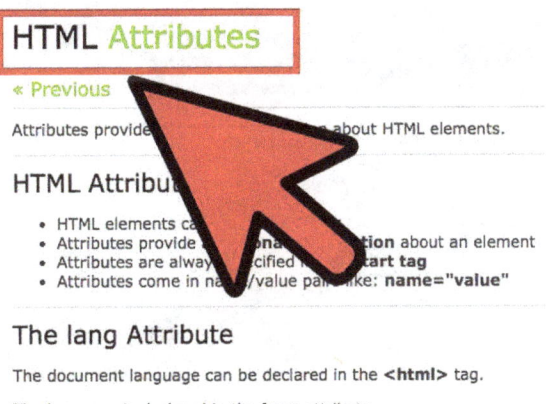

1. Learn about attributes. Attributes are placed within the tag itself, making additional alterations

to the "element content" between the start and end tag. They never stand alone. They are written in the format name="value", where name is the name of the attribute (for instance "color"), and value describes this specific instance (for instance "red").

- You've actually seen attributes before, if you followed the tutorial in the basic HTML section. <img> tags use the src attribute, anchors use the name attribute, and links use the href attribute. See how those all follow the ____= "____" format?

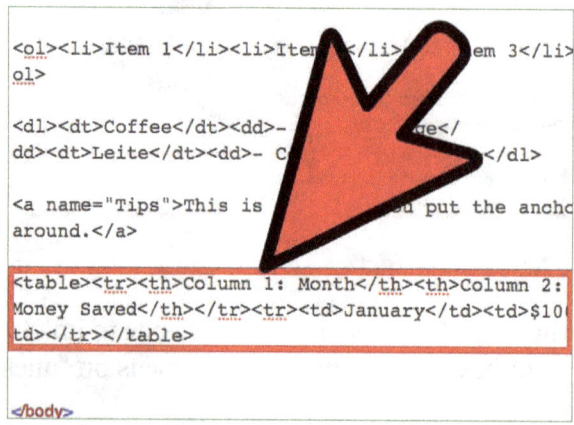

2. Experiment with HTML tables. Making a table, or chart, requires several different tags. Play with these tags, or learn about HTML tables in more detail.

- Start with table tags around the entire table:<table></table>
- Row tags around the contents of each row: <tr>
- Column headers in the first row: <th>
- Cells in subsequent rows: <td>
- Here's an example of how it all fits together:
  <table><tr><th>Column 1: Month</th><th>Column 2: Money Saved</th></tr><tr><td>January</td><td>$100</td></tr></table>

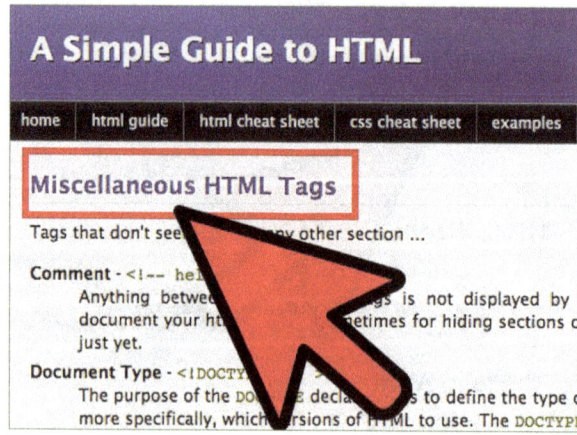

3. Learn the miscellaneous head tags. You've already learned the <head> tag, which shows up at the start of each document. Besides the <title> tag, it can include the following types of tags:

- Meta tags, which are used to provide *metadata* about a web page. This data can be used by search engines when the robot scours the internet to locate and list websites. To make your website more visible on search engines, use one or more <meta> start tags (no end tags necessary), each with exactly one name attribute and one content attribute, for example: <meta name="description" content="write a description here">; or <meta name="keywords" content="write a list of keywords, each separated by a comma">

- <link> tags are used to associate other files with the page. This is mainly used to link to CSS stylesheets, which are made using a different type of coding to alter your HTML page by adding color, aligning your text, and many other things.

- <script> tags are used to link the page to JavaScript files, which can cause the page to change as the user interacts with it.

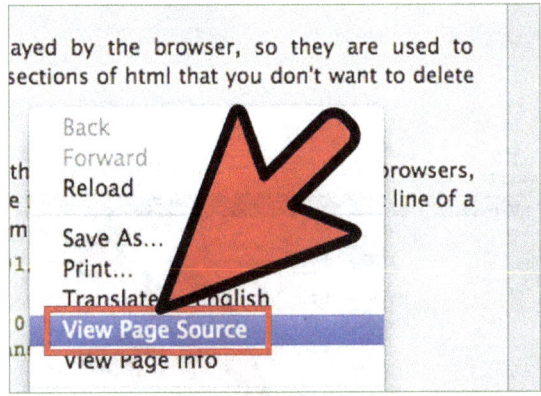

4. Play around with HTML found on websites. A great way to expand your knowledge is by looking into the HTML source of webpages. You can do this by right clicking the page and selecting "View Source," "View Page Source," or a similar option, or by going to the *View* section in the top menu of your browser. Try to figure out what each unfamiliar HTML tag does, or look it up online for the answer.

- While you cannot edit other people's web sites, you can copy the HTML you find into your own document, then play with it to see what different options do. Note that, without the CSS stylesheet that website links to, you may not be able to see all of the colors or formatting.

5. Learn more advanced web design from comprehensive guides. There are various resources on the internet that you can use to learn about many more HTML tags, such as W3Schools or

Codecademy. You may also find books with tutorials about HTML, but make sure you use one that was published within the last couple years, since there are occasional updates and changes. Better yet, learn CSS to have much more control over your web page's layout and appearance. Once you have CSS down, the next step for web designers is typically Javascript.

How to create CSS

A Cascading Style Sheet (CSS) is a system for website coding that allows designers to manipulate several features at once by assigning certain elements to groups. For instance, by using a code for the website background, designers can change the background color or image on all pages of the website with one change to the CSS file. Here's how to create CSS for a basic website.

Part 1

Writing Inline CSS

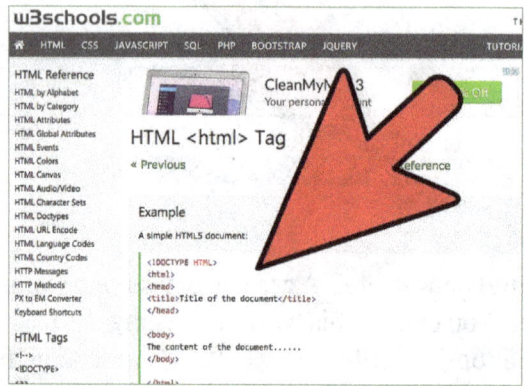

1. Be sure you have a basic understanding of HTML tags. You should know how tags work and of the src and href attributes.

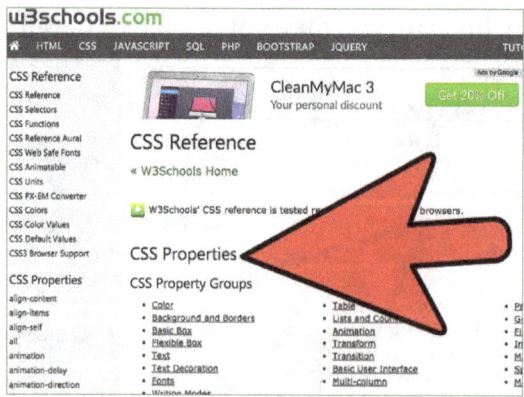

2. Learn some of the basic CSS properties. You will find that there are very many properties. However, it is not necessary to learn them all.

- Some good basic CSS properties to know are color and font-family.

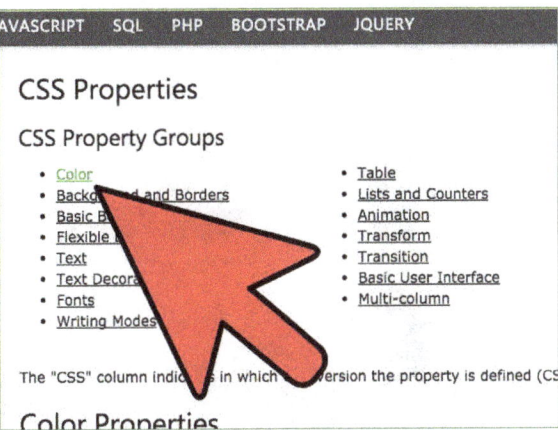

3. Learn about values for each respective property. All properties need a value. For the color property, for example, you might put the red value.

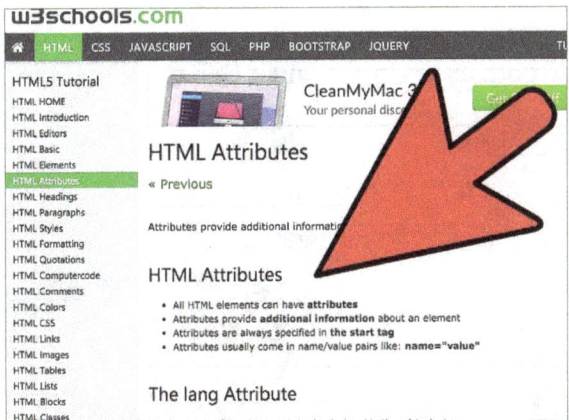

4. Learn about the style HTML attribute. It is used within an element like href or src. To use it, within the quotation marks after the equal sign, put the CSS attribute, a colon, and then the value of the property. This is known as a CSS rule.

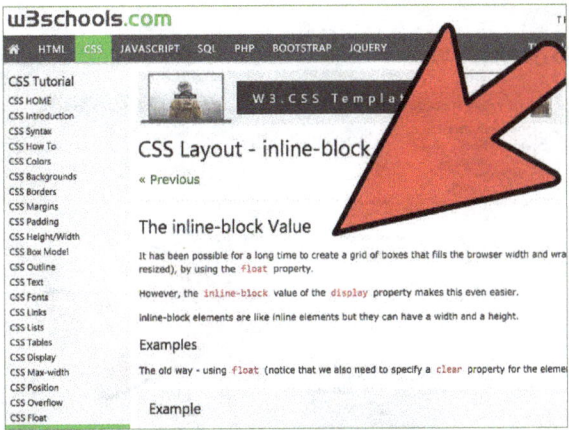

5. Understand that inline CSS is not usually used for websites by professional web developers. Inline CSS can add unnecessary clutter to an HTML document. However, it is a great way to get introduced to how CSS works.

Part 2
Writing Basic CSS

1. Launch the program you desire to use. It should allow you to create HTML and CSS files.

   - If you don't have a special program installed, you can use Notepad or another text editor. Simply save your file both as a text file and a CSS file.

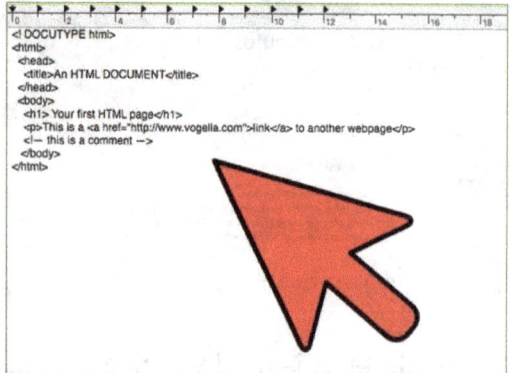

2. Open the HTML file for your website. You should open this with an HTML editor as well, if you have one installed.

   - HTML editors allow you to edit HTML and CSS at the same time.

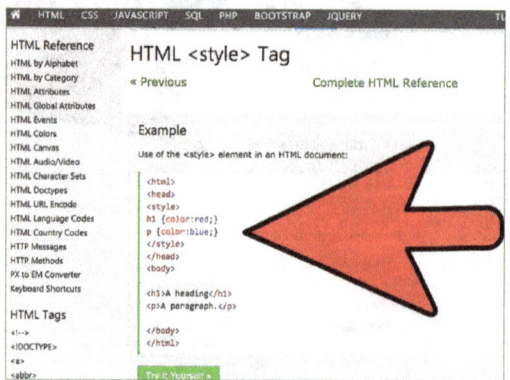

3. Create a <style> tag within your HTML head. This will let you write CSS without the need for a separate file.

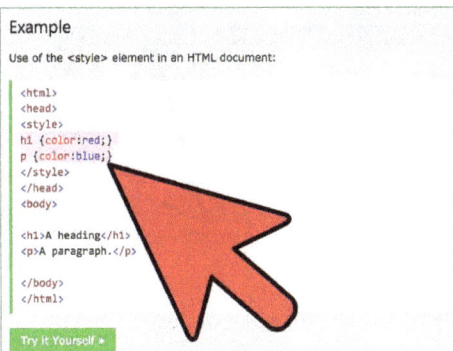

4. Choose an element you want to add styling to and type the name of the element followed by a set of curly braces ({ }). To make your code more legible, always put the second curly brace on its own line.

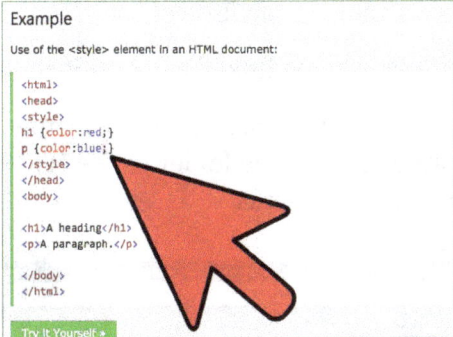

5. Between the braces, type your CSS rules as you would using the style attribute. Each line *must* end with a semicolon (;). To make your code legible, each rule should start on its own line and each line should be indented.

- It is very important to note that this styling will affect *all* elements of the selected type on the page. More specific styling will be covered.

Part 3
More Advanced CSS

1. Create a CSS file, not an HTML file and save it using the .css extension. Open your HTML file as well.

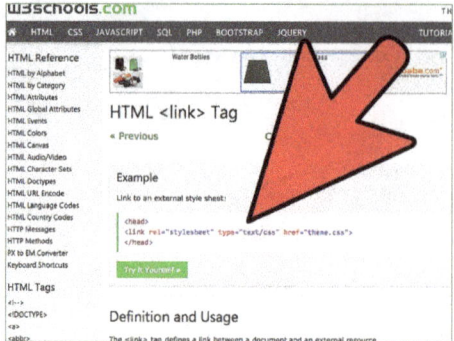

2. Create a `<link>` tag in your HTML head. This will allow you to link a separate CSS file to your HTML document. Your link tag needs three attributes: rel, type, and href.

- rel means "relationship" and tells the browser what the relationship is to the HTML document. Here it should have a value of "stylesheet".
- type tells what type of media is being linked to. Here it should have a value of "text/css"
- href here is used similarly to how it is used in an `<a>` element, but here it must link to a CSS file. If the CSS file is located in the same folder as the HTML file, only the file name needs to be written within the quotation marks.

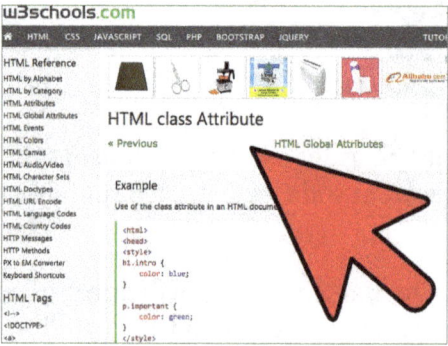

3. Select elements of different types you want to add the same styling to. Add a class attribute to these elements and set them equal to a class name of your choice. This will give your elements the same styling.

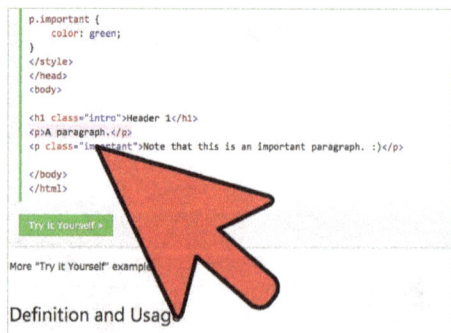

4. Assign what styling a class will receive. Type the class name in your CSS file with a period (.) preceding it (i.e. class).

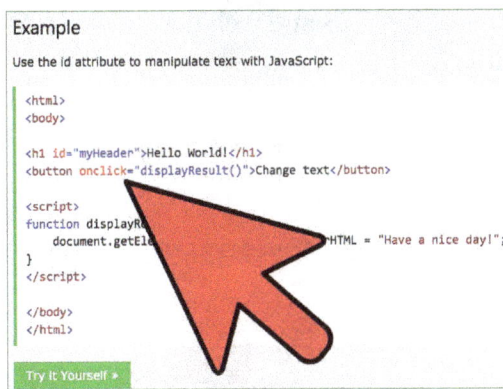

5. Select single elements you want to add special styling to and add an id attribute. Id's are created in CSS using a pound symbol (#) rather than a period.

- Id's are more specific than classes, so an id will override any class styling if it has an attribute with a different value than the class.

Part 4
Learning More

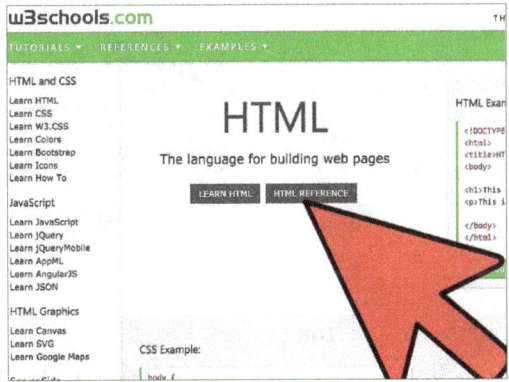

1. Visit the w3 schools. It is an official website aimed at teaching web development skills. The w3 has plenty of references listed for HTML and CSS, as well as other web languages.

2. Find other sites specifically aimed at learning and teaching HTML and CSS. Sites like CSS tricks.

com specifically are aimed at teaching CSS and web design skills. Finding reputable sources will help you on your learning journey.

3. Get in touch with web designers and developers. Their experience and know-how can teach you valuable knowledge and skills.

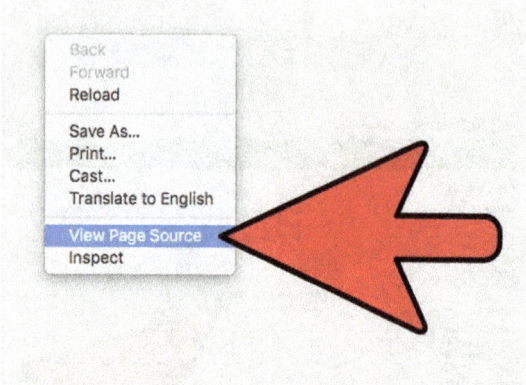

4. View the source code of websites you come across. Viewing the CSS of well-developed websites can show you ways to design parts of websites. Copying it down *as practice* and fiddling with the code can help you learn how to use different CSS attributes.

Tools and Techniques used in Web Designing

Websites can be created using various packages such as Microsoft Word, Wordpress, Adobe Photoshop, etc. Links, forms, templates, etc. are some of the most basic elements found on websites. Tools and techniques are an important component of this field of study. The following chapter elucidates the various tools and techniques that are related to web designing.

How to make a Website with Word

While it is possible to generate an HTML page with Word, it's generally recommended that you do not do so if you intend for the page to be used in any professional or widespread manner. Making your own website with Word is like building your own house with LEGO blocks: it works well enough if you don't have the expertise to do a proper job of it, but using the right tools or hiring a professional will yield immeasurably better results.

Word is made for creating paper documents, which have a fixed page size, typeface, and layout, whereas the page size, typeface and layout available to someone viewing your website may be completely different than yours. Because Word is purpose-built for fixed paper formatting, the web page code it creates is loaded with non-standard, paper-based styling which may not appear as you intend it to in any browsers other than Microsoft's own Internet Explorer.

Steps

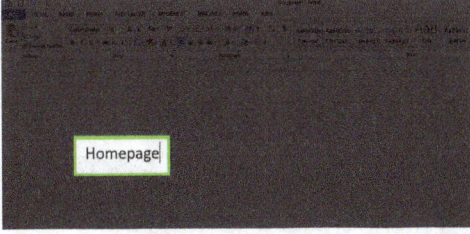

1. Load Word.

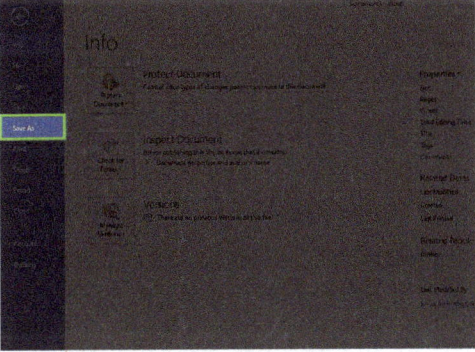

2. Type "Homepage" into the page.

3. Click File > Save as Webpage. In Office 2007, click the Office button > Save As > Other Formats.

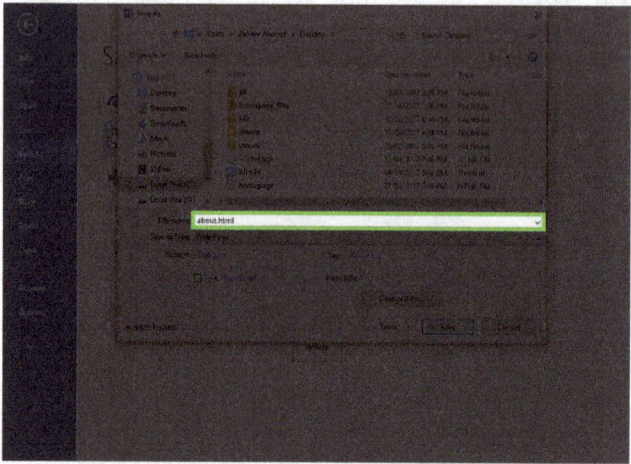

4. Save your page as index.html. In 2007, change "Save as type" to "Web Page."

5. You will see now that the page doesn't look like a normal Word document - you are now in web layout mode.

6. Add some additional text; try typing "This is my home page."

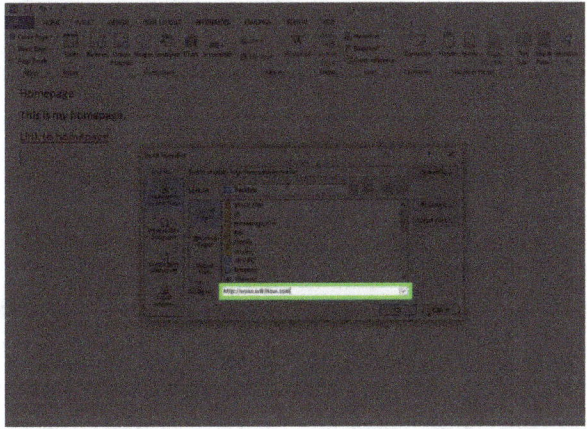

7. Save your work frequently (just click the save icon - Word will remember it's a web page.)

8. Do the same to make the other pages (keep reading to make a hyperlink).

9. Type "Link to homepage" under the text.

10. Highlight the text.

11. Click Insert > Hyperlink (All versions.)

12. Find index.html.

13. When you find it, select it and click OK.

14. Note that you have just created a hyperlink. This means that in a browser you can click that hyperlink and go to another page in your site.

15. You can add a hyperlink to another website - in the "Insert Hyperlink" dialog, in the "Address" text box, type the address of the web page.

16. Keep doing this until your website is complete.

17. Good job making your website. Remember the information in the introduction.

How to make a Website using Wordpress

It wasn't long ago that having your own website was an expensive luxury. If one wanted his or her own website, they would probably hire professionals and spend thousands of dollars. Nowadays, anyone can create their own website, and purchase the space and all the tools they need, for less than the price of a good video game.

Steps

1. Get a web host. Although you can have a "free" website these days, free means many limitations. Free sites will limit your design and function abilities, and there may be ads placed on your website. You will get a sub domain with a free website, instead of a domain. In other words, instead of yourspace.com, you will get yourspace.freesite.com. Why does that make a difference? First of all, everyone has come to recognize these sites as free websites and they will assume that they are inferior. Most importantly, these free websites will not generally get the respect of the search engines. Your free website will not get much traffic from the search engines. So, get yourself a web host.

2. Create the website. Create the website with Wordpress. Wordpress is a great program to make websites and blogs, and it comes with your web hosting plan. Wordpress is a new breed of website creators known as "CMS", or "Content Management Systems". These web creators require no HTML or any other programming language. Most of the design elements of the website are controlled by an intuitive menu, or icons.

Tools and Techniques used in Web Designing | 113

3. Select the design theme from thousands of available themes. Plug in the content. The bottom line here is that you can create a very professional looking website that will generate traffic, without having to learn any programming languages. Instead, you can work on the content of your website. That is the two steps to creating your own website. Instead of needing professional help and paying thousands, you can create your own website in a short time, and pay as little as forty dollars or less. Your website can be as professional looking as any you've seen, and if you wish, this website could very well become a source of income for you.

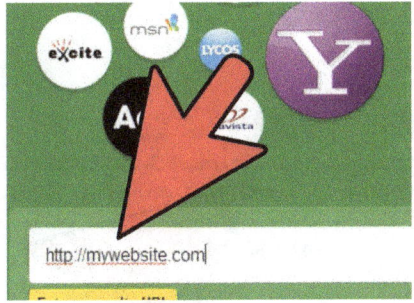

4. Market your website. Wordpress takes care of some of the SEO work automatically. It broadcasts every addition you make to your website and Google search is known to like WordPress websites.

How to use Photoshop to Design a Website

There are many ways for creating websites, Photoshop is one of them.

Steps

1. Download and install Photoshop.

114 | Web Designing

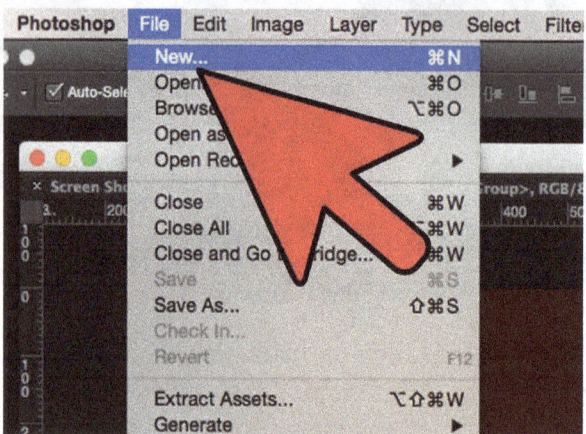

2. Open your Photoshop version on your personal computer and create a new document with the height and width set to what you choose (normal width is 800px-900px, normal height is 1200px-1500px).You can name the folder (optional).

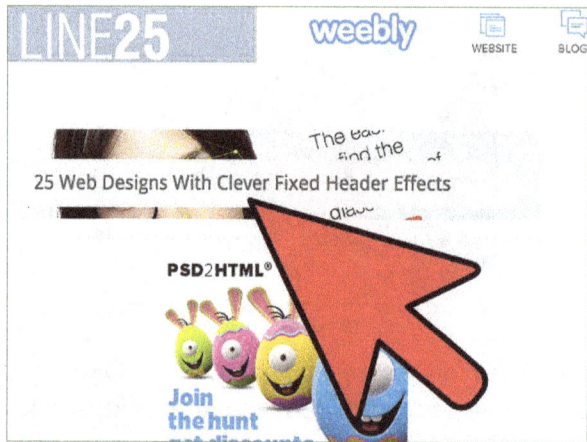

3. Create a header for your site (from an existing image or from scratch) and with your website's logo embedded into it.

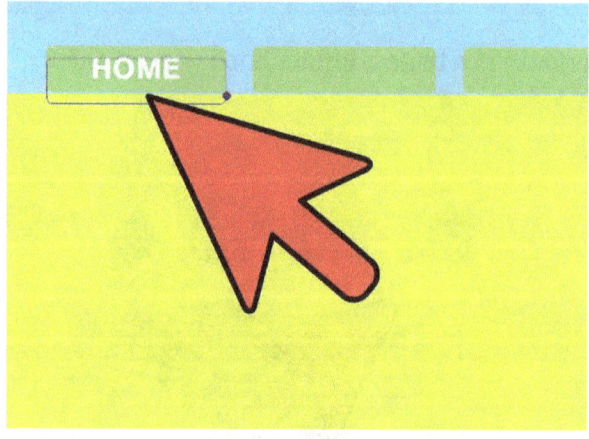

4. Create your site's menu buttons (shape and color, space between them, as an upper menu, bottom menu, right or left side menu or a combination of two or three sets of menus, etc.)

5. Create the content area, the footer area, a place to put banners on, a place for a photo gallery and so on, until you have finished the general looks of your site.

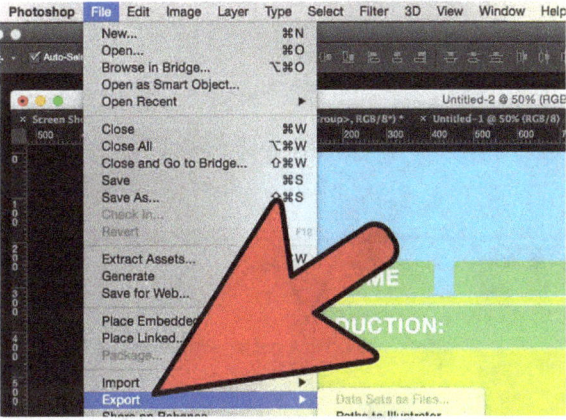

6. Now for the hard part: in Photoshop, slice and export your finished site, by giving names to all the slices before exporting (for example: mark the area that is the header with the slicing tool and name it "header", mark the area of the Home button and name it "home button" and so on to every separate part of the website).

7. It is advised to leave the content area empty as you are only saving it as image slices and the text will show up as a part of the image, when empty, you can add each page's content separately.

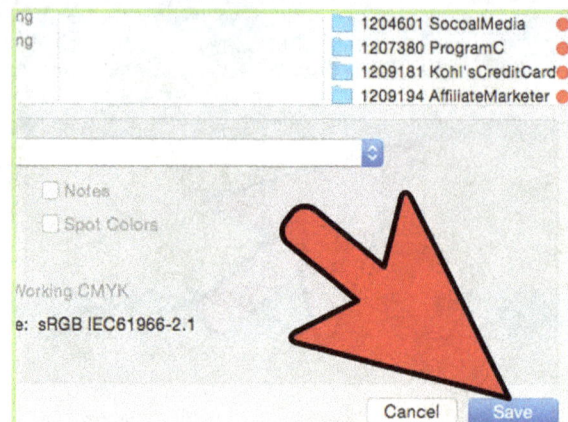

8. Export it to a new file on your desktop, the export will create an HTML file (which will be your internet page, not yet centered and without content), a CSS file, and an Images folder with all the different slices and images inside it.

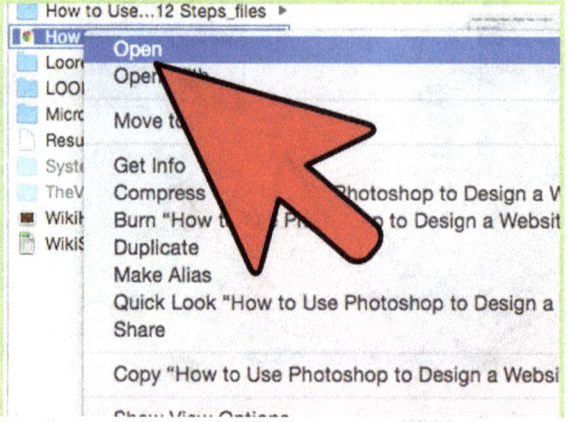

9. Open the HTML file with OneNote or Notepad and make your changes in HTML (center the whole page, set a background color to the whole page, put the content in a div tag where the content image is sitting, or create a few paragraphs by using the P tag inside the div tag, create the meta data for key words, content and so on).

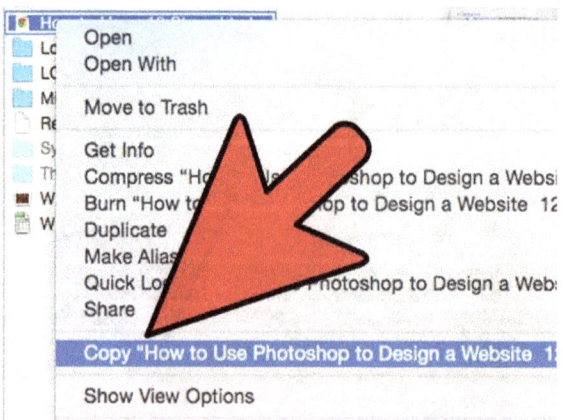

10. Copy and paste the same HTML page as many times as the number of the webpages you have,

but then be careful to rename them to the related pages (ie.Home.html, AboutUs.html, ContactUs.html and so on).

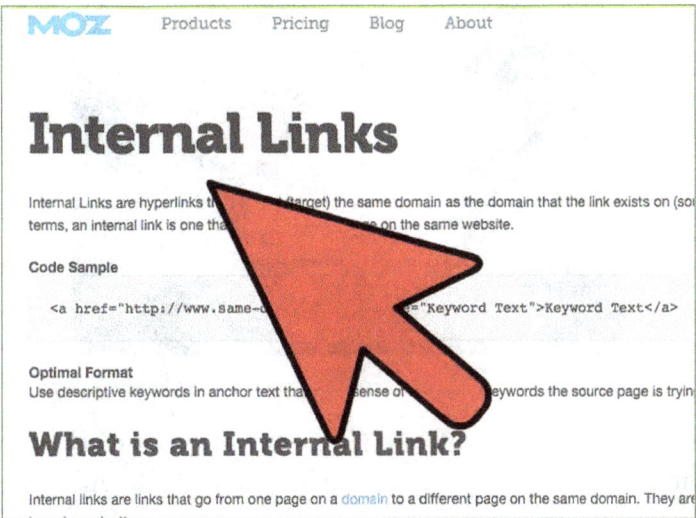

11. Create internal links for the pages in the HTML files (or do it before creating more pages so you won't have to repeat yourself) where the button image code is by creating divs and giving the buttons link addresses.

12. Upload your finished site's files to the host.

How to make a Website Fast by using Templates

The very first requirement for an online presence is having a website of your own. And as building a full-fledged website one needs a lot of time, more and more people are using ready made templates. In web site templates there are pre-made website designs which you can use along and by simply adding the content and images you can create a great looking website.

Steps

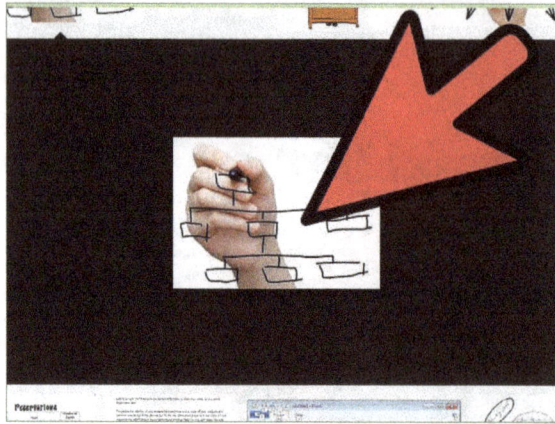

1. Write down the ideas for creating a website. Research well your competitor's websites to get an idea about what are the things that you might need in your website. All these tidbit of information help you in the later stage.

2. Identify your target audience and the market. Until the targeted market is analyzed properly, it is impossible to finalize the look and feel of a website. Go for an idea that is both profitable and practical.

3. Now decide the time and money that you can invest for building a website. The price for creating

a website depends on a lot of factor such as the design, advanced features, maintenance, web hosting charges and lots more.

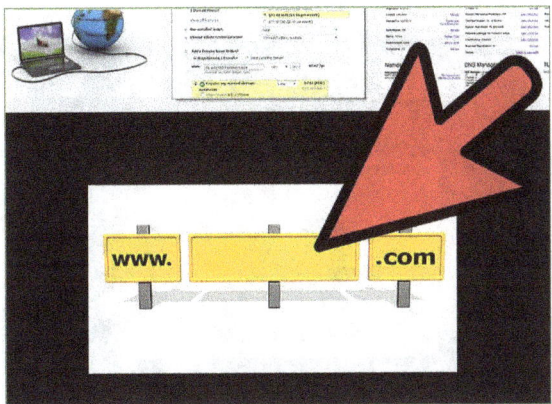

4. Next register a domain name and choose a web hosting service provider. If time is constrain for you select a company where the registration of the domain name and hosting of the web site can be done.

5. Search major search engines for online companies dealing with website templates to create your website within one day. There are many reputed website templates that can give a professional impression if you have the eye to choose a design that looks great and attractive.

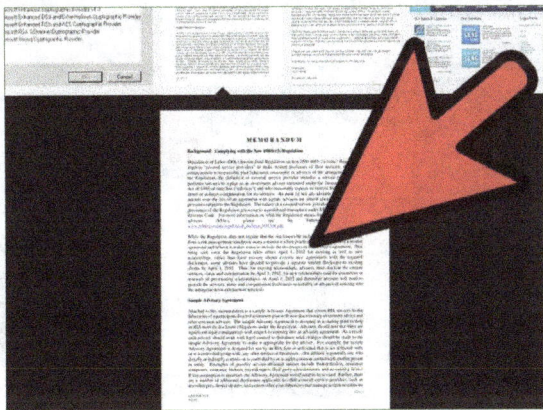

6. Read the instructions provided for using the template by the service providers. You should make

sure that you understand the instructions and are comfortable with the directions given before finalizing anything.

7. After finalizing the service provider take your time looking for a simple design layout that highlights your business. Avoid selecting sophisticated templates for creating a website until and unless you have some designing or programming skills.

8. Purchase the template and use it to create the website to give yourself or your business an online presence.

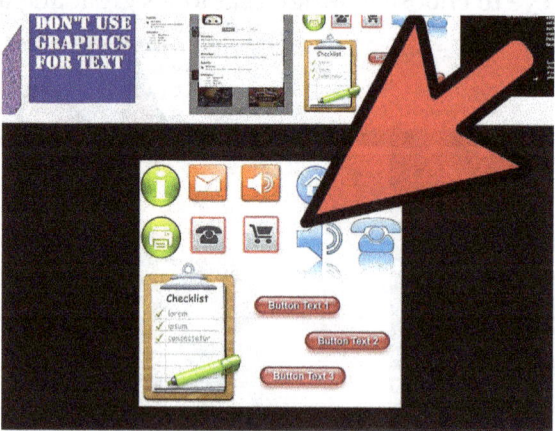

9. Write down the text for your website and keep the pictures or graphics to be used in the website

ready. By keeping the materials ready the process of creating a web site will become comfortable for you. Make sure the text and graphics to be used in the website is copyright free.

10. While writing the content for the website, use keywords throughout the text for a better search engine ranking.

11. Add your company's logo (if any), the images of your product and the relevant and informative content in the pre-defined template design.

12. After you are satisfied with your creativity go for final testing to check the usability and mend the mistakes if there are any.

13. When everything is working fine, it is time to upload your website.

14. Submit your site to major search engines and do everything for promoting it well so that people can get to know about your site.

How to make a Website using a Web Editing Program

Need a website for business or personal use, but not sure how to make one? It's easier than you think. There are several web editing programs out there; Frontpage is one of the easiest. It's simple to use and has lots of help articles in case you get lost along the way. And you really don't have to know complicated HTML to get a professional looking website.

Steps

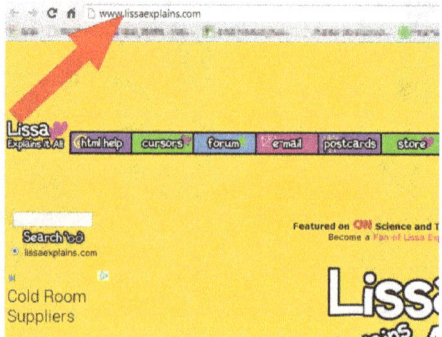

1. Get yourself a little bit familiar with HTML and web design in general.

Tools and Techniques used in Web Designing | 123

2. Consider who your website is for. Ask yourself the following questions:

    - What kind of colors and/or graphics will fit your audience?
    - Are you entertaining or trying to do business?
    - Should the website be built for ease-of-use or design?

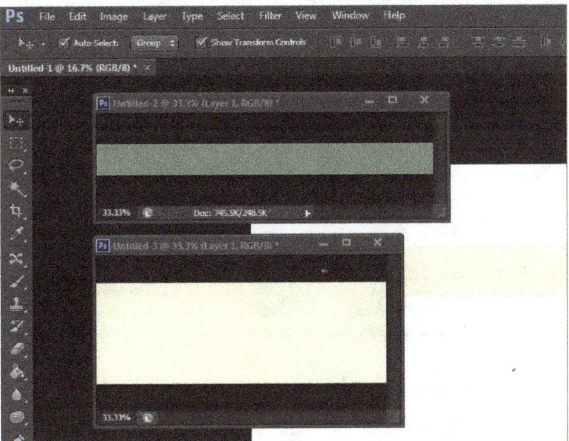

3. Open your graphic editing program (this example uses Paint Shop Pro but there is also GimPhoto). Let's make your graphics first (or if you have your own already, skip to the next step).

    - To make a simple button, select New from the file menu. When the dialog box pops up, select 88 x 31 Micro Button from the Presets menu, or type in your own dimensions. Flood fill your button with your desired color, and add any desired text on now. Then go click the Effects menu, select 3D effects, and then Buttonize. You can mess around with the variables if you like, but once you're done, click okay, and viola. There is your button.
    - To make a matching divider, mess with the picture size dimensions until it's the size and length you want and do the same thing.
    - If you need backgrounds, search the web for royalty free images, there are *tons* of them out there.

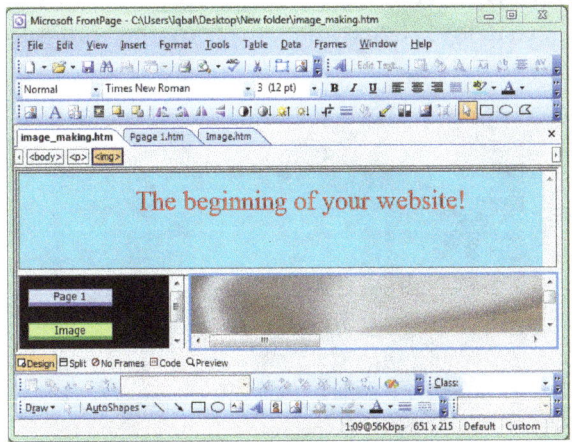

4. Open up your web editor (in this example we use Front Page but there is also Kompozer and Sea

Monkey Composer). Your website likely has more than one page, so let's make a frames page as your index.

- Select New from the File menu, If a Templates dialog does not open, check to your right, and select More page templates.

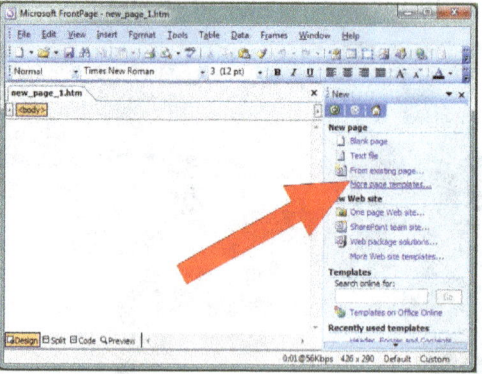

- Click the Frames Pages tab, and find the one that suits you and your website. For this example, we'll use the Banner and Contents.

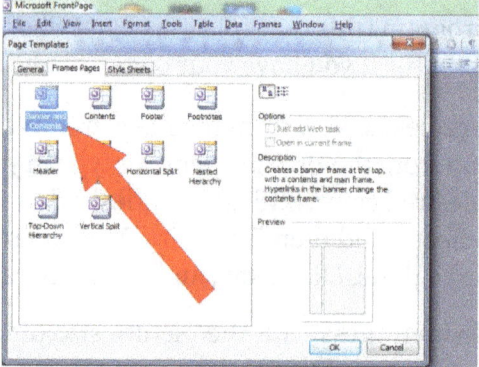

- To adjust the frame sizes, drag near the borders where the little arrow pops up, until the size you want is reached. If you want to keep the frames as resizeable in the browser, leave them alone. Otherwise, right click on the page and select Frame Properties. Down the the bottom, uncheck where it says Resizeable and browser, and presto.

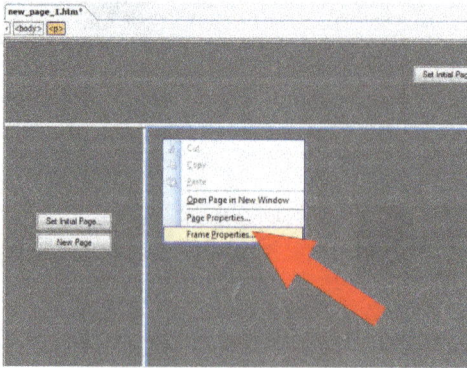

- To set the backgrounds on your newly created pages, right click anywhere in the white and select Page properties. Click the Formatting tab and select either the color you want or the image you wish to use. Generally, your menu bar (or button links) are stationary in one or more of the frames pages, with the center page being the one that displays your linked pages.

- To add your buttons, pick your menu page and select Insert, Picture, From File, and get it from your computer. Don't worry about linking right now, we'll get to that later.

- If you want to get rid of the scroll bar, right click on the page, and select Frame Properties. At the bottom where it says Options, choose between Never, If Needed, and Always.

- Add your homepage content. You may want to consider adding a link back to your homepage if there is any important information on it.

- Name your frame pages. Right click anywhere on each page, and select Frame Properties. Right at the top is Name; name them whatever you want (i.e. home, menu, banner, etc.) Save everything, making sure that you name your Frame set index (index is the page that your browser will automatically link to when opening a website).

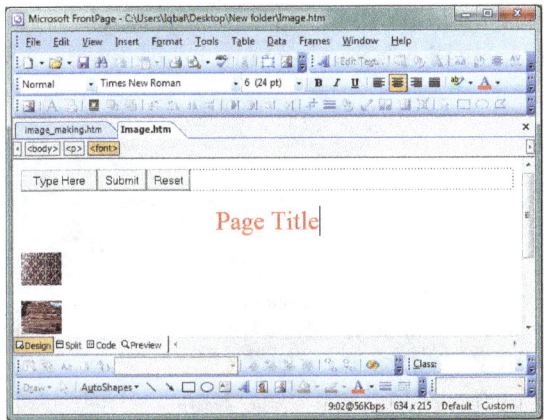

5. Get one of your "linked pages" started. Your linked pages are the pages that your buttons will be leading to. Select New and keep it a blank page; this will go inside the page you set as your homepage in the frame set. Add your content and save.

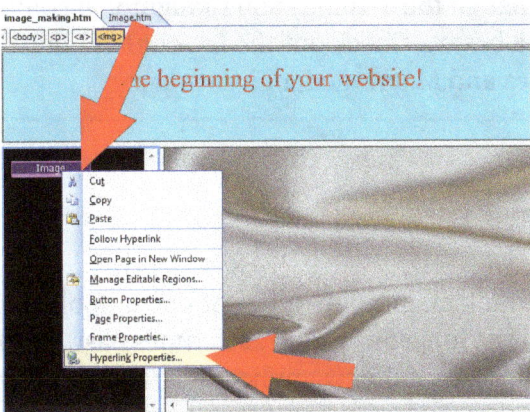

6. Go back to your frame set. To link a button to your page, right click on it, and select Hyperlink.

Find the page you created for this button, highlight it, and on the right hand side, select Target Frame...From here, highlight the frame you want your page to be displayed in, and hit ok. Test out your link; right click on your button, and select Follow Hyperlink...if you did it right, you linked page will be displayed where your homepage was before! Sometimes, FrontPage can be goofy, so if that doesn't work, try linking to Parent Frame instead.

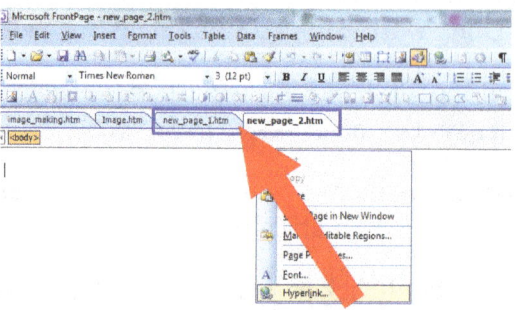

7. Create the rest of your pages, and link them up the same way! To get links to open in a new window, do the same thing, only instead of selecting your home frame, select New Window.

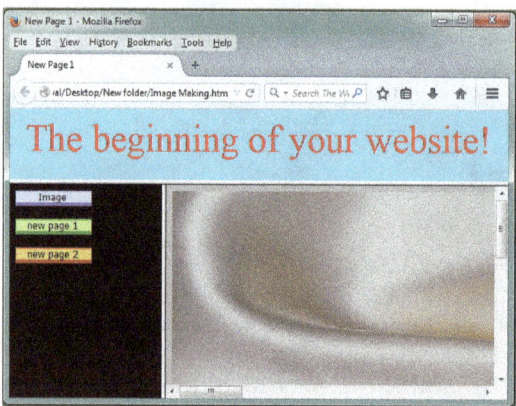

8. Publish the page. The FrontPage help file should explain it pretty well. Once you start doing this more and more, you'll find that all those things you thought you couldn't do, you can, and making really great websites will be a breeze. Check out the Layout land link for a great tutorial on how to create websites using iFrames and Macromedia Fireworks.

How to Design a Form

Designing a form is a common task in many types of office applications. At times, the task is to update an older format that is no longer as useful as in times past. In some cases, the goal is to start fresh and create something for a brand new application or task. With both scenarios, there are a few basic steps that will make it easier to design a form that is well organized, easy to read and will fulfill its purpose.

Steps

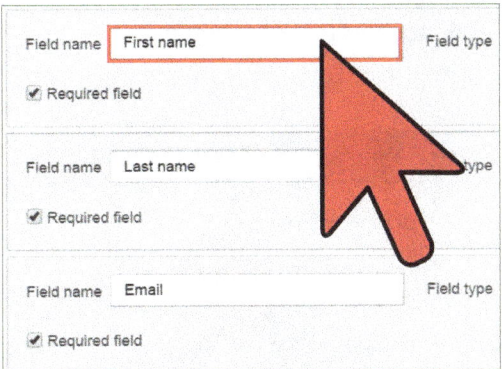

1. Determine the types of information that must be captured in the fields of the form. This is governed by the intended use of the document. Identify how many different pieces of information must be captured, and relate that to the number of fields required to provide adequate space for that data.

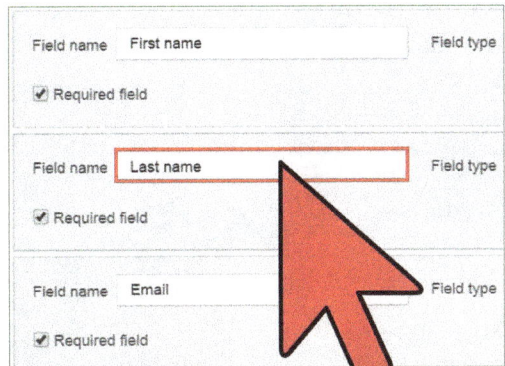

2. Arrange those information types in a logical sequence. The idea is to create a flow from 1 field to the next that simply makes sense to those who will make use of the document. A very simple form that is intended to capture basic contact information may follow a sequence of date, first name, last name, address, city, state or province, zip or postal code, telephone and fax numbers and a field for an email address.

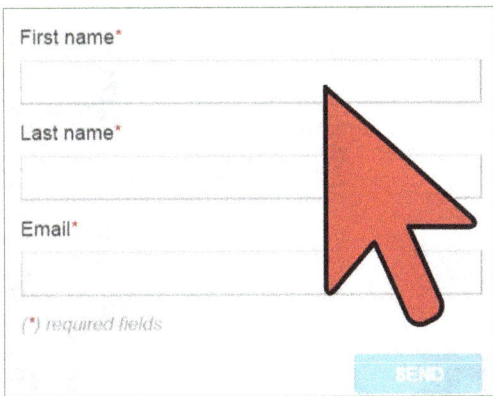

3. Apply that arrangement to the creation of a form template. Software applications typically make

it easy to create fields that can be situated by using a computer mouse to drag the field into position on a blank document. Create and place fields that correspond to the data that must be captured on the form in the same logical sequence identified earlier.

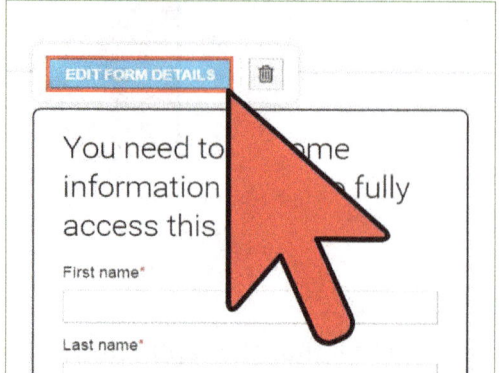

4. Customize each field on your form template. Most software programs that aid in creating forms make it possible to adjust the length and width of each field, as well as restrict the type of characters that are allowed in each field. This makes it possible to ensure that dates and telephone numbers are entered in a uniform manner.

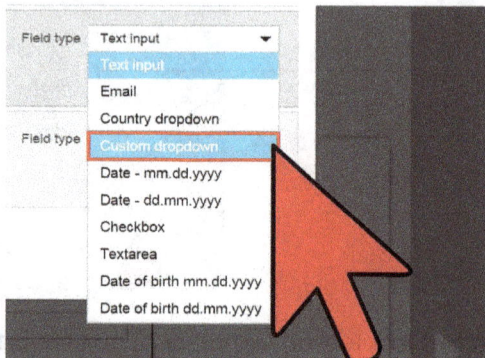

5. Add drop down menus when appropriate. If the form is to be used in an online environment or part of a template in a database, adding drag down menus will often require creating a table and associating it with the appropriate field. Specific instructions in how to accomplish this can be found in the support materials that came with the software.

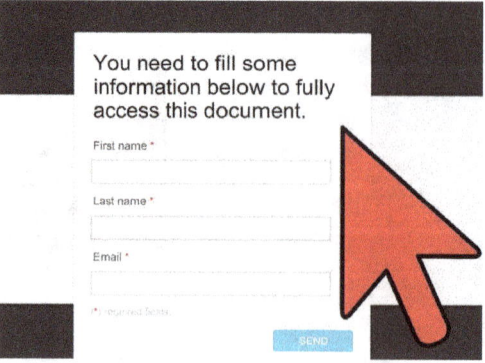

6. Test-drive your form. Before releasing the form for general use, take the time to enter some data

and make sure the result is within your expectations. Should the data fail to capture properly, or 1 or more fields do not function as anticipated, return to the form template and make adjustments.

How to create a Link

Hyperlinks, usually referred to simply as "links," are a crucial part of the Internet as a whole and each website in particular. Links allow users to click on a piece of text or an image and be propelled towards another web page. They are therefore integral to the experience of web browsing. Creating hyperlinks as part of your website requires only a short snippet of HTML code. You can create a basic link quickly and then add modifiers to that link by using this code.

Method 1

Creating a Basic Link

1. Create the text or image you want to use as a link. Links are created using a simple HTML tag when editing the code of your website. First, however, you should create the content that will be placed inside the tag. This can be text, an image, or another HTML element, though the example used here is text.

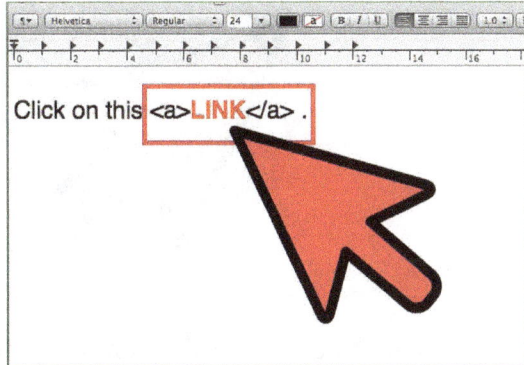

2. Surround the content you created with the tags. Hyperlinks are indicated using a simple tag, closed with the corresponding tag. These tags won't be functional if used without any attributes, but you can add those soon.

- For example, your link might currently look like this: Click here to visit my new page.

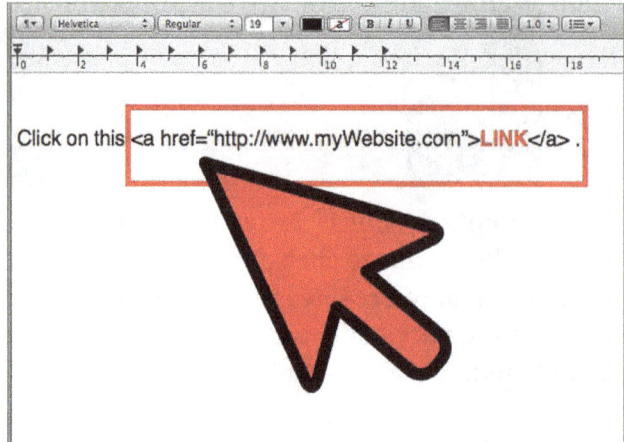

3. Add the "href" attribute to indicate the hyperlink destination. The "href" attribute tells the browser where to direct the user once the link is clicked. It is followed by an equals sign, which is followed by the destination web address in quotations.

- Continuing with the example above, your link might now look like this: Click here to visit my new page.

- Note that if the link's destination is an external website, you must include the entire URL (which likely begins with "http"). If only the page name is specified, as above, the directory of the current page will be used as the parent directory.

Method 2
Adding Modifiers

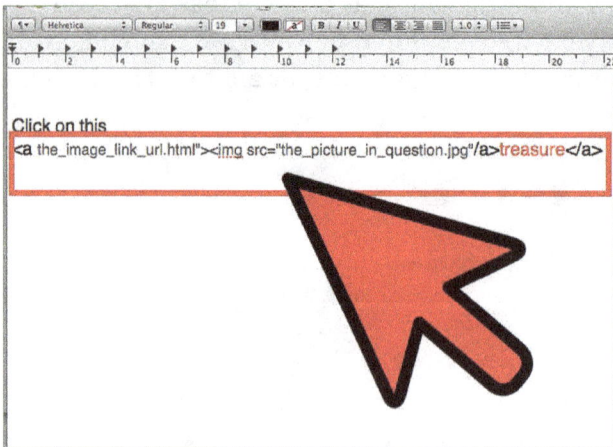

1. Create an image link. This is done by simply adding an image tag within the link tags. You will need the address of the hosted image, however (such as its location on your server or another server). Here is what an example image link might look like:

- <a href="the_intended_link_url.html"><img src="the_picture_in_question.jpg" /></a>

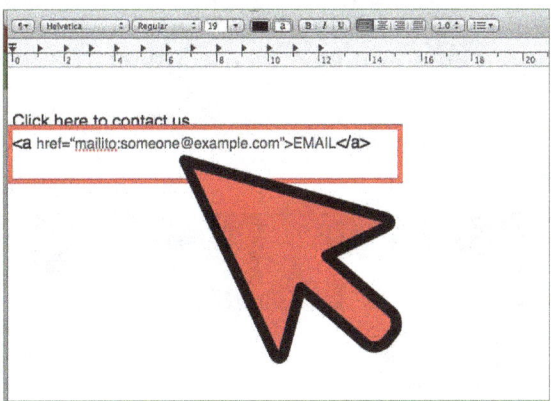

2. Create an email link using the "mailto:" modifier. To create a link which will begin composing an email message to a particular address, use the "mailto:" modifier just before the person's email address.

- For example, an email link might look like this: Click here to ask a question or voice a concern.

3. Create anchors within a large web page to be referenced later. If you need to link to a specific portion of a web page, you need to use an anchor. Anchors are useful in large pages with a table of contents; each section of the text can be assigned an anchor to which the table of contents can link. Anchors are created using the "name" attribute.

- To create an anchor, insert the following tag at the appropriate location on the page: Chapter 3 - Using Anchors in HTML
- To link to the anchor you created, use the # sign.

How to make a Web Browser

While there are many Internet browsers such as Internet Explorer, Firefox and Google Chrome that can be downloaded and installed on your computer for free, creating web browsers yourself gives you more control over how you want to browse the Internet. With a custom web browser you can not only decide how the appearance should be but also add custom buttons and features. Visual Basic is one of the most common programs used to make a web browser on the Windows operating system.

Steps

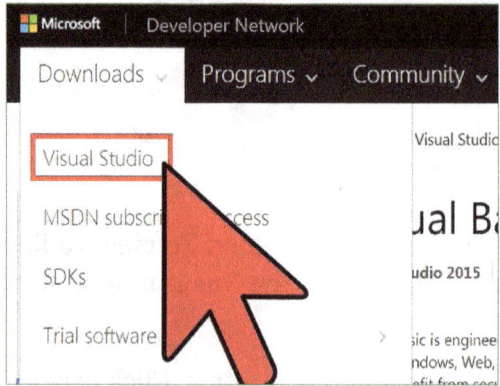

1. Install Visual Basic on your computer by either downloading the software from the Visual Basic Developer Center website or using an installation disk.

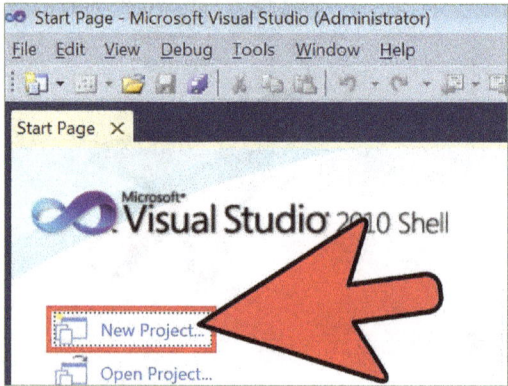

2. Run Visual Basic and start a new project by going to the File menu and clicking on "New Project."

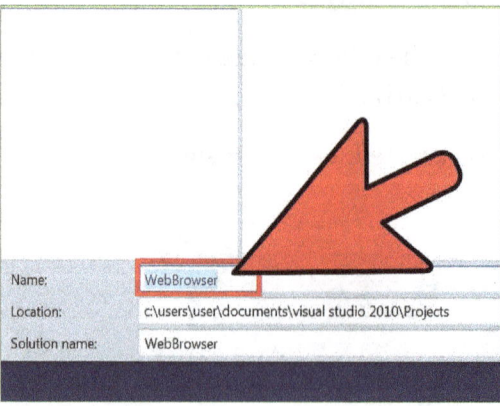

3. Browse over "Text" and select "Web Browser" in the form page that appears.

Tools and Techniques used in Web Designing | 133

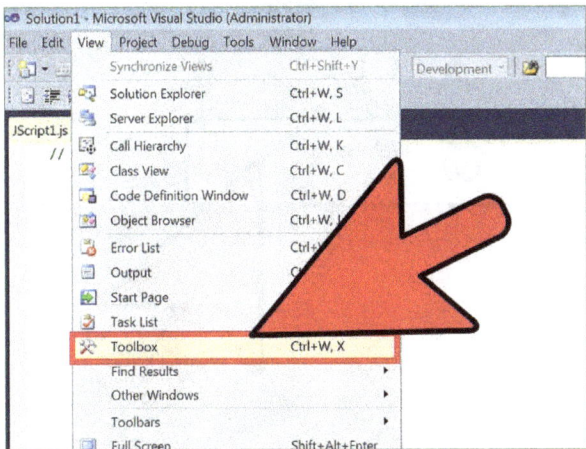

4. Go to "View" in the top menu bar, browse over "Other Windows" and click on "Toolbox." This will display the Visual Basic toolbox.

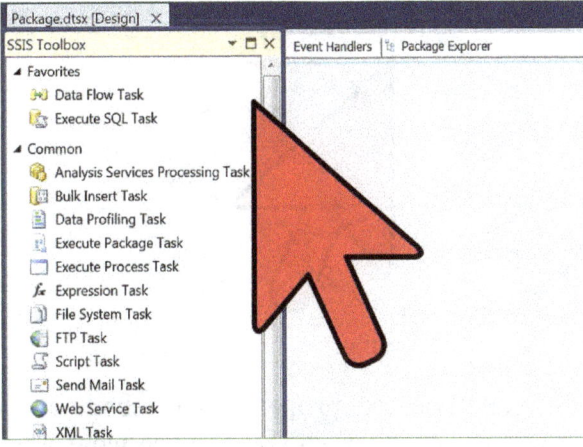

5. Double-click on the Web browser tool in the toolbox.

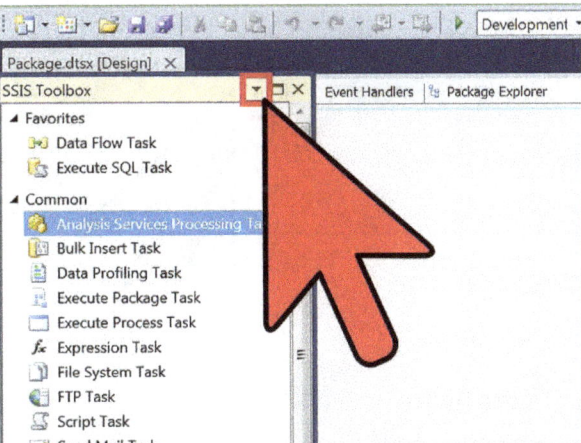

6. Press the right arrow icon on the top-right of the form and click on "Undock in Parent Container." This will change the view of the form from full-screen to a smaller window within the Visual Basic interface.

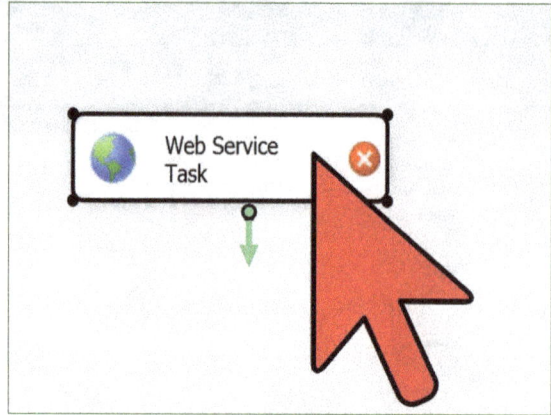

7. Resize the web browser form to your desired size using the clickable outline around it.

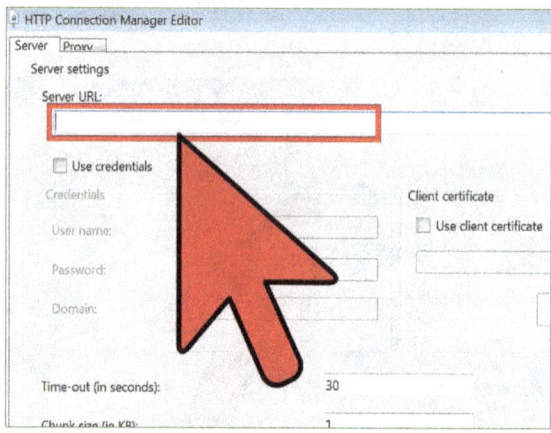

8. Set the URL (Uniform Resource Locator) property to a website address that you wish to visit. This will open up a default website on open so you can see what a website will look like when opened through your Internet browser.

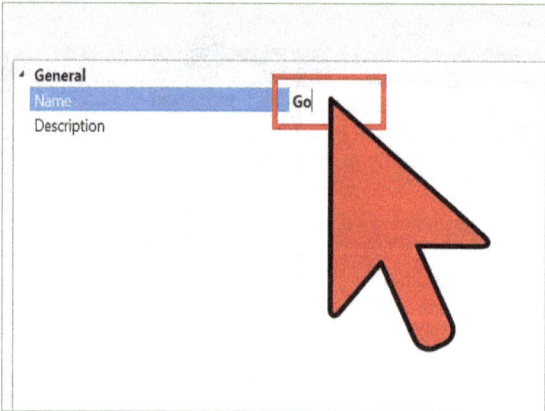

9. Create a new button and assign the following properties to it.

- The text on the button should say "Go."
- Name the button "GoBtn."

Tools and Techniques used in Web Designing | 135

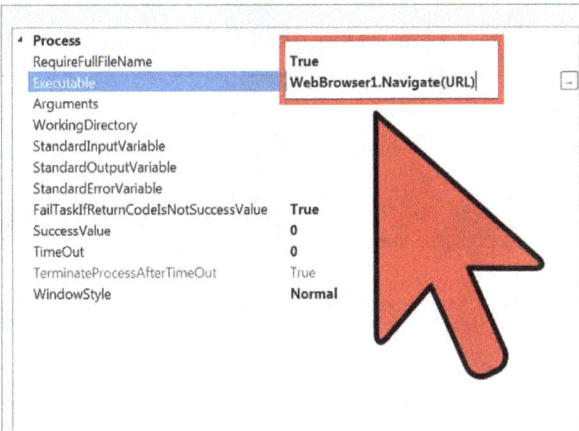

10. Trigger the button by double-clicking on it. This will pop up a private sub. Enter the following code between the private and end subs (you can replace "URL" with any website address).

- WebBrowser1.Navigate(URL)

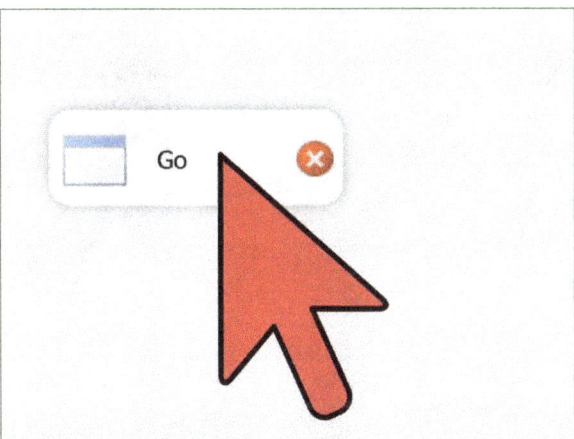

11. Test the button by clicking on it. It should take you away from the default website to the destination website assigned for the button.

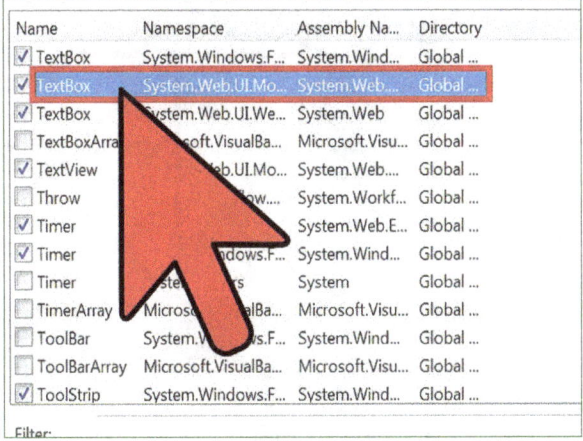

12. Select the TextBox tool from the toolbox.

136 | Web Designing

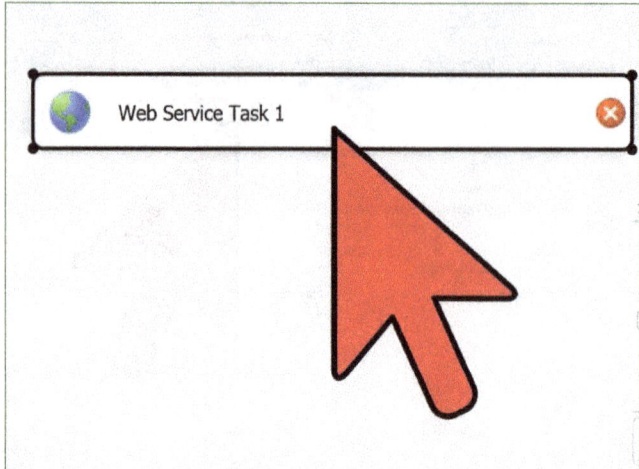

13. Drag the TextBox tool and drop it on the custom web browser form that you are creating.

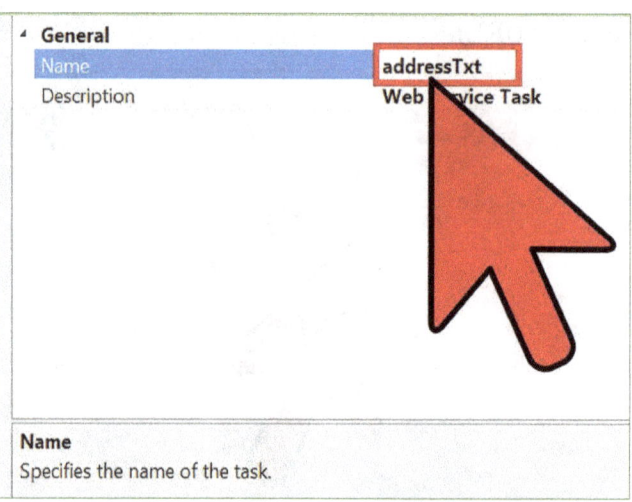

14. Name the text box as "addressTxt."

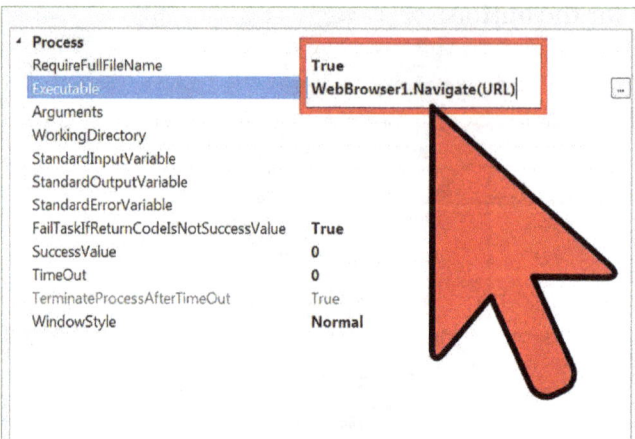

15. Go back to the button you created earlier and replace the URL with "addressTxt.Text." This indicates that you want to use the button to go to whatever URL is typed in the address bar.

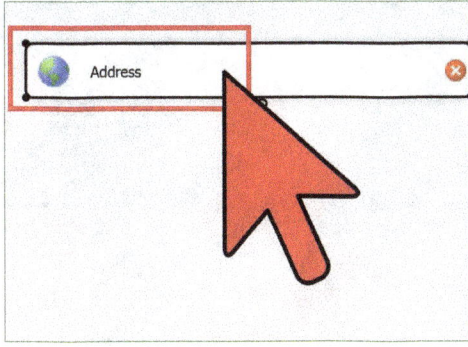

16. Test the address bar by using it to visit different websites.

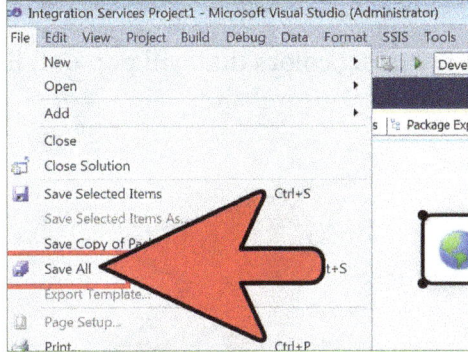

17. Save the web browser that you have just created as a program through Visual Basic by selecting the option to save through the File menu.

How to Design a Website Template

This is an in-depth guide for those who know HTML and CSS but are clueless in how to make your layout.

Steps

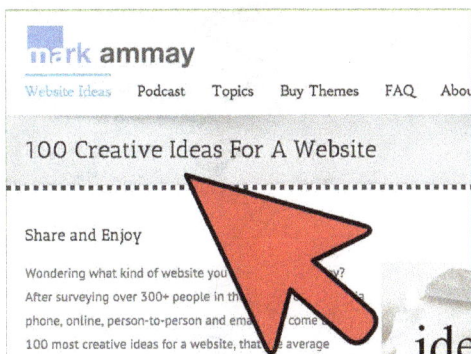

1. Decide what your website topic is. There are millions of different kinds of websites that you can choose to your liking.

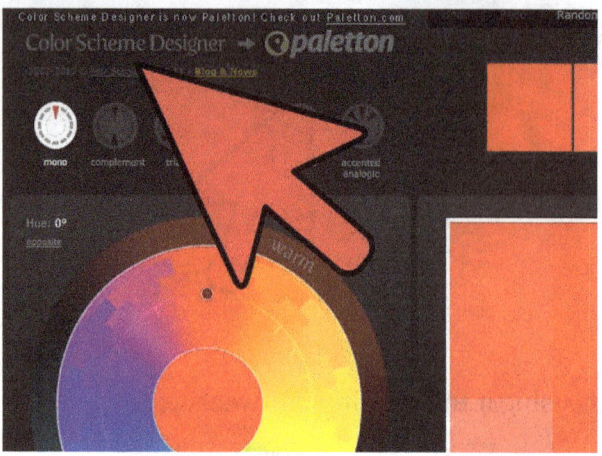

2. Find the right color scheme. Try using colors that will pop out, like blue, purple or orange. You can also adjust the color to the topic of your website.

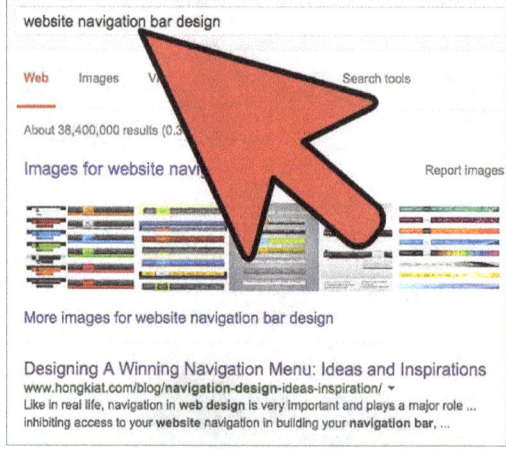

3. Decide what kind of navigation bar to use. Make sure it has useful resources, such as home, comments, and more.

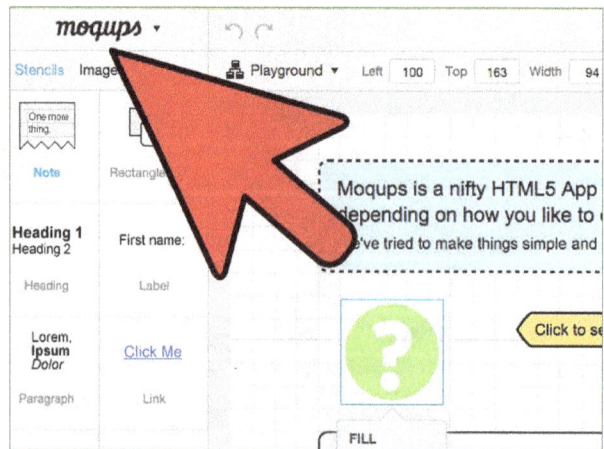

4. Mock up how your website will be laid out in a graphic editing program. Just like the topics, there are wide choices on how you would like the layout of each page to be.

5. Create the page in HTML. You can also create it by going onto Google websites. Be sure to pick a creative name too.

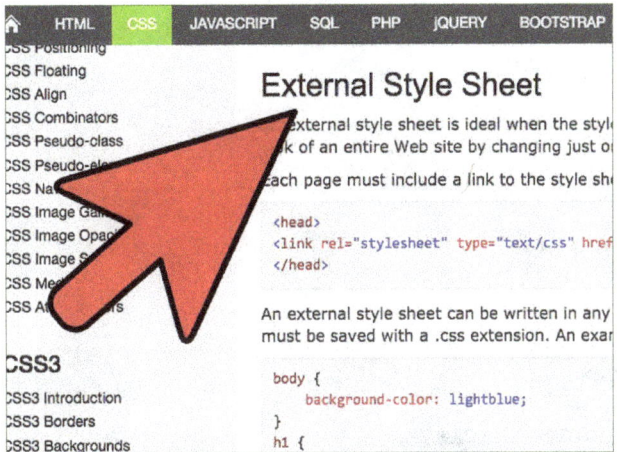

6. Create a style sheet in CSS.

7. Duplicate the HTML page for the other pages and add content. This topic is just an in-depth for layouts.

How to create a Secure Login Script in PHP and MySQL

Nowadays, with more and more stories of cracking in the news, developers are looking for the best ways of securing their sites. If your site has a member system, it could be at risk from being cracked and your users' data could be compromised. This guide will show you one attempt at making a secure login using PHP. The code is as good as we can make it, but security and especially encryption are complex subjects that are changing all the time, and we can't claim to have the entire field mastered. Therefore we may have missed a few tricks in our code. If we have, please let us know and we'll try to incorporate any improvements into what we have.

Writing a login system is a complex topic and not something to be undertaken by those who are not intimately familiar with a wide variety of security topics. The login system presented here is to be used for educational purposes, not a production environment. If you need a login system for a production environment, please locate a prepacked and vetted system.

Following this guide will help guard against many types of attack that crackers can use to gain control of other users' accounts, delete accounts and/or change data. Below is a list of possible attacks this guide tries to defend against:

- SQL Injections
- Session Hijacking
- Network Eavesdropping
- Cross Site Scripting
- Brute Force Attacks
- Covert Timing Channel Attacks

The approach is to use a mixture of data filtering, encryption and other methods to make the lifes of the bad guys just that little bit more difficult.

We're continually trying to improve this script. The very latest version of the code is available from github. There may be some differences between the code you download in this way from the code quoted in this topic. You should also know that we have made no attempt to make the HTML pages output by the application look at all pretty.

You may also notice that we do not close PHP tags in files containing only PHP code. This is in line with most code formatting recommendations.

Finally, you need to know that we ask you to create all the application's non-HTML files in various directories within the application's root directory. The easiest way to get the correct directory structure is to download the latest code by following one of the links above.

Please feel free to use this application as a basis for your own implementation, but don't use it as any kind of example of good coding practice.

Things you'll Need

As we will be using the mysqli_* set of PHP classes to access our MySQL database you will need the following versions of PHP and mySQL.

- PHP version 5.3 or later
- MySQL version 4.1.3 or later

You will also need, of course, a web server configured to use PHP, to host your pages. This will most likely be your Web Host's web server, unless you are hosting the site yourself.

To check the version of PHP and MySQL on your server use the phpinfo(); function.

Part 1

Configure your Server

1. Install a Web Server, PHP and MySQL on your server. Most web hosting services will have PHP and MySQL already installed. You will just have to check they have the most recent versions of PHP and MySQL for this guide to work. If they don't have at least PHP5.3 and MySQL5 you might like to ask a few questions about their commitment to security. Keeping your software up-to-date is a part of the security process.

If you have your own server or computer, you should install the required software in the normal way for your system. Generally speaking, if you are not going to use the setup for production purposes and you are developing under Windows or OS/X, installing an XAMPP stack is the way to go.

But please note that you should under no circumstances use XAMPP to create a production server environment for you.

Under Linux, use your package manager to download and install the necessary packages. Some distributions, like Ubuntu, package all the necessary applications into one bundle. Just do the following from a terminal window in Ubuntu:

sudo apt-get install lamp-server^ phpmyadmin

However you install the necessary elements, please ensure you configure MySQL with a secure root password.

Part 2

Configure the MySQL Database

1. Create a MySQL database.

Log into your database as an administrative user (usually root) In this guide we will create a database called "secure_login".

You can either use the code below or do the same thing in phpMyAdmin/your favourite GUI MySQL client, if you prefer:

```
CREATE DATABASE `

secure_login`;
```

Note: Some hosting services don't allow you to create a database through phpMyAdmin, Learn how to do it in cPanel.

2. Create a user with only SELECT, UPDATE and INSERT privileges.

Creating a user with restricted privileges means that if there was ever a breach of security in our script the hacker couldn't delete or drop anything from our database. Using these privileges, you can get by doing pretty much anything you would want to in your application. If you are really paranoid, create a user for each function.

Of course you will need to be logged into MySQL as a user with sufficient privileges in order to create a user. This user will usually be root. These are the details of the user we created:

- User: "sec_user"
- Password: "eKcGZr59zAa2BEWU"

Note: it is a good idea to change the password from the one given above when running on your own server. Make sure, if you do this, that you also change the code below, and your PHP database connection code in the application we are creating.

Remember it doesn't need to be a password that you can remember so make it as complicated as possible. Here's a random password generator

Given below is the SQL code for creating the database user and granting it the necessary permissions. Or you can do this in a GUI database client like phpmyadmin if you prefer:

```
CREATE USER 'sec_user'@'localhost' IDENTIFIED BY 'eKcGZr59zAa2BEWU';

GRANT SELECT, INSERT, UPDATE ON `secure_login`.* TO 'sec_user'@'localhost';
```

If you see yourself deleting records from either of the tables in this module, you may want to add DELETE to the list of privileges, or you may prefer to create a different user with just the DELETE privilege, and only on the table from which you want to delete records if you don't want to delete from both. You do not need to grant DELETE privileges at all for anything in this example script.

3. Create a MySQL table named "members".

The code below creates a table with four fields (id, username, email, password). We use the BINARY datatype to store the password because it will be encrypted using BCrypt, which has an output length of 60 characters. To store it more efficiently, we store it in the BINARY format:

IMPORTANT: If you have attempted to use this script with SHA512 hashing and had problems with logging in, you need to change the PASSWORD field to CHAR(128) as the original

BINARY(60) cropped out 68 crucial characters at the end of the hashed password, this causes the password to mismatch when attempting to login.

```
CREATE TABLE `secure_login`.`members` (
    `id` INT NOT NULL AUTO_INCREMENT PRIMARY KEY,
    `username` VARCHAR(30) NOT NULL,
    `email` VARCHAR(50) NOT NULL,
    `password` CHAR(128) NOT NULL
) ENGINE = InnoDB;
```

As we've said before, you can do this in whatever type of client you prefer.

4. Create a table to store login attempts.

We will use this table to store login attempts for a user. This is one way in which we will make brute force attacks more difficult:

```
CREATE TABLE `secure_login`.`login_attempts` (
    `user_id` INT(11) NOT NULL,
    `time` VARCHAR(30) NOT NULL
) ENGINE=InnoDB
```

5. Create a test row in table "members".

It will be important to be able to test your login script, so below is the script to create a user with known details:

- Username: test_user
- Email: test@example.com
- Password: 6ZaxN2Vzm9NUJT2y

The code you need in order to be able to log in as this user is:

```
INSERT INTO `secure_login`.`members` VALUES(1, 'test_user', 'test@example.com',
'$2y$10$IrzYJi10j3Jy/K6jzSLQtOLif1wEZqTRQoK3DcS3jdnFEhL4fWM4G');
```

Part 3

Create Database Connection Page

1. Create a global configurations page Create a folder called "includes" in the root directory of the application and then create a new PHP file in that directory. Call it psl-config.php. In a production

environment you'll probably want to locate this file and all your other include files, outside of the web server's document root. If you do that, and we strongly suggest that you do, you will need to alter your include or require statements as necessary, so that the application can find the include files.

Locating your include files outside of the web server's document root means that your file cannot be located using a URL. So, if someone mistakenly dropped the 'php' extension, say, or messed up the file permissions the file still could not be displayed as text in a browser window.

The file contains global configuration variables. Things like whether anyone can register, whether or not it's a secure (HTTPS) connection, and other stuff as well as the database details could also go here...

```php
<?php
/**
 * These are the database
login details
 */
define("HOST", "localhost");     // The host you want to connect to.
define("USER", "sec_user");      // The database username.
define("PASSWORD", "eKcGZr59zAa2BEWU");   // The database password.
define("DATABASE", "secure_login");    // The database name.


define("CAN_REGISTER", "any");
define("DEFAULT_ROLE", "member");


define("SECURE", FALSE);    // FOR DEVELOPMENT ONLY!!!!
?>
```

2. Create the database connection page. This is the PHP code that we will use to connect to our mySQL database. Create a new PHP file called db_connect.php in the application's includes directory and add the code below. You can then include the file onto any page you wish to connect to the database.

```php
<?php
include_once 'psl-config.php';   // As functions.php is not included
$mysqli = new mysqli(HOST, USER, PASSWORD, DATABASE);
```

Part 4

Create the PHP Functions

These functions will do all the processing of the login script. Add all of the functions to a page called functions.php in the includes directory of the application.

1. Securely start a PHP session.

PHP sessions are known not to be secure, therefore it is important not just to put "session_start();" at the top of every page on which you want to use PHP sessions. We are going to create a function called "sec_session_start()", this will start a PHP session in a secure way. You should call this function at the top of any page in which you wish to access a PHP session variable. If you are really concerned about security and the privacy of your cookies, have a look at this topic: Create-a-Secure-Session-Managment-System-in-Php-and-Mysql.

This function makes your login script a whole lot more secure. It stops crackers accessing the session id cookie through JavaScript (for example in an XSS attack). Also the "session_regenerate_id()" function, which regenerates the session id on every page reload, helps prevent session hijacking. Note: If you are using HTTPS in your login application set the "$secure" variable to true. In a production environment it is essential that you use HTTPS.

Create a new file called functions.php in your application's includes directory and add the following code to it:

```php
<?php
include_once 'psl-config.php';


function sec_session_start() {
    $session_name = 'sec_session_id';   // Set a custom session name
    $secure = SECURE;
    // This stops JavaScript being able to access the session id.
    $httponly = true;
    // Forces sessions to only use cookies.
    if (ini_set('session.use_only_cookies', 1) === FALSE) {
        header("Location: ../error.php?err=Could not initiate a safe session (ini_set)");
        exit();
    }
```

```php
    // Gets current cookies params.
    $cookieParams = session_get_cookie_params();
  session_set_cookie_params($cookieParams["lifetime"], $cookieParams["path"], $cookieParams["domain"], $secure, $httponly);
    // Sets the session name to the one set above.
    session_name($session_name);
    session_start();            // Start the PHP session
     session_regenerate_id();    // regenerated the session, delete the old one.
}
```

2. Create the Login Function.

This function will check the email and password against the database. Using the password_verify function rather than comparing the strings helps to prevent timing attacks. It will return true if there is a match. Add this function to your functions.php file:

```php
function login($email, $password, $mysqli) {
    // Using prepared statements means that SQL injection is not possible.
    if ($stmt = $mysqli->prepare("SELECT id, username, password
        FROM members
      WHERE email = ?
        LIMIT 1")) {
        $stmt->bind_param('s', $email);   // Bind "$email" to parameter.
        $stmt->execute();    // Execute the prepared query.
        $stmt->store_result();

        // get variables from result.
        $stmt->bind_result($user_id, $username, $db_password);
        $stmt->fetch();

            if ($stmt->num_rows == 1) {
```

```php
// If the user exists we check if the account is locked
// from too many login attempts


if (checkbrute($user_id, $mysqli) == true) {
    // Account is locked
    // Send an email to user saying their account is locked
    return false;
} else {
    // Check if the password in the database matches
    // the password the user submitted. We are using
    // the password_verify function to avoid timing attacks.
    if (password_verify($password, $db_password)) {
        // Password is correct!
        // Get the user-agent string of the user.
        $user_browser = $_SERVER['HTTP_USER_AGENT'];
        // XSS protection as we might print this value
        $user_id = preg_replace("/[^0-9]+/", "", $user_id);
        $_SESSION['user_id'] = $user_id;
        // XSS protection as we might print this value
        $username = preg_replace("/[^a-zA-Z0-9_\-]+/",
                                                    "",
                                                $username);
        $_SESSION['username'] = $username;
        $_SESSION['login_string'] = hash('sha512',
                $db_password . $user_browser);
        // Login successful.
        return true;
    } else {
```

```
                    // Password is not correct
                    // We record this attempt in the database
                    $now = time();
                    $mysqli->query("INSERT INTO login_attempts(user_id, time)
                                    VALUES ('$user_id', '$now')");
                    return false;
                }
            }
        } else {
            // No user exists.
            return false;
        }
    }
}
```

3. The Brute Force Function.

Brute force attacks are when a hacker tries thousands of different passwords on an account, either randomly generated passwords or from a dictionary. In our script if a user account has more than five failed logins their account is locked.

Brute force attacks are hard to prevent. A few ways we can prevent them are using a CAPTCHA test, locking user accounts and adding a delay on failed logins, so the user cannot login for another thirty seconds.

We strongly recommend using a CAPTCHA. As yet we have not implemented this functionality in the example code, but hope to do so in the near future, using SecureImage, since it does not require registration. You may prefer something better known such as reCAPTCHA from Google.

Whichever system you decide on, we suggest you only display the CAPTCHA image after two failed login attempts so as to avoid inconveniencing the user unnecessarily.

When faced with the problem of brute force attacks, most developers simply block the IP address after a certain amount of failed logins. But there are many tools to automate the process of making attacks like these; and these tools can go through a series of proxies and even change the IP on each request. Blocking all these IP addresses could mean you're blocking legitimate users as well. In our code we'll log failed attempts and lock the user's account after five failed login attempts. This should trigger the sending of an email to the user with a reset link, but we have not implemented this in our code. Here is the code for the checkbrute() function at the time of writing. Add it to your functions.php code:

```php
function checkbrute($user_id, $mysqli) {
    // Get timestamp of current time
    $now = time();

    // All login attempts are counted from the past 2 hours.
    $valid_attempts = $now - (2 * 60 * 60);

    if ($stmt = $mysqli->prepare("SELECT time
                    FROM login_attempts
                    WHERE user_id = ?
                    AND time > '$valid_attempts'")) {
        $stmt->bind_param('i', $user_id);

        // Execute the prepared query.
        $stmt->execute();
        $stmt->store_result();

        // If there have been more than 5 failed logins
        if ($stmt->num_rows > 5) {
            return true;
        } else {
            return false;
        }
    }
}
```

4. Check logged in status. We do this by checking the "user_id" and the "login_string" SESSION variables. The "login_string" SESSION variable has the user's browser information hashed together with the password. To check if they are equal, we use the hash_equals function to prevent timing attacks. We use the browser information because it is very unlikely that the user will change their browser mid-session. Doing this helps prevent session hijacking. Add this function to your functions.php file in the includes folder of your application:

```php
function login_check($mysqli) {
    // Check if all session variables are set
    if (isset($_SESSION['user_id'],
                $_SESSION['username'],
                $_SESSION['login_string'])) {

        $user_id = $_SESSION['user_id'];
        $login_string = $_SESSION['login_string'];
        $username = $_SESSION['username'];

        // Get the user-agent string of the user.
        $user_browser = $_SERVER['HTTP_USER_AGENT'];

        if ($stmt = $mysqli->prepare("SELECT password
                                      FROM members
                                      WHERE id = ? LIMIT 1")) {
            // Bind "$user_id" to parameter.
            $stmt->bind_param('i', $user_id);
            $stmt->execute();    // Execute the prepared query.
            $stmt->store_result();

            if ($stmt->num_rows == 1) {
                // If the user exists get variables from result.
                $stmt->bind_result($password);
                $stmt->fetch();
```

```
            $login_check = hash('sha512', $password . $user_browser);

                if (hash_equals($login_check, $login_string) ){
                    // Logged In!!!!
                    return true;
                } else {
                    // Not logged in
                    return false;
                }
            } else {
                // Not logged in
                return false;
            }
        } else {
            // Not logged in
            return false;
        }
    } else {
        // Not logged in
        return false;
    }
}
```

5. Sanitize URL from PHP_SELF. This next function sanitizes the output from the PHP_SELF server variable. It is a modificaton of a function of the same name used by the WordPress Content Management System:

```
function esc_url($url) {

    if ('' == $url) {
        return $url;
    }
```

```php
        $url = preg_replace('|[^a-z0-9-~+_.?#=!&;,/:%@$\|*\'()\\x80-\\xff]|i', '', $url);


    $strip = array('%0d', '%0a', '%0D', '%0A');
    $url = (string) $url;


    $count = 1;
    while ($count) {
        $url = str_replace($strip, '', $url, $count);
    }


    $url = str_replace(';//', '://', $url);


    $url = htmlentities($url);


    $url = str_replace('&amp;', '&#038;', $url);
    $url = str_replace("'", '&#039;', $url);


    if ($url !== '/') {
        // We're only interested in relative links from $_SERVER['PHP_SELF']
        return '';
    } else {
        return $url;
    }
}
```

The trouble with using the server variable unfiltered is that it can be used in a cross site scripting attack. Most references will simply tell you to filter it using htmlentities(), however even this appears not to be sufficient hence the belt and braces approach in this function.

Others suggest leaving the action attribute of the form blank, or set to a null string. Doing this, though, leaves the form open to an iframe clickjacking attack.

Part 5

Create Processing Pages

1. Create the login processing page (process_login.php) Create a file to process logins, called process_login.php in the application's includes directory. It goes in this directory because it contains no HTML markup.

We will use the mysqli_* set of PHP functions as this is one of the most up-to-date mySQL extensions.

```php
<?php
include_once 'db_connect.php';
include_once 'functions.php';

sec_session_start(); // Our custom secure way of starting a PHP session.

if (isset($_POST['email'], $_POST['p'])) {
    $email = $_POST['email'];
    $password = $_POST['p']; // The hashed password.

    if (login($email, $password, $mysqli) == true) {
        // Login success
        header('Location: ../protected_page.php');
    } else {
        // Login failed
        header('Location: ../index.php?error=1');
    }
} else {
    // The correct POST variables were not sent to this page.
    echo 'Invalid Request';
}
```

2. Create a logout script. Your logout script must start the session, destroy it and then redirect to somewhere else. Note: it might be a good idea to add CSRF protection here in case someone sends a link hidden in this page somehow. For more information about CSRF you could visit Coding Horror.

The current code for logging out the user, which you should add to a file called logout.php in the application's includes directory, is:

```php
<?php
include_once 'functions.php';
sec_session_start();

// Unset all session values
$_SESSION = array();

// get session parameters
$params = session_get_cookie_params();

// Delete the actual cookie.
setcookie(session_name(),
        '', time() - 42000,
        $params["path"],
        $params["domain"],
        $params["secure"],
        $params["httponly"]);

// Destroy session
session_destroy();
header('Location: ../index.php');
```

3. Registration Page. The registration code is included in two new files, called register.php in the application's root directory and register.inc.php in the includes directory. It does the following things:

- Obtains and validates the username the user wishes to adopt
- Obtains and validates the user's email address
- Obtains and validates the password the user wants to use
- Hashes the password and passes it back to the register.php page (i.e. it posts to itself)

Most of the validation is done in JavaScript, client side. This is because the user has no motivation to circumvent these checks. Why would a user want to create an account that would be less secure than otherwise? We will discuss the JavaScript in the next section.

TIP: $error_msg can be changed into an array instead of simply making it one long string of errors. This is as simple as setting $error_msg = array(); at the top of the file. Then replacing every $error_msg .= to $error_msg[] =. It would also be recommended to remove the html from the $error_msg so all of the errors are in plain text inside of the array. If you want to be able to use the array on the page which you are posting to you can set a posting variable to equal the array like this: $_POST['error_msg'] = serialize($error_msg);, the serialize turns the array into a single string so the post is able to use it. To use this post on the page after registering, simply do: $error_variable = unserialize($_POST['error_msg']);, of course you should always use an if(isset($_POST['error_msg'])) {$error_variable = unserialize($_POST['error_msg']);} as this checks if the variable is actually set.

For now, just create the register.php file and include the following code in it:

```php
<?php
include_once 'includes/register.inc.php';
include_once 'includes/functions.php';
?>
<!DOCTYPE html>
<html>
    <head>
        <meta charset="UTF-8">
        <title>Secure Login: Registration Form</title>
        <script type="text/JavaScript" src="js/sha512.js"></script>
        <script type="text/JavaScript" src="js/forms.js"></script>
        <link rel="stylesheet" href="styles/main.css" />
    </head>
    <body>
```

```
<!-- Registration form to be output if the POST variables are not
set or if the registration script caused an error. -->
<h1>Register with us</h1>
<?php
if (!empty($error_msg)) {
    echo $error_msg;
}
?>
<ul>
    <li>Usernames may contain only digits, upper and lowercase letters and underscores</li>
    <li>Emails must have a valid email format</li>
    <li>Passwords must be at least 6 characters long</li>
    <li>Passwords must contain
        <ul>
            <li>At least one uppercase letter (A..Z)</li>
            <li>At least one lowercase letter (a..z)</li>
            <li>At least one number (0..9)</li>
        </ul>
    </li>
    <li>Your password and confirmation must match exactly</li>
</ul>
<form action="<?php echo esc_url($_SERVER['REQUEST_URI']); ?>"
    method="post"
    name="registration_form">
    Username: <input type='text'
        name='username'
        id='username' /><br>
```

```
            Email: <input type="text" name="email" id="email" /><br>
            Password: <input type="password"
                            name="password"
                            id="password"/><br>
            Confirm password: <input type="password"
                                    name="confirmpwd"
                                    id="confirmpwd" /><br>
            <input type="button"
                value="Register"
                onclick="return regformhash(this.form,
                                this.form.username,
                                this.form.email,
                                this.form.password,
                                this.form.confirmpwd);" />
        </form>
        <p>Return to the <a href="index.php">login page</a>.</p>
    </body>
</html>
```

The register.inc.php file in the includes directory should contain the following code:

```php
<?php
include_once 'db_connect.php';
include_once 'psl-config.php';

$error_msg = "";

if (isset($_POST['username'], $_POST['email'], $_POST['p'])) {
    // Sanitize and validate the data passed in
    $username = filter_input(INPUT_POST, 'username', FILTER_SANITIZE_
```

```php
STRING);

    $email = filter_input(INPUT_POST, 'email', FILTER_SANITIZE_EMAIL);

    $email = filter_var($email, FILTER_VALIDATE_EMAIL);

    if (!filter_var($email, FILTER_VALIDATE_EMAIL)) {

        // Not a valid email

        $error_msg .= '<p class="error">The email address you entered is not valid</p>';

    }


    $password = filter_input(INPUT_POST, 'p', FILTER_SANITIZE_STRING);

    if (strlen($password) != 128) {

        // The hashed pwd should be 128 characters long.

        // If it's not, something really odd has happened

        $error_msg .= '<p class="error">Invalid password configuration.</p>';

    }


    // Username validity and password validity have been checked client side.

    // This should should be adequate as nobody gains any advantage from

    // breaking these rules.

    //


    $prep_stmt = "SELECT id FROM members WHERE email = ? LIMIT 1";

    $stmt = $mysqli->prepare($prep_stmt);


   // check existing email

    if ($stmt) {

        $stmt->bind_param('s', $email);
```

```php
        $stmt->execute();

        $stmt->store_result();


        if ($stmt->num_rows == 1) {

            // A user with this email address already exists

            $error_msg .= '<p class="error">A user with this email address already exists.</p>';

                        $stmt->close();

        }

    } else {

        $error_msg .= '<p class="error">Database error Line 39</p>';

            $stmt->close();

    }


    // check existing username

    $prep_stmt = "SELECT id FROM members WHERE username = ? LIMIT 1";

    $stmt = $mysqli->prepare($prep_stmt);


    if ($stmt) {

        $stmt->bind_param('s', $username);

        $stmt->execute();

        $stmt->store_result();


                if ($stmt->num_rows == 1) {

                    // A user with this username already exists

                    $error_msg .= '<p class="error">A user with this username already exists</p>';

                        $stmt->close();

            }
```

```php
        } else {
            $error_msg .= '<p class="error">Database error line 55</p>';
            $stmt->close();
        }


    // TODO:
    // We'll also have to account for the situation where the user doesn't have
    // rights to do registration, by checking what type of user is attempting to
    // perform the operation.


    if (empty($error_msg)) {

        // Create hashed password using the password_hash function.
        // This function salts it with a random salt and can be verified with
        // the password_verify function.
        $password = password_hash($password, PASSWORD_BCRYPT);


        // Insert the new user into the database
        if ($insert_stmt = $mysqli->prepare("INSERT INTO members (username, email, password) VALUES (?, ?, ?)")) {
            $insert_stmt->bind_param('sss', $username, $email, $password);
            // Execute the prepared query.
            if (! $insert_stmt->execute()) {
                header('Location: ../error.php?err=Registration failure: INSERT');
            }
```

```
        }
        header('Location: ./register_success.php');
    }
}
?>
```

If there is no POST data passed into the form, the registration form is displayed. The form's submit button calls the JavaScript function regformhash(). This function does the necessary validation checks and submits the form when all is well.

If the POST data exists, some server side checks are done to sanitise and validate it. NOTE that these checks are not complete at the time of writing. Some of the issues are mentioned in the comments in the file. At present, we just check that the email address is in the correct format, that the hashed password is the correct length and that the user is not trying to register an email that has already been registered.

If everything checks out, the new user is registered by writing a new record into the members table.

Part 6

Create Javascript Files

1. Create sha512.js file

This file is an implementation in JavaScript of the hashing algorithm sha512. We will use the hashing function so our passwords don't get sent in plain text.

The file can be downloaded from pajhome.org.uk

(It is also saved in the github repository)

Store your copy of this file in a directory called "js", off the root directory of the application.

2. Create forms.js file

This file, which you should create in the js directory of the application, will handle the hashing of the passwords for the login (formhash()) and registration (regformhash()) forms:

```
function formhash(form, password) {
    // Create a new element input, this will be our hashed password field.
    var p = document.createElement("input");


    // Add the new element to our form.
```

```
    form.appendChild(p);

    p.name = "p";

    p.type = "hidden";

    p.value = hex_sha512(password.value);


    // Make sure the plaintext password doesn't get sent.

    password.value = "";


    // Finally submit the form.

    form.submit();
}


function regformhash(form, uid, email, password, conf) {

    // Check each field has a value

    if (uid.value == ''         ||

        email.value == ''       ||

        password.value == ''    ||

        conf.value == '') {


        alert('You must provide all the requested details. Please try again');

        return false;

    }


    // Check the username


    re = /^\w+$/;

    if(!re.test(form.username.value)) {

        alert("Username must contain only letters, numbers and underscores.
```

Please try again");

    form.username.focus();

    return false;

}

// Check that the password is sufficiently long (min 6 chars)

// The check is duplicated below, but this is included to give more

// specific guidance to the user

if (password.value.length < 6) {

    alert('Passwords must be at least 6 characters long. Please try again');

    form.password.focus();

    return false;

}

// At least one number, one lowercase and one uppercase letter

// At least six characters

var re = /(?=.*\d)(?=.*[a-z])(?=.*[A-Z]).{6,}/;

if (!re.test(password.value)) {

    alert('Passwords must contain at least one number, one lowercase and one uppercase letter. Please try again');

    return false;

}

// Check password and confirmation are the same

if (password.value != conf.value) {

    alert('Your password and confirmation do not match. Please try again');

    form.password.focus();

    return false;

```
    }

    // Create a new element input, this will be our hashed password field.
    var p = document.createElement("input");

    // Add the new element to our form.
    form.appendChild(p);
    p.name = "p";
    p.type = "hidden";
    p.value = hex_sha512(password.value);

    // Make sure the plaintext password doesn't get sent.
    password.value = "";
    conf.value = "";

    // Finally submit the form.
    form.submit();
    return true;
}
```

In both cases, the JavaScript hashes the password and passes it in the POST data by creating and populating a hidden field.

Part 7

Create HTML Pages

1. Create the login form (index.php).

This is an HTML form with two text fields, named "email" and "password". The form's submit button calls the JavaScript function formhash(), which will generate a hash of the password, and send "email" and "p" (the hashed password) to the server. You should create this file in the application's root directory.

When logging in, it is best to use something that is not public, for this guide we are using the email as the login id, the username can then be used to identify the user. If the email is not displayed on any pages within the wider application, it adds another unknown for anyone trying to crack the account.

Note: even though we have encrypted the password so it is not sent in plain text, it is essential that you use the HTTPS protocol (TLS/SSL) when sending passwords in a production system. It cannot be stressed enough that simply hashing the password is not enough. A man-in-the-middle attack could be mounted to read the hash being sent and use it to log in.

```php
<?php
include_once 'includes/db_connect.php';
include_once 'includes/functions.php';

sec_session_start();

if (login_check($mysqli) == true) {
    $logged = 'in';
} else {
    $logged = 'out';
}
?>
<!DOCTYPE html>
<html>
    <head>
        <title>Secure Login: Log In</title>
        <link rel="stylesheet" href="styles/main.css" />
        <script type="text/JavaScript" src="js/sha512.js"></script>
        <script type="text/JavaScript" src="js/forms.js"></script>
    </head>
    <body>
        <?php
        if (isset($_GET['error'])) {
            echo '<p class="error">Error Logging In!</p>';
        }
        ?>
         <form action="includes/process_login.php" method="post" name="
```

```
login_form">
            Email: <input type="text" name="email" />
            Password: <input type="password"
                            name="password"
                            id="password"/>
            <input type="button"
                value="Login"
                onclick="formhash(this.form, this.form.password);" />
    </form>


<?php
    if (login_check($mysqli) == true) {
                echo '<p>Currently logged ' . $logged . ' as ' . htmlentities($_SESSION['username']) . '.</p>';

        echo '<p>Do you want to change user? <a href="includes/logout.php">Log out</a>.</p>';
        } else {
                echo '<p>Currently logged ' . $logged . '.</p>';
                echo "<p>If you don't have a login, please <a href='register.php'>register</a></p>";
        }
?>
    </body>
</html>
```

2. Create the register_success.php page

Create a new PHP web page called register_success.php, in the root directory of the application. This is the page to which the user is redirected after successfully registering. Of course you can make this page anything you like or redirect to another page entirely (or even not at all). It's up to you. The page should be located in the root directory of the application. The current register_success.php page that we have written looks like this:

```
<!DOCTYPE html>
```

```
<html>
    <head>
        <meta charset="UTF-8">
        <title>Secure Login: Registration Success</title>
        <link rel="stylesheet" href="styles/main.css" />
    </head>
    <body>
        <h1>Registration successful!</h1>
        <p>You can now go back to the <a href="index.php">login page</a> and log in</p>
    </body>
</html>
```

3. Create the error page

Create a new HTML page in the root directory of the application. Call it error.php This is the page to which users will be directed if an error occurs during the login or registration process, or when trying to establish a secure session. The code given below simply provides a bare bones error page. You will probably need something a bit more sophisticated. However, please note that the input into the page must be properly filtered to guard against XSS attacks. The example page code is:

```
<?php
$error = filter_input(INPUT_GET, 'err', $filter = FILTER_SANITIZE_STRING);

if (! $error) {
    $error = 'Oops! An unknown error happened.';
}
?>
<!DOCTYPE html>
<html>
    <head>
        <meta charset="UTF-8">
        <title>Secure Login: Error</title>
        <link rel="stylesheet" href="styles/main.css" />
    </head>
```

```
            <body>
                <h1>There was a problem</h1>
                <p class="error"><?php echo $error; ?></p>
            </body>
</html>
```

Part 8

Protecting Pages

1. Page Protection Script

One of the most common problems with authentication systems is the developer forgetting to check if the user is logged in. It is very important you use the code below on every protected page to check that the user is logged in. Make sure you use this function to check if the user is logged in.

```
// Include database connection and functions here.
sec_session_start();
if(login_check($mysqli) == true) {
        // Add your protected page content here!
} else {
        echo 'You are not authorized to access this page, please login.';
}
```

As an example of what you should do, we have included a sample protected page. Create a file called protected_page.php in the root directory of the application. The file should contain something like the following:

```
<?php
include_once 'includes/db_connect.php';
include_once 'includes/functions.php';

sec_session_start();
?>
<!DOCTYPE html>
<html>
    <head>
        <meta charset="UTF-8">
```

```
        <title>Secure Login: Protected Page</title>
        <link rel="stylesheet" href="styles/main.css" />
    </head>
    <body>
        <?php if (login_check($mysqli) == true) : ?>
            <p>Welcome <?php echo htmlentities($_SESSION['username']); ?>!</p>
            <p>
                This is an example protected page.  To access this page, users
                must be logged in.  At some stage, we'll also check the role of
                the user, so pages will be able to determine the type of user
                authorised to access the page.
            </p>
            <p>Return to <a href="index.php">login page</a></p>
        <?php else : ?>
            <p>
                <span class="error">You are not authorized to access this page.</span> Please <a href="index.php">login</a>.
            </p>
        <?php endif; ?>
    </body>
</html>
```

Our application redirects to this page after a successful login. Your own implementation does not have to do this, of course.

How to set up a Local Testing Server

This is a short guide about setting up WAMP as a local testing server for web site development and using SkyDrive to sync the server files between your computers.

Steps

1. Install WAMP using the default settings. You can download it from here.

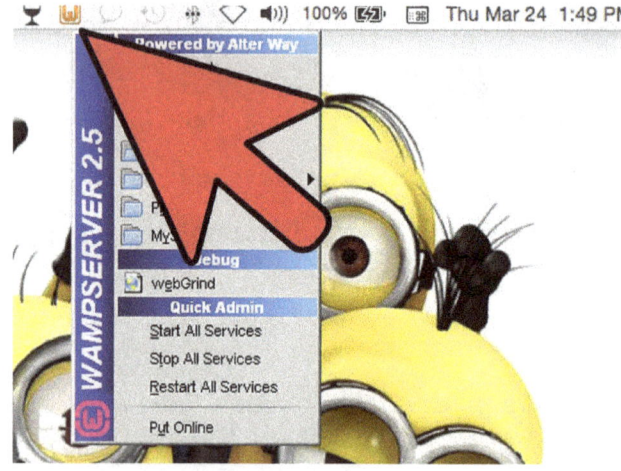

2. Start it. The icon in the notification area should turn green.

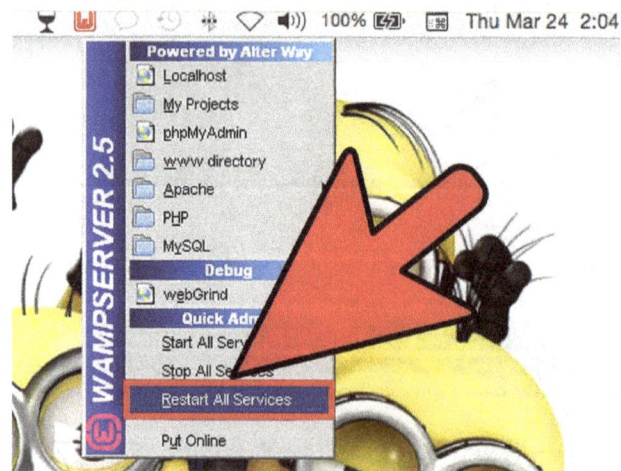

3. Left click the icon and stop all services. The icon should turn red.

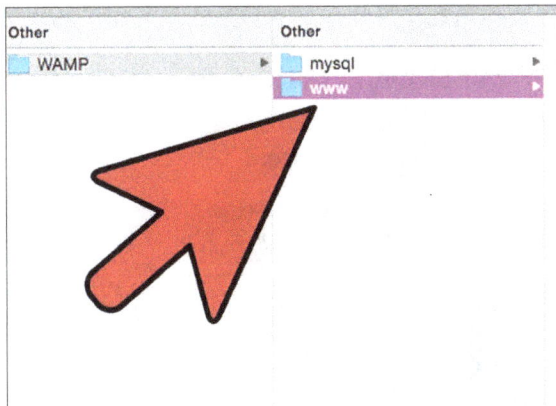

4. In your SkyDrive folder create another folder named WAMP. In this folder create two subfolders called www and mysql.

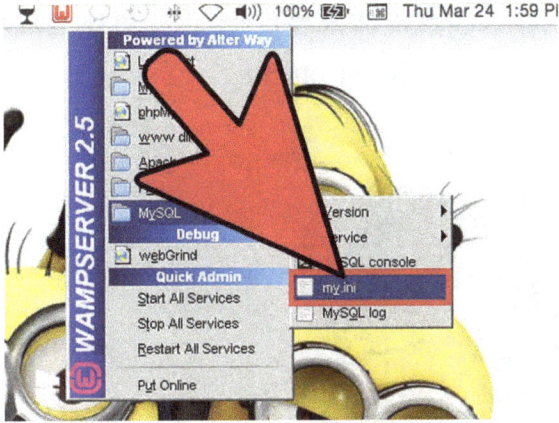

5. There are two files to edit in your WAMP installation. Left-click the WAMP icon. Select MySQL, my.ini. This opens a file in notepad. Edit the line below using your location of the mysql folder you created in the previous step. Save the file.

- datadir=C:/Users/Your Name/SkyDrive/Wamp/mysql

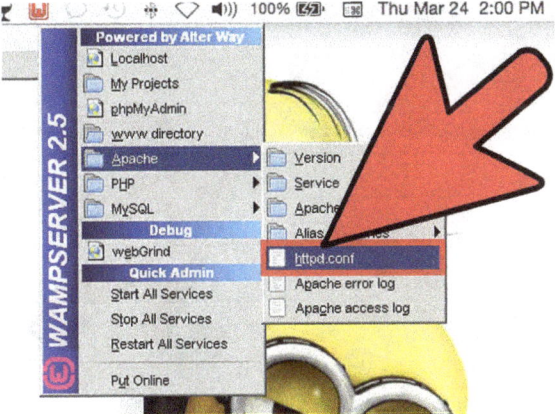

6. Left-click the WAMP icon again. Select Apache, httpd.conf . Edit these lines in this file. Use the location of the www folder you created previously. Save the file.

- DocumentRoot "C:/Users/Your Name/SkyDrive/Wamp/www"
- <Directory "C:/Users/Your Name/SkyDrive/Wamp/www">

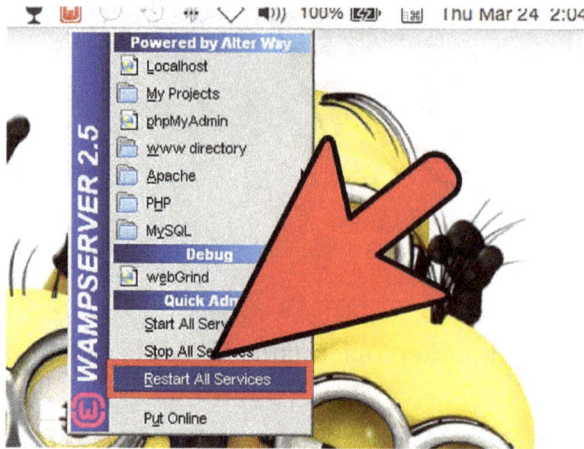

7. Restart all services. Test WAMP server by opening a browser and entering localhost in the address bar.

8. Setting up Dreamweaver to use the testing server.

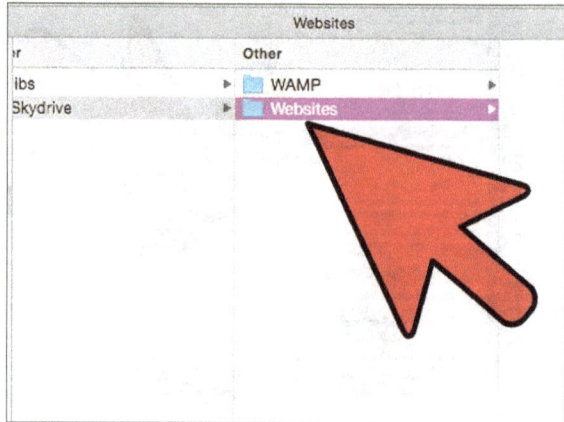

9. Create a folder on SkyDrive to hold your local site files and assets (eg. graphics, fonts, etc.) This

could be a subfolder of a main folder if you have many web sites. Name it for your site. Create a subfolder in your site folder and name it images.

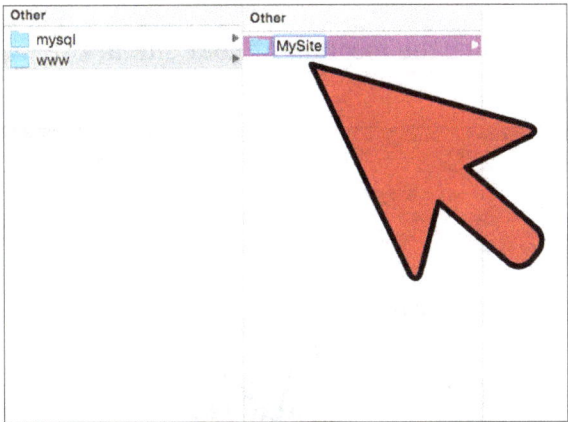

10. Create a folder in your www folder on SkyDrive and name it for your site.

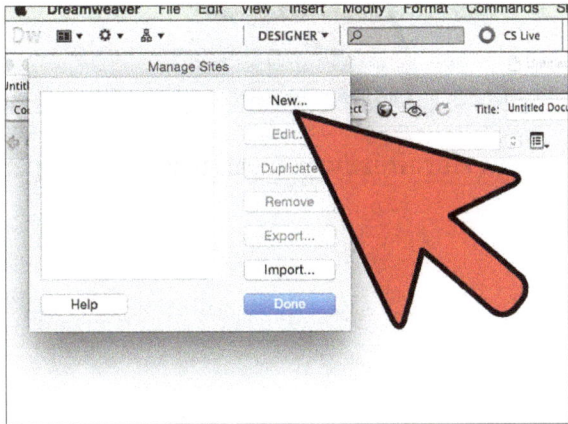

11. Open Dreamweaver. From top menu, select Site and click Manage Sites. Select new site.

- Name your site. Enter the location of the folder you just created for your local site files (not your WAMP server files).

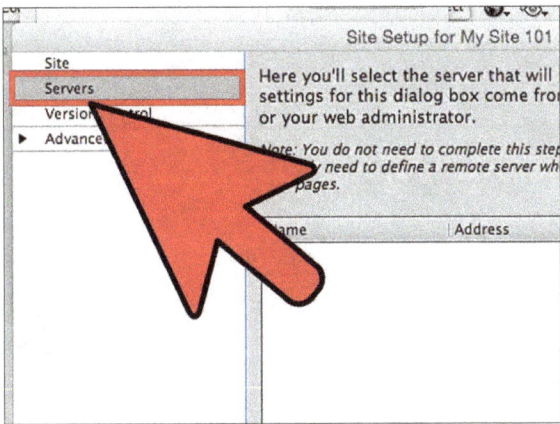

12. Select server from left side. Click the plus sign to add a server.

- Under Server Name, put Testing server.

- For Connect using, select local/network.

- For the Server Folder, enter the location of your site in the www folder on SkyDrive you created earlier.

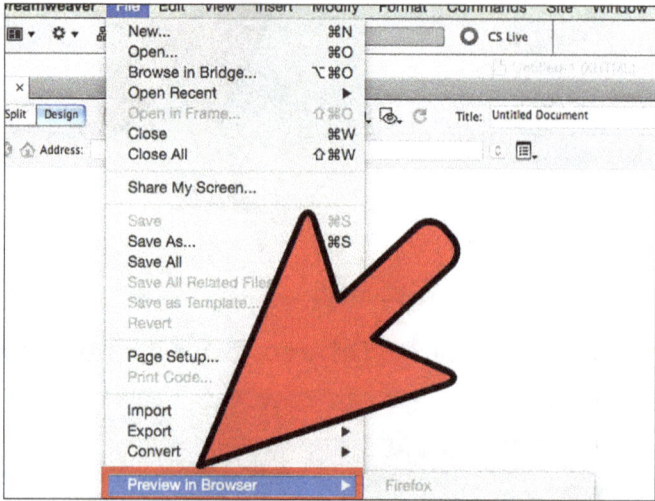

13. If you have a web page in your site already, you can test it now. Open it in Dreamweaver. Press F12 to preview in your browser.

Search Engine Optimization 5

A commercial website needs to be visible and provide relevant information that users are looking for. Search Engine Optimization (SEO) compliant websites prove to have more views and visitors. Trending keywords direct traffic towards websites where these keywords are available. This chapter will provide an integrated understanding of search engine optimization.

How to develop a Commercial Website

When you develop a commercial website, it is important to follow some general guidelines. You want your website to look professional, be easy to navigate, have quality content and, perhaps most importantly, you want it to show up favorably in search engine results. If you understand how to develop a commercial website by implementing all necessary aspects into your site, you will increase its chances of being a success.

Steps

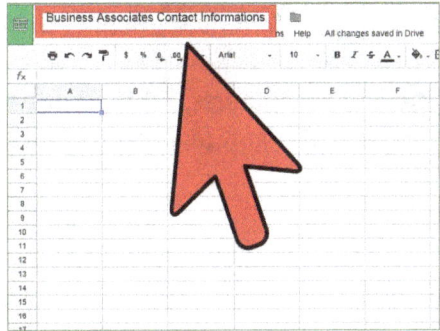

1. Decide the scope of your website, and plan to meet the needs of your potential customers. Be sure to obtain the correct amount bandwidth to accommodate your expected traffic. If your business sells merchandise, be sure to develop a fully fledged set of product pages that are easy to navigate--if you sell services be sure to list the contact information of the appropriate business associates corresponding to the particular services described.

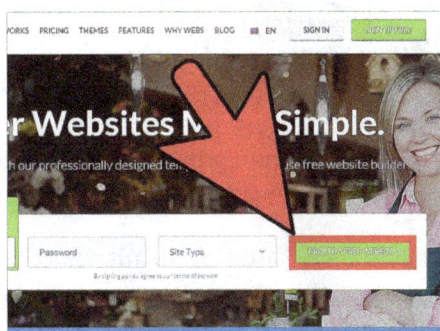

2. Focus on making your website look professional. People, in general, will take your website more

seriously and appreciate it if your website has a clean, professional look. Nothing should distract from the content of your website or make it more difficult to navigate.

- Bright colors with too-high contrast and too much saturation of pictures and videos are examples of what can detract from your website's focus. Also poor quality photos, disorganized information, and a haphazard design can make a website look unprofessional and amateurish.

3. Create quality content so that potential customers are able to learn what they need to know by visiting your website. If you make the effort to show people you know what you are talking about and prove to them that you can help them understand the knowledge related to your company's purpose, they will be more likely to trust you and feel comfortable buying from you.

- Develop your product information so that it is both informative and easy to understand.

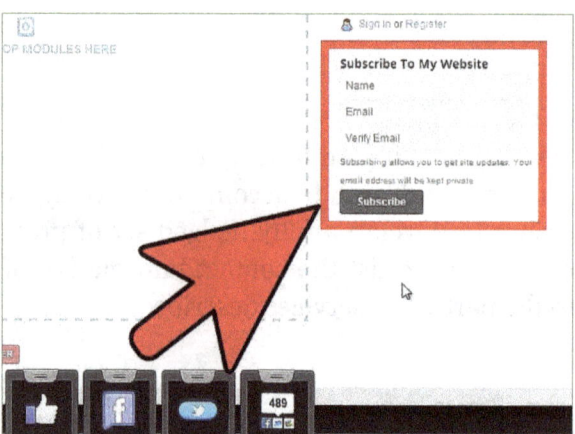

4. Prioritize having a website that is easy to navigate. Ideally, visitors should be able to find what they are looking for in a half dozen clicks or less, starting from your website's homepage.

- Focus to make your website's navigation as intuitive as possible, which lessens the time visitors must invest to find what they need. If a person cannot find what they need within your website in around half a minute, then there is a good chance that they will visit a competitor's website instead of continuing to trudge through yours.

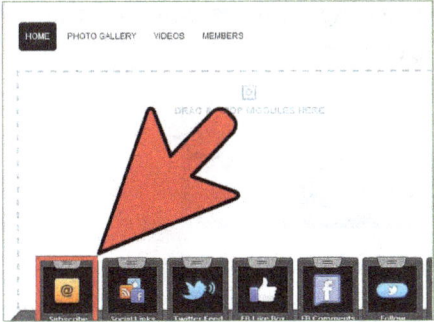

5. Implement a product selection and purchasing system that is easy for your customers to navigate so shopping with you is a simple process.

- Display your products with photos and complete descriptions so all your products are easy to find and learn about. The selection process needs to be easy as well, making it also simple to remove items the customer has selected in case they change their minds.

- Utilize a shopping cart system that is easy to use. If feasible, take as many forms of payment as possible, including credit cards and online payment methods.

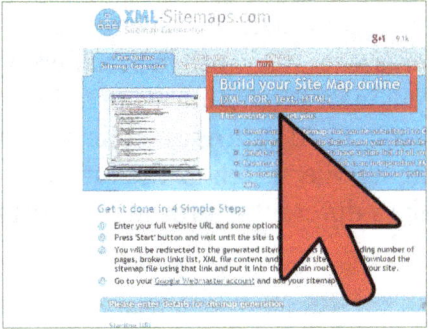

6. Implement search engine optimization techniques so that your website displays favorably in search engines. Ideally, you want your website to show up on the first page when a person performs a search using keywords appropriate to your website's purpose.

- Strive to be one of the first few websites displayed when a user searches for your types of products or services. Creating a sitemap and utilizing both Meta and ALT tags will help your website display favorably.

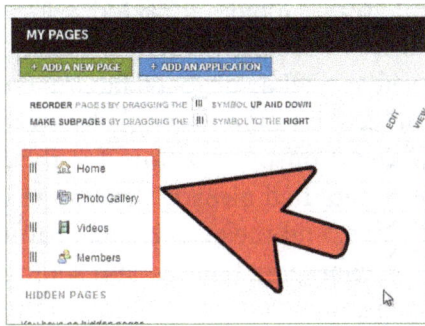

7. Dedicate yourself to keeping your website as up-to-date as possible. Doing so will help ensure

that existing customers continue visiting your website and that new visitors will find their way to your website and want to become customers.

Search Engine Optimization

Search engine optimization (SEO) is the process of affecting the visibility of a website or a web page in a web search engine's unpaid results—often referred to as "natural", "organic", or "earned" results. In general, the earlier (or higher ranked on the search results page), and more frequently a site appears in the search results list, the more visitors it will receive from the search engine's users; these visitors can then be converted into customers. SEO may target different kinds of search, including image search, video search, academic search, news search, and industry-specific vertical search engines. SEO differs from local search engine optimization in that the latter is focused on optimizing a business' online presence so that its web pages will be displayed by search engines when a user enters a local search for its products or services. The former instead is more focused on national searches.

As an Internet marketing strategy, SEO considers how search engines work, what people search for, the actual search terms or keywords typed into search engines and which search engines are preferred by their targeted audience. Optimizing a website may involve editing its content, HTML, and associated coding to both increase its relevance to specific keywords and to remove barriers to the indexing activities of search engines. Promoting a site to increase the number of backlinks, or inbound links, is another SEO tactic. By May 2015, mobile search had surpassed desktop search. Google is developing and pushing mobile search as the future in all of its products. In response, many brands are beginning to take a different approach to their internet strategies.

Relationship with Google

In 1998, Graduate students at Stanford University, Larry Page and Sergey Brin, developed "Backrub", a search engine that relied on a mathematical algorithm to rate the prominence of web pages. The number calculated by the algorithm, PageRank, is a function of the quantity and strength of inbound links. PageRank estimates the likelihood that a given page will be reached by a web user who randomly surfs the web, and follows links from one page to another. In effect, this means that some links are stronger than others, as a higher PageRank page is more likely to be reached by the random surfer.

Page and Brin founded Google in 1998. Google attracted a loyal following among the growing number of Internet users, who liked its simple design. Off-page factors (such as PageRank and hyperlink analysis) were considered as well as on-page factors (such as keyword frequency, meta tags, headings, links and site structure) to enable Google to avoid the kind of manipulation seen in search engines that only considered on-page factors for their rankings. Although PageRank was more difficult to game, webmasters had already developed link building tools and schemes to influence the Inktomi search engine, and these methods proved similarly applicable to gaming PageRank. Many sites focused on exchanging, buying, and selling links, often on a massive scale. Some of these schemes, or link farms, involved the creation of thousands of sites for the sole purpose of link spamming.

By 2004, search engines had incorporated a wide range of undisclosed factors in their ranking algorithms to reduce the impact of link manipulation. In June 2007, *The New York Times'* Saul Hansell stated Google ranks sites using more than 200 different signals. The leading search engines, Google, Bing, and Yahoo, do not disclose the algorithms they use to rank pages. Some SEO practitioners have studied different approaches to search engine optimization, and have shared their personal opinions. Patents related to search engines can provide information to better understand search engines.

In 2005, Google began personalizing search results for each user. Depending on their history of previous searches, Google crafted results for logged in users.

In 2007, Google announced a campaign against paid links that transfer PageRank. On June 15, 2009, Google disclosed that they had taken measures to mitigate the effects of PageRank sculpting by use of the nofollow attribute on links. Matt Cutts, a well-known software engineer at Google, announced that Google Bot would no longer treat nofollowed links in the same way, in order to prevent SEO service providers from using nofollow for PageRank sculpting. As a result of this change the usage of nofollow leads to evaporation of PageRank. In order to avoid the above, SEO engineers developed alternative techniques that replace nofollowed tags with obfuscated Javascript and thus permit PageRank sculpting. Additionally several solutions have been suggested that include the usage of iframes, Flash and Javascript.

In December 2009, Google announced it would be using the web search history of all its users in order to populate search results.

On June 8, 2010 a new web indexing system called Google Caffeine was announced. Designed to allow users to find news results, forum posts and other content much sooner after publishing than before, Google caffeine was a change to the way Google updated its index in order to make things show up quicker on Google than before. According to Carrie Grimes, the software engineer who announced Caffeine for Google, "Caffeine provides 50 percent fresher results for web searches than our last index…"

Google Instant, real-time-search, was introduced in late 2010 in an attempt to make search results more timely and relevant. Historically site administrators have spent months or even years optimizing a website to increase search rankings. With the growth in popularity of social media sites and blogs the leading engines made changes to their algorithms to allow fresh content to rank quickly within the search results.

In February 2011, Google announced the Panda update, which penalizes websites containing content duplicated from other websites and sources. Historically websites have copied content from one another and benefited in search engine rankings by engaging in this practice, however Google implemented a new system which punishes sites whose content is not unique. The 2012 Google Penguin attempted to penalize websites that used manipulative techniques to improve their rankings on the search engine. Although Google Penguin has been presented as an algorithm aimed at fighting web spam, it really focuses on spammy links by gauging the quality of the sites the links are coming from. The 2013 Google Hummingbird update featured an algorithm change designed to improve Google's natural language processing and semantic understanding of web pages.

Getting Indexed

The leading search engines, such as Google, Bing and Yahoo!, use crawlers to find pages for their algorithmic search results. Pages that are linked from other search engine indexed pages do not need to be submitted because they are found automatically. The Yahoo! Directory and DMOZ, two major directories which closed in 2014 and 2017 respectively, both required manual submission and human editorial review. Google offers Google Search Console, for which an XML Sitemap feed can be created and submitted for free to ensure that all pages are found, especially pages that are not discoverable by automatically following links in addition to their URL submission console. Yahoo! formerly operated a paid submission service that guaranteed crawling for a cost per click; this was discontinued in 2009.

Search engine crawlers may look at a number of different factors when crawling a site. Not every page is indexed by the search engines. Distance of pages from the root directory of a site may also be a factor in whether or not pages get crawled.

Preventing Crawling

To avoid undesirable content in the search indexes, webmasters can instruct spiders not to crawl certain files or directories through the standard robots.txt file in the root directory of the domain. Additionally, a page can be explicitly excluded from a search engine's database by using a meta tag specific to robots. When a search engine visits a site, the robots.txt located in the root directory is the first file crawled. The robots.txt file is then parsed and will instruct the robot as to which pages are not to be crawled. As a search engine crawler may keep a cached copy of this file, it may on occasion crawl pages a webmaster does not wish crawled. Pages typically prevented from being crawled include login specific pages such as shopping carts and user-specific content such as search results from internal searches. In March 2007, Google warned webmasters that they should prevent indexing of internal search results because those pages are considered search spam.

Increasing Prominence

A variety of methods can increase the prominence of a webpage within the search results. Cross linking between pages of the same website to provide more links to important pages may improve its visibility. Writing content that includes frequently searched keyword phrase, so as to be relevant to a wide variety of search queries will tend to increase traffic. Updating content so as to keep search engines crawling back frequently can give additional weight to a site. Adding relevant keywords to a web page's meta data, including the title tag and meta description, will tend to improve the relevancy of a site's search listings, thus increasing traffic. URL normalization of web pages accessible via multiple urls, using the canonical link element or via 301 redirects can help make sure links to different versions of the url all count towards the page's link popularity score.

White Hat Versus Black Hat Techniques

SEO techniques can be classified into two broad categories: techniques that search engines recommend as part of good design, and those techniques of which search engines do not approve. The search engines attempt to minimize the effect of the latter, among them spamdexing. Industry commentators have classified these methods, and the practitioners who employ them, as either white hat SEO, or black hat SEO. White hats tend to produce results that last a long time, whereas black hats anticipate that their sites may eventually be banned either temporarily or permanently once the search engines discover what they are doing.

An SEO technique is considered white hat if it conforms to the search engines' guidelines and involves no deception. As the search engine guidelines are not written as a series of rules or commandments, this is an important distinction to note. White hat SEO is not just about following guidelines but is about ensuring that the content a search engine indexes and subsequently ranks is the same content a user will see. White hat advice is generally summed up as creating content for users, not for search engines, and then making that content easily accessible to the spiders, rather than attempting to trick the algorithm from its intended purpose. White hat SEO is in many ways similar to web development that promotes accessibility, although the two are not identical.

Black hat SEO attempts to improve rankings in ways that are disapproved of by the search engines, or involve deception. One black hat technique uses text that is hidden, either as text colored similar to the background, in an invisible div, or positioned off screen. Another method gives a different page depending on whether the page is being requested by a human visitor or a search engine, a technique known as cloaking.

Another category sometimes used is grey hat SEO. This is in between black hat and white hat approaches where the methods employed avoid the site being penalized however do not act in producing the best content for users, rather entirely focused on improving search engine rankings.

Search engines may penalize sites they discover using black hat methods, either by reducing their rankings or eliminating their listings from their databases altogether. Such penalties can be applied either automatically by the search engines' algorithms, or by a manual site review. One example was the February 2006 Google removal of both BMW Germany and Ricoh Germany for use of deceptive practices. Both companies, however, quickly apologized, fixed the offending pages, and were restored to Google's list.

As a Marketing Strategy

SEO is not an appropriate strategy for every website, and other Internet marketing strategies can be more effective like paid advertising through pay per click (PPC) campaigns, depending on the site operator's goals. Search engine marketing (SEM), is practice of designing, running, and optimizing search engine ad campaigns. Its difference from SEO is most simply depicted as the difference between paid and unpaid priority ranking in search results. Its purpose regards prominence more so than relevance; website developers should regard SEM with the utmost importance with consideration to PageRank visibility as most navigate to the primary listings of their search. A successful Internet marketing campaign may also depend upon building high quality web pages to engage and persuade, setting up analytics programs to enable site owners to measure results, and improving a site's conversion rate. In November 2015, Google released a full 160 page version of its Search Quality Rating Guidelines to the public, which now shows a shift in their focus towards "usefulness" and mobile search.

SEO may generate an adequate return on investment. However, search engines are not paid for organic search traffic, their algorithms change, and there are no guarantees of continued referrals. Due to this lack of guarantees and certainty, a business that relies heavily on search engine traffic can suffer major losses if the search engines stop sending visitors. Search engines can change their algorithms, impacting a website's placement, possibly resulting in a serious loss of traffic. According to Google's CEO, Eric Schmidt, in 2010, Google made over 500 algorithm changes – almost 1.5 per day. It is considered wise business practice for website operators to liberate themselves from dependence on search engine traffic.

In addition to accessibility in terms of web crawlers (addressed above), user web accessibility has become increasingly important for SEO.

International Markets

Optimization techniques are highly tuned to the dominant search engines in the target market. The search engines' market shares vary from market to market, as does competition. In 2003, Danny Sullivan stated that Google represented about 75% of all searches. In markets outside the United States, Google's share is often larger, and Google remains the dominant search engine worldwide as of 2007. As of 2006, Google had an 85–90% market share in Germany. While there were hundreds of SEO firms in the US at that time, there were only about five in Germany. As of June 2008, the marketshare of Google in the UK was close to 90% according to Hitwise. That market share is achieved in a number of countries.

As of 2009, there are only a few large markets where Google is not the leading search engine. In most cases, when Google is not leading in a given market, it is lagging behind a local player. The most notable example markets are China, Japan, South Korea, Russia and the Czech Republic where respectively Baidu, Yahoo! Japan, Naver, Yandex and Seznam are market leaders.

Successful search optimization for international markets may require professional translation of web pages, registration of a domain name with a top level domain in the target market, and web hosting that provides a local IP address. Otherwise, the fundamental elements of search optimization are essentially the same, regardless of language.

Legal Precedents

On October 17, 2002, SearchKing filed suit in the United States District Court, Western District of Oklahoma, against the search engine Google. SearchKing's claim was that Google's tactics to prevent spamdexing constituted a tortious interference with contractual relations. On May 27, 2003, the court granted Google's motion to dismiss the complaint because SearchKing "failed to state a claim upon which relief may be granted."

In March 2006, KinderStart filed a lawsuit against Google over search engine rankings. KinderStart's website was removed from Google's index prior to the lawsuit and the amount of traffic to the site dropped by 70%. On March 16, 2007 the United States District Court for the Northern District of California (San Jose Division) dismissed KinderStart's complaint without leave to amend, and partially granted Google's motion for Rule 11 sanctions against KinderStart's attorney, requiring him to pay part of Google's legal expenses.

How to Improve Search Engine Optimization

Showing up on search engines is one of the most critical ways to increase website traffic and expose your content, product or service to people who might be interested in what you have to offer. This means that you'll want to practice a little SEO (search engine optimization).

Most of the major search engines utilize an algorithm to determine where a website ranks. The criteria are different for every engine, but all engines share several commonalities. It all boils down to the type and amount of content provided on a given website, the level of optimization done on the site, and the popularity of the website.

Method 1

Taking Advantage of Google

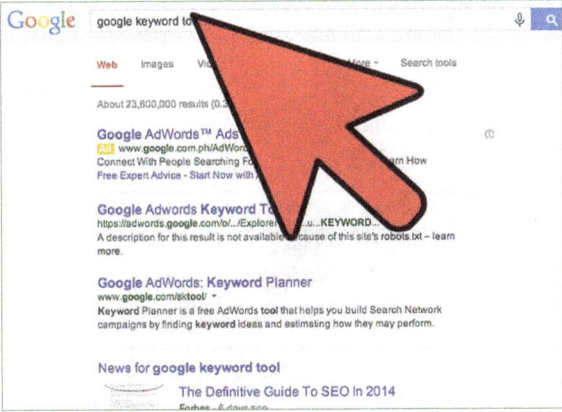

1. Use Keywords. Google Keywords, a tool within the Google AdSense website, allows you to track keywords and find keyword suggestions. Browse the site and get familiar with how it works and then use it to your advantage. Find keywords that will help you maximize your website's viewership.

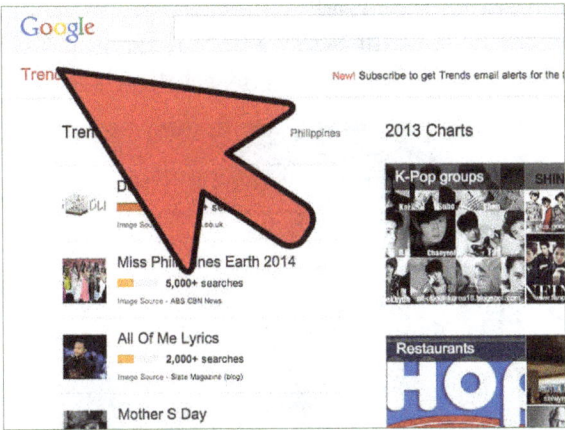

2. Use Trends. Google Trends tells you how searches in a subject change over time. You can use it to predict spikes and slumps as well as to know when you should update and change pages for the season or switch to using different keywords. You can look at and compare several different terms at a time.

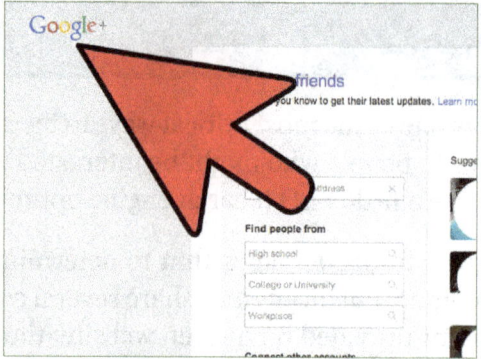

3. Add yourself to Google. Google will reward Google Plus users and also businesses which are registered on Google Maps. Take advantage and join Google, as it is the most popular search engine by far.

Method 2

Creating your Content

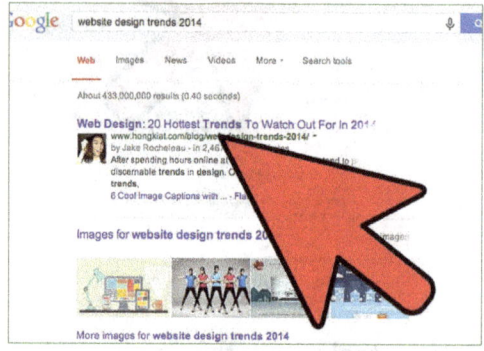

1. Have quality content. Quality content, in other words lots of original, error-free text organized well on a modern-looking website, is what matters most in terms of SEO that you can control. Hiring a professional website designer can help with the cosmetics and get you taken seriously by your visitors. You'll also want to be sure that you're not misleading visitors, they should be getting what was advertised when they looked at the site's description.

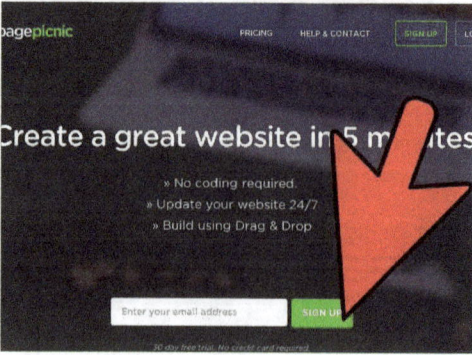

2. Create original content. You also create quality content by making sure that your content is original. This means that not only should each page of your site have different content than every

other page of your site, but it also means that you'll be docked for stealing the content of others. Make your text original.

3. Incorporate appropriate images. Quality images, tagged with good keywords, can also help your rankings with search engines.

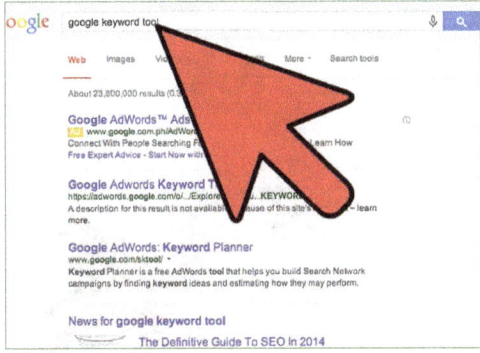

4. Use keywords. Find the most relevant and search keywords that relate to the content you provide and then add those keywords to your site text. Use the word a few times within the page in a way that relates to the rest of the text and is natural. Going over the top with the word-drops or pairing them with content that is irrelevant will get you punished in the rankings, however.

5. Target niche keywords with low competition. This involves at least a little bit of figuring out what makes your business unique. Maybe you're not just a clothing designer, but you're a geeky clothing designer. Maybe you're not just an auto shop but you're an auto shop in Seattle. Try to use Google Adwords to check how competitive your keywords are before deciding on them. Be sure that the keywords have at least some searches. You will want to try using broader key words too.

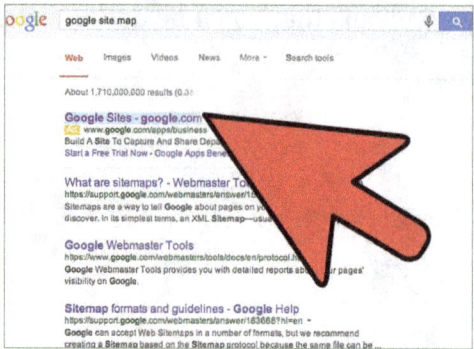

6. Have a site map. Create a site map that tells people where everything is on your site. You will get about a 1% click through rate to your site map. However, it will do wonders for those who know what site maps do, and the Search Engines will like it as well.

Method 3

Creating your Code

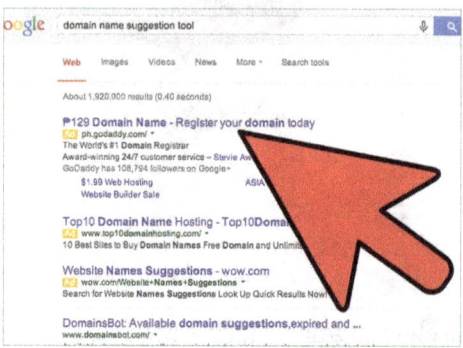

1. Choose a good domain name. Keywords as the first word in a domain name will boost your traffic a little. Using a country TLD (top level domain) will boost your rankings locally but hurt you internationally so use that with caution. Avoid dated domain naming techniques like replacing words with numbers. Being a subdomain (like a something.tumblr.com) will also hurt you.

- Keywords in your own subpages and subdomains also help. Your subpages especially should always have a descriptive title.

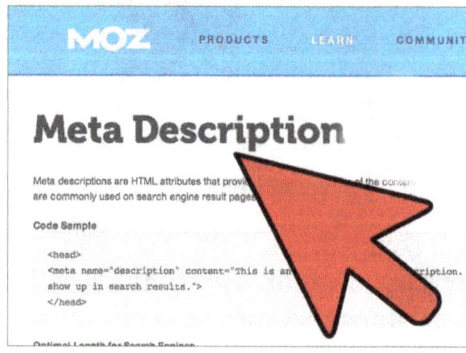

2. Use descriptions and Meta tags. Descriptions are a tagged part of your website code which

describe the content on the page. Having one at all will help your rankings and having one which contains good keywords will help even more. If your site is using the same tags for all the pages, you are not helping search engines figure out the subject or relevance of your individual pages. Regarding Meta Tags, there are 2 very important fields:

- Title Tag - arguably the most important SEO tag for any website. Google supports approx. 60 characters in the title, while Yahoo allows for up to 110 characters in the title. It is important to target the most critical keywords in the Title. Every page should have a unique Title.

- META Description Tag - These were once important but are no longer. Some engines do display the description defined, while others do not. Some search engines do read the description tag, and do utilize the content found within in the ranking process. Google, MSN and Yahoo give very little weight to no weight for these.

3. Use headers. Headers are similar to descriptions and the same rules apply: having one at all helps and having one with keywords is even better. Use them.

4. Keep it simple. Keep the structure, navigation and URL structure of your site simple enough for search engines to follow. Remember that search engines cannot parse your navigation if it's using flash or javascript. So try to stay close to standard HTML when it comes to Navigation. URLs with dynamic parameters (?, &, SIDs) usually do not perform when it comes to search engine rankings.

Method 4
Making Connections

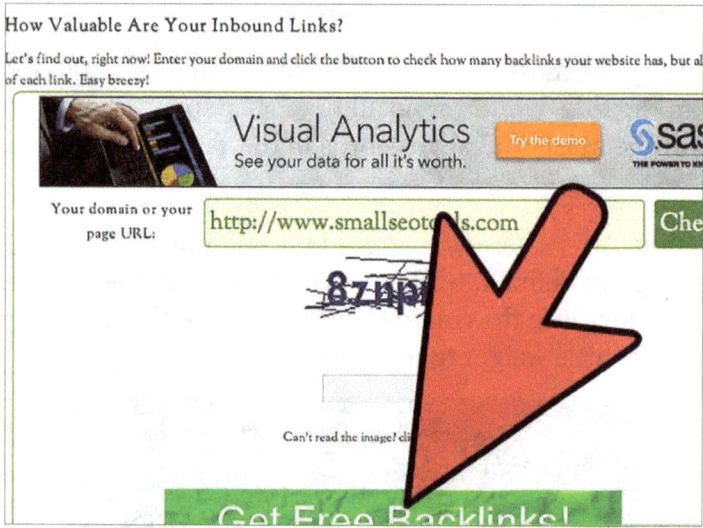

1. Create quality backlinks. Backlinks are when another website links to your page. It works in your favor if the website is one that gets more hits than yours does. The best types of "link building" are directory registration, text link advertising, and press release distribution, but you can also build links by doing a link exchange, cross promotion, or guest blogging for a relevant blog.

   - Try to offer valuable information or tools so that other people are motivated to link to your site. This will increase the chances of natural backlinks.

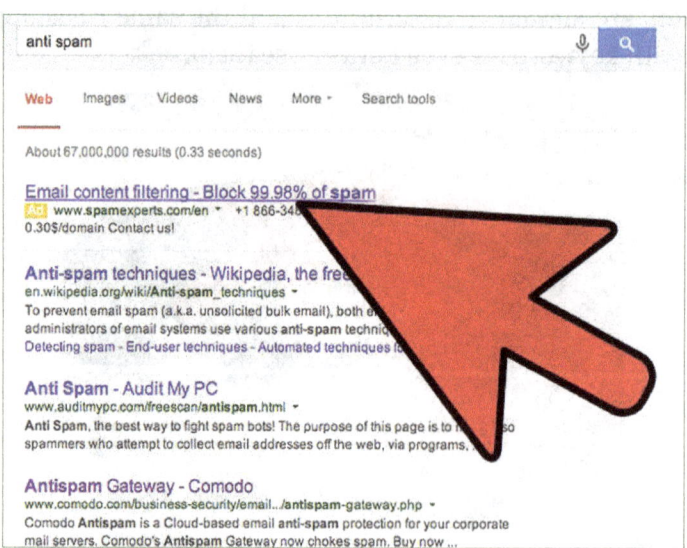

2. Do NOT spam. Spamming comment sections and other website areas will actually make Google and other search engines dock you severely or remove you entirely. Do not spam people to build backlinks for yourself. Search engines will also punish you if your name is attached to spamming complaints or if you operate your website anonymously.

3. Do that social media thing. Right now, social media share and likes are the activity which is most rewarded by Google and other search engines. especially for subjects that are currently relevant. Create social media accounts with the major sites and update them regularly. Avoid being spammy by not just posting ads: post pictures of customers, events that you attend relating to your business, and other content that your fans might enjoy.

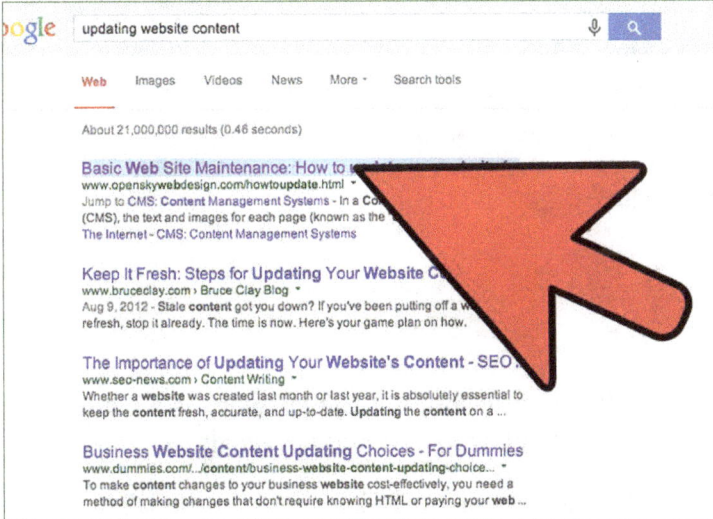

4. Update your site regularly. Most search engines reward websites which see regular or at least recent updates.

How to Design a Website for SEO

Learning to design an excellent SEO incorporated website is not a joke, it requires a systematic approach. Anyone who is design a SEO friendly website has to keep in mind few things which hold relevance from the search engine optimization point of view.

Steps

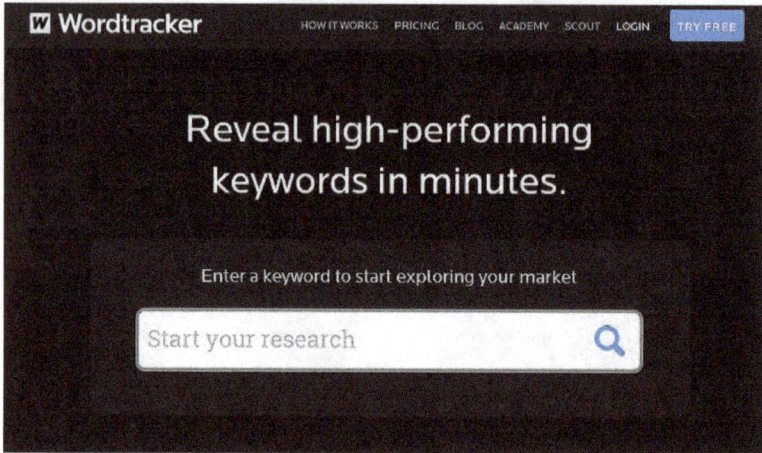

1. Research keywords. When designing a search engine friendly site, carry out the research for keywords. Make effective use of a word tracker. A word tracker is a keyword research tool from which one can find relevant databases that could help one grab the attention of prospective audience. The two main things to remember are competition search and the misspelling search.

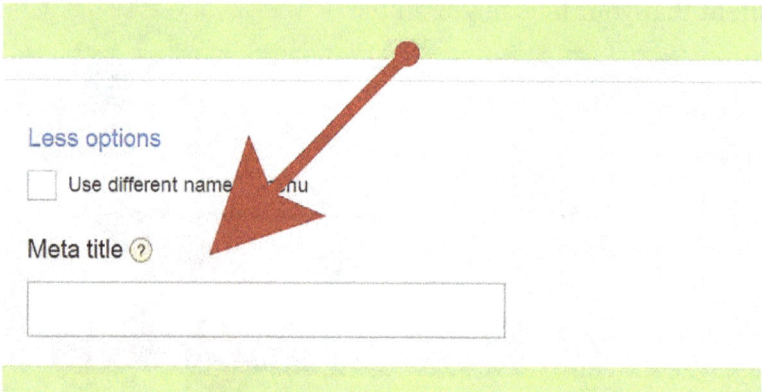

2. Place keywords strategically. Researching for the keyword is a complex chore, but what holds more complexity is correct placement of researched keywords.

- Place keywords in the URL. Inclusion of keywords in the URL of the website is optimal. If you have multiple words that need to be placed in the URL, then appropriately separated dashes should be used.

- Focus on areas that register well with search engines, including bold headings, near the top of the page and at the end of the page.

- Embed keywords in the anchor text used to describe links, your domain name and title and Meta tags.

- Use keywords to create a theme throughout the content on your site. Search engines tend to look for a theme or common topic on a Website in an effort to deliver more relevant results for searchers.

- Place your keywords as closely together as possible, while making sure your sentences remain clear.
- Ensure a proper keyword density or weight. The greater the percentage of keywords, in relation to other text, the better.

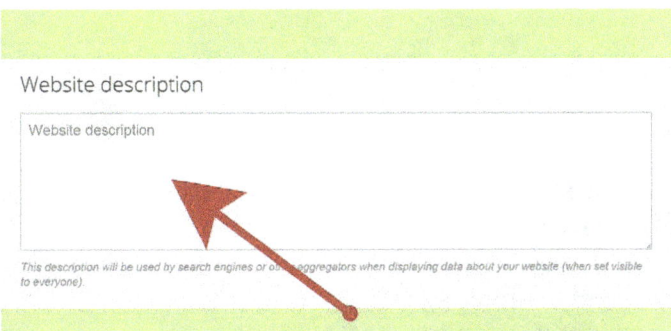

3. Include Meta and title tags. Some search engines still use Meta Keyword, Meta Description and Title tags to catalog and rank Web pages. Be sure to place a title tag at the top of each page to identify the document's overall content. You should also write an accurate Meta description tag. Don't neglect to include a Meta keyword tag to reveal the most important keywords for each page to search engine spiders.

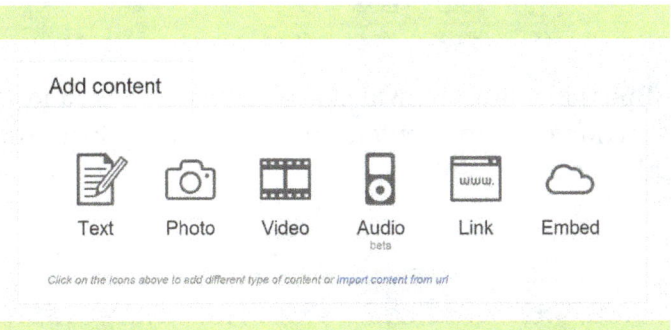

4. Keep your content updated. This lets search engines know the content on your site isn't stale, plus it will keep your site appealing to visitors looking for the latest information.

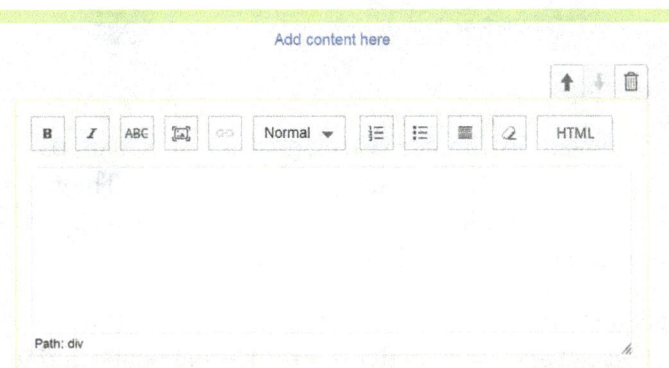

5. Provide enough content. Major search engines typically require you to have at least 200 to 250 words on each page.

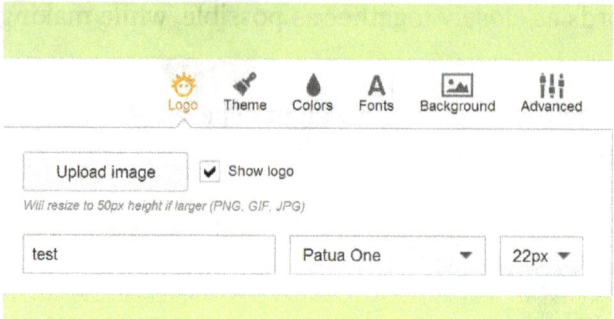

6. Use images sparingly. Apart from the logo or any other specific symbol, the text of the website should be kept away from images. The size and the placement of the image also need to be watched.

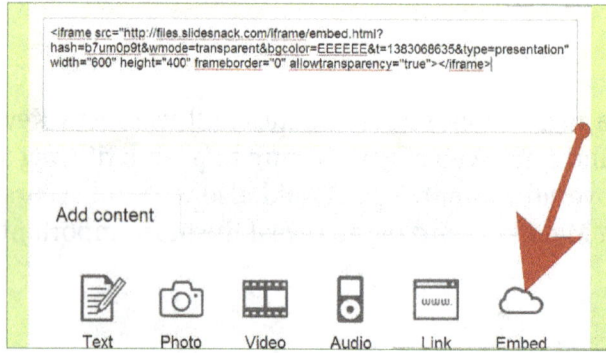

7. Avoid using frames if possible. Frames, which are being used less and less, enable you to split a page into pieces and section off static content to decrease download times. However, they can cause navigation difficulties and prevent search engines from being able to access every page on your website.

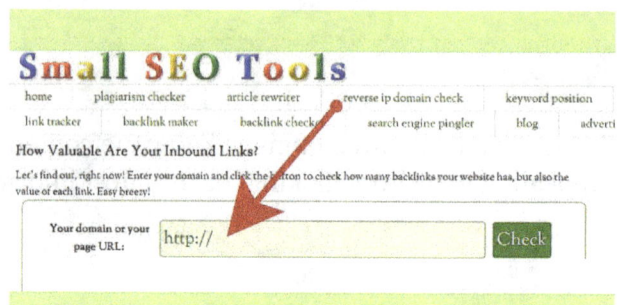

8. Build incoming or back links. Most major search engines rank Web pages based on the number and the quality of links that point to the Website (link popularity). They do so because it's very difficult for Web masters to "fake" good links. As a result, link analysis gives search engines a useful means of determining which pages are good for particular topics.

- Listing your Website with relevant directories and portals is an ideal way to build valuable incoming links. You can also write articles, forum/blog posts, and testimonials and include a link pointing back to your site. In addition, you can trade links with Websites that complement yours. Just make sure they're not competing Websites. The main objective is to link to sites that are closely related to your site's topic.

- Keep in mind that search engines look for websites that are useful for site visitors. If your linking structure indicates that it is helpful and informative, you'll generate more favorable search engine rankings. You'll also enjoy a steady stream of targeted traffic from your link partners.

How to create a Quality Website

Web design is the planning and creation of websites. This includes the information architecture, user interface, site structure, navigation, layout, colors, fonts, and imagery. All of these are combined with the principles of design to create a website that meets the goals of the owner and designer.

Steps

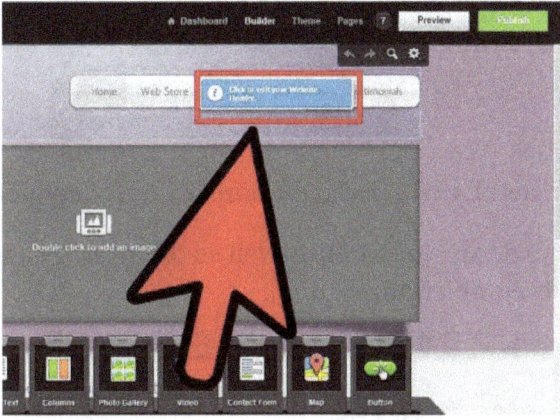

1. Consider how easy it is to use the site. It's no use having a website you can't navigate yourself.

2. Make sure that your website is user-friendly and easy to navigate. This will attract the attention of your potential customers.

- Focusing on logical reasoning, which is needed to achieve good quality web design. That being said, the best sites will also stir up an emotional response.

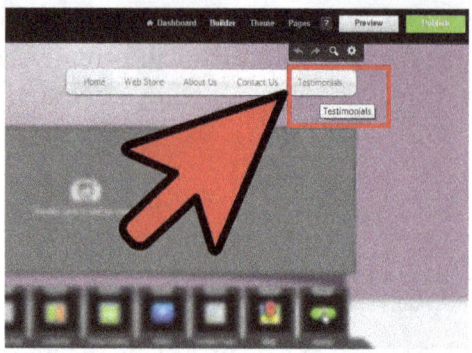

3. Consider getting the services of a Web Design Company or independent web designer.

- Describe your website design in detail, as well as the strategy and tactics you have planned in order to achieve its completion.

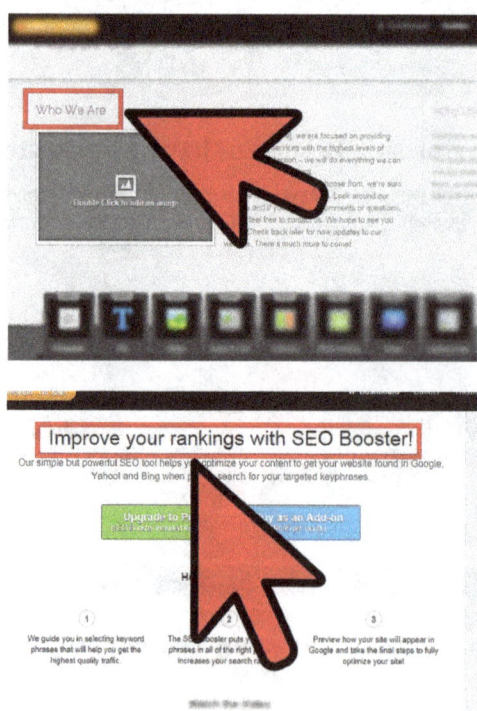

4. Make necessary upgrades and adjustments to your website from time to time. You will want

Search Engine Optimization | 195

your designer to be up to date on Search Engine Optimization so that your site can get good rankings and be easily found in search engines. Keep these tips for quality web design in mind in order to achieve the goals of your online business.

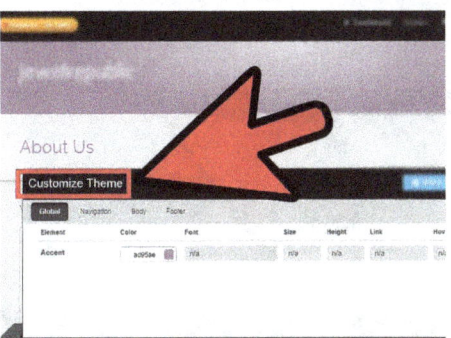

5. Site owners want a website that they can edit easily without paying more every time. We can help!"The next generation in custom website design" means advanced code for a great looking website now that will still display well for years to come into the future. Fully custom websites for static sites, content management, and e-commerce. Matching custom blog designs and templates created in various blog formats. Low overhead means small business website designs for low cost solutions. Custom web graphics for websites, blogs, audio players, and video production.

6. In good web design, less is almost always more. Common mistakes are to wow the user better to focus on central message. Find quality images 1 large quality image on the main page is worth 200 bad images inside. When you design the website it's not you who you want to please but your users that u want to please and it's not your website that is you want necessary to impress them but what you do the product that you offer or the service that you offer.

7. Tailor the website to be clean, crisp, focus, honest and sometimes a little unpredictable. Start

with that information which you want to convey to the public write it down organizes it then design the website around the information that you want to convey and not the other way round.

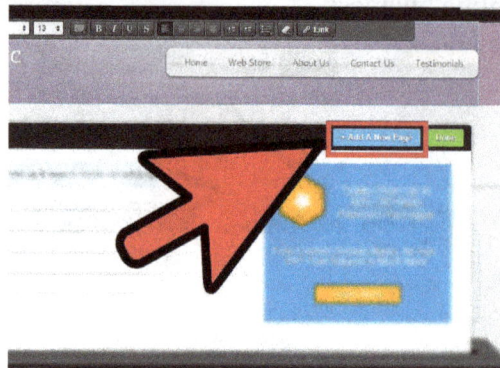

8. Create a place where many people start with the website and think of it as a perfect picture within the frame. When they build the picture and think it is great and two weeks later they want to add something and the realization that they can't without completely destroying the picture.

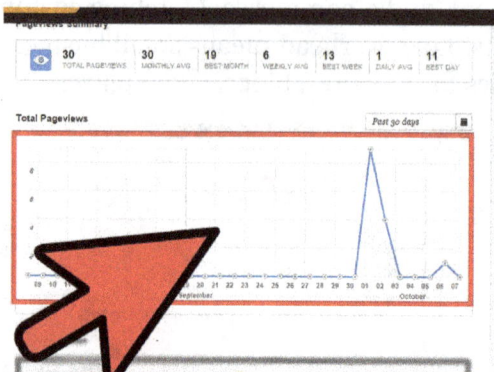

9. Know that the life span of the average new website is incredibly short. In two weeks, millions of people are opening new websites, every day. The majority of them don't touch it again, and the website dies and goes down nest. If you want to keep your website in top 10 or 20 rankings, update it with valuable information which users will be impressed by and will want to come back.

10. Understand the first page of your website is far more important visually than all the other pages of your website as that's the first impression. Putting together a website is a very frustrating experience, but it also can be very very rewarding.

Web Designing as a Career

Professional web design and development is an important industry. Almost all businesses, organizations and companies have a presence on the Internet. Familiarity with various Internet tools, programming languages and multimedia editing is a must for making a career in this field. Professional web designing is best understood in confluence with the major topics listed in the following chapter.

How to become a Professional Web Designer and Programmer

Web designers and web developers are two of the most sought-after professions these days, and it's not as hard as it may seem to become one. With some free time, a keen interest, and a lot of practice and patience, you could find yourself making world-class websites and earning a nice income by doing so.

Steps

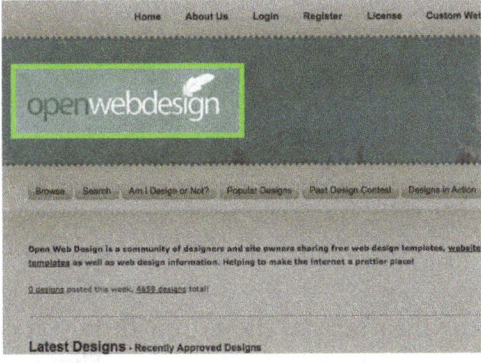

1. Learn from other great web designers and programmers. Take a look at other well-designed websites, and note how a menu or content area is laid out and then use that knowledge in your designs.

2. Get the right tools. Start by getting a good vector graphics editor such as Adobe Illustrator.

Making images using vector graphics is the easiest way to grasp graphics design, so spending some money on something like Illustrator or Fireworks will be a great help. Inkscape is a nice free and open-source alternative for beginners.

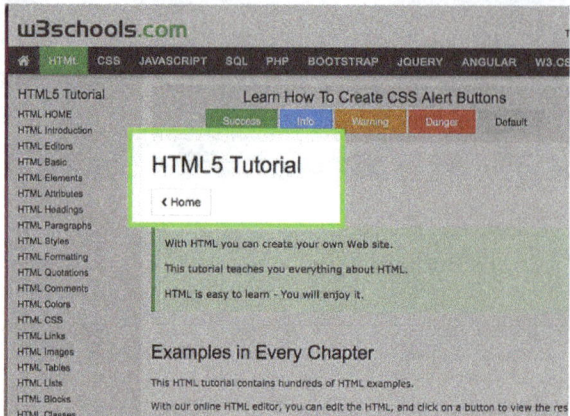

3. Learn the skills you'll need. These skills include:

- HTML
- CSS
- JavaScript
- jQuery
- PHP
- SQL
- Bootstrap

Of course there are many tutorials on the Web where you can learn these languages. But we want to know about the best place for learning. The most famous place (if you search on Google) is W3Schools. The six languages listed above are enough for a start. However there is no end of learning, especially in a Web Developer's life. The main purposes of these languages are:

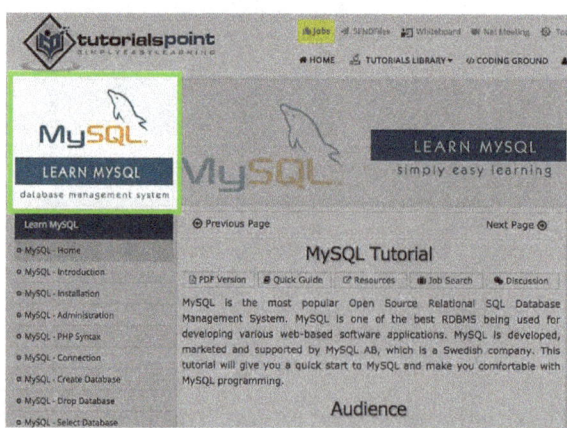

- HTML: For the main content of the webpage,
- CSS: For the page style,
- JavaScript: For dynamic content,
- jQuery: For easy JavaScript scripting,
- PHP: For server side scripting,
- SQL: For database management.
- BootStrap: Rapid development for websites that is mobile ready first.

Please find and study these tutorials on W3Schools. Also you should study other stuff in W3schools as well, because they are extremely helpful.

4. Create dynamic websites using PHP and MySQL. These technologies will enable you to create a website that does not require you to make individual HTML pages but allow you to use templates to display multiple pages within the same design.

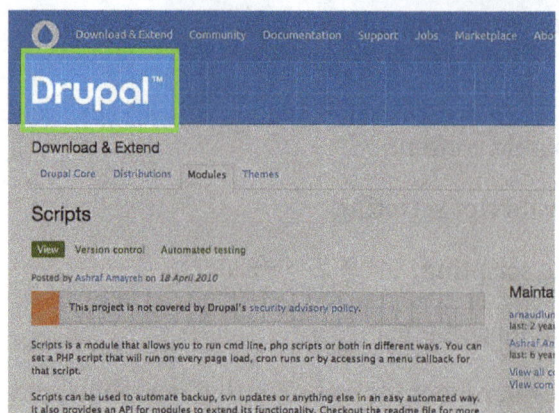

5. Consider using a dynamic web service to improve the user experience (UX). Create a web site that uses AJAX so you can utilise the server-side power of PHP without having to refresh the page thus saving bandwidth and enabling you to create 'interactive' web applications.

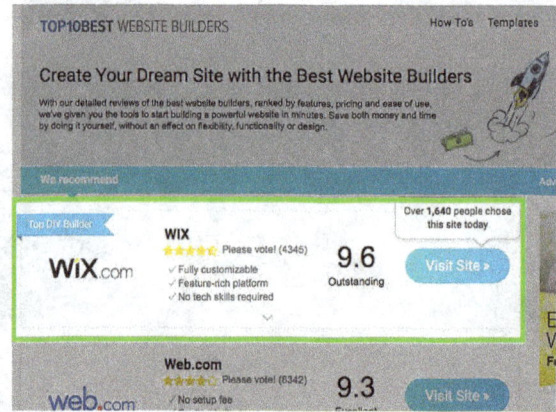

6. Set up your computer as a productive website development environment. Install a web server on your Computer so that you can work on scripts locally without an Internet connection. If you choose the PHP . If you use ASP.NET use IIS available on most versions of windows.

7. Practice using coding examples. Get yourself some script examples to "tinker" with: Finding a script to dissect is the best way to learn. Try CMS's like Drupal and Joomla

8. Be bold by starting a project when you have idea and some time. The best time to start making websites is as soon as possible, for two reasons; they can take a lot of time to complete, and you learn a lot just by making them. Don't worry too much about making it perfect the first time; one of the best things about websites is that they can always be improved at any time.

How to develop a Portfolio for Web Design

Your web design portfolio should ideally be your own website that represents your best work, features projects you have worked on, and informs potential clients about your exact services. Though you may want to burn a copy of your portfolio onto a disk or make prints of screenshots, the most accepted form of presentation for a web design portfolio remains your own website. Developing a portfolio for web design involves creating a unique and functional website, featuring websites you've worked on, including client testimonials, providing information about you and your services, and giving potential clients an easy way to contact you. Read the following steps to find out how to develop a portfolio for web design.

Steps

1. Design your own website.

   - Because you're developing a portfolio for web design, you want to avoid using templates.

   - Create your own unique design, but keep it clear and simple. Make the site easy-to-navigate and functional.

   - Put your logo at the top of each page and link it to your home page.

   - Write a tagline that says something about your work as a web designer and is catchy enough for people to remember. Include it beneath your logo.

2. Clearly feature other websites you've worked on.

   - Whether you've worked for many different clients or have only finished a few student projects, you should feature your best work on your website.

- Offer a screenshot of each website with a link through to the live website. If possible, add a description of each, as well as what the client's wishes were, and what approach you took in designing their sites.

3. Add testimonials from clients.

- Ask clients who were pleased with your work for some short testimonials. Request that they say something about your professional approach and conduct, as well as the results.

4. Include publicity. If you've been featured in any publications either online or in print, include links to them or excerpts from the articles.

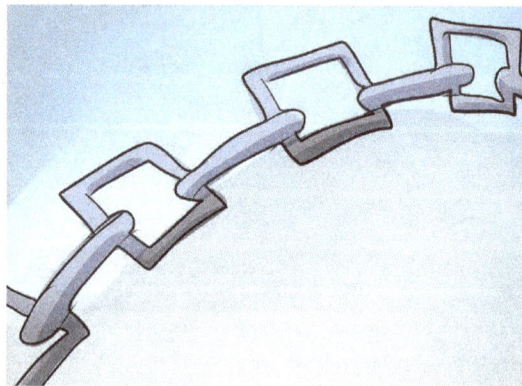

5. Link to your blog. If you maintain a blog that clearly demonstrates your expertise in the field of web design, link to it.

6. Create an "About" page. This page should tell visitors to your site about you, your education, and your experience in web design. Though people generally like to hear a brief reference to your hobbies or interest, the main focus should be on web design.

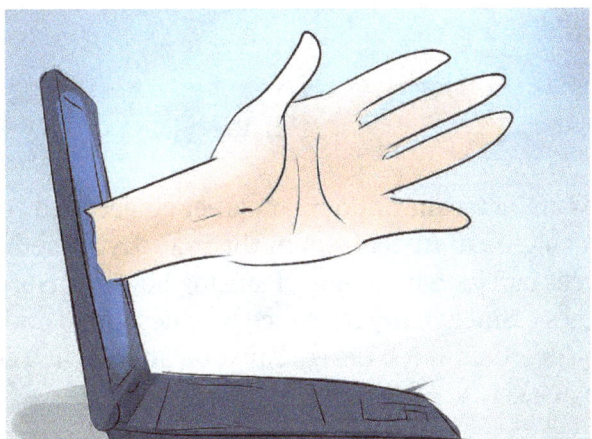

7. Add a services page. This should include the specifics of your web design, such as programming languages and software programs you use. If you do graphic design as a part of your web design, include that too.

8. Create a contact page.

- Include your email address and phone number.
- You can also create a contact form that allows the visitor to include some information about why they are contacting you.

9. Include a prominently displayed "Hire Me" link. Link this to your contact page.

How to Advertise your Web Design Business

The Web design industry is an increasingly popular career choice, and competition could be fierce in your area due to a high volume of freelancers in the industry. Whether you are the owner of a firm with multiple employees or a lone freelancer, learning how to advertise your web design business is critical to your success. Since many freelance web designers and firms market locally and nationally, if not globally, advertising web design must be approached seriously and creatively to reach your segment of the market.

Method 1

Advertise your Website Online

You can use paid advertising, free advertising, social media, and a variety of other techniques to spread the word about your business.

1. Work on your own website. Websites are important for any business to have as the Internet

continues to pull in consumers in nearly every industry, but since websites are your business, your company definitely needs one. How you structure your website is up to you, but you should have a clear focus on what your skill is while providing the information potential customers need. Your website doesn't have to include your rates, but it should include your services, examples of previous work, contact information, and supporting educational information such as if you attended a web design degree program of any kind.

2. Pay for online advertising. You could ad listings on high-traffic websites, or do a pay-per-click campaign with the large search engines. Pay for listings in business directories for web designers.

3. Become active in social media and in other online communities. These are places you may find your customers. Facebook, Twitter, FourSquare, and other social networking websites give you another avenue to connect to both current and prospective clients while also giving them a way to connect with and learn about you before, during, and after the sale. Become active in places where you know your target market is and in industry-related communities to establish yourself as an expert.

4. Focus on search engine optimization (SEO). Let the search engines do some of the work for you

naturally at all hours of the day. If you are not familiar with SEO, you can either research and try your hand at it or hire someone to help you. Clients want to know their website is going to be seen, so if you can offer SEO services to your customers, then you have more value.

Method 2

Advertise your Website Offline

You can do this via newspaper ads, business cards and fliers, radio and/or TV spots, and through general face-to-face interaction.

1. Attend industry-related conferences. This may not bring in more customers unless some of the attendees are looking for services, but you may find other people to network with. Networking may help you offer more to customers or may help you handle e a higher customer volume. Industry conferences will also have valuable information to keep you on top of the latest trends and technology in the field, enabling you to provide more value to customers.

2. Read industry-related magazines. One of the magazines is Website Magazine, which has a free and paid edition, and offers valuable information to designers and others who run online businesses. The magazine also offers ad spots, and since it targets Internet marketers and other online professionals, advertising web design services there could prove profitable.

3. Reach out to small businesses in your area and suggest helping each other. Offer to help them grow their business if they use your services. Offer them a free consultation to show them where they can improve and how you can help.

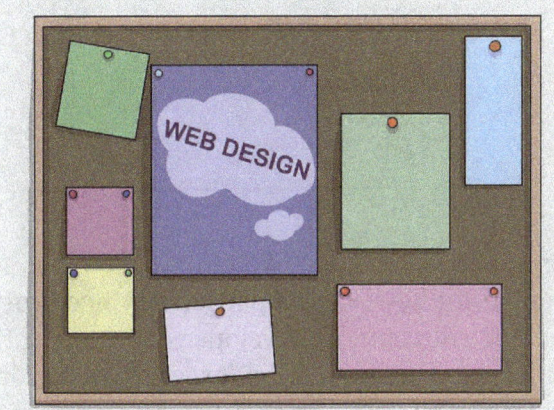

4. Print fliers and business cards. Pass these out at local events you attend, as long as you are allowed to do so. Hang fliers up at local businesses with permission. Leave business cards with other local businesses. Always have these on hand so if you strike up a conversation with someone while you are away from your office, your contact information is readily available to hand out.

5. Run a client referral incentive program both online and off. Advertising and marketing go

hand-in-hand. By marketing a web design business to existing customers and offering an incentive to them for bringing in more customers, you have an advertising team working for you.

How to become a Successful Web Designer

Becoming a successful web designer goes beyond just learning about web design. To be successful, you need to master skills in design, business tactics, and interpersonal communication.

Steps

1. Develop effective communication skills. Effective communication is one of all the skills used that may build or break you in any field; however it's particularly necessary in internet style whether you interact with a shopper, stage director, or developer. Communication will dictate the success of a project. It's quite possible that artistic souls don't seem to be intuitively chatty in nature. But, once it involves presenting yourself and marketing your work, one needs to be daring and clear in his communication with the shopper.

- You wish to be able to speak showing intelligence concerning your style selections – why you selected them and why your particular style alternative the right one for his or her business. Also, lots of little disputes can be resolved simply if you are sensible in your actions. So, communicate and communicate well, so as to survive and achieve success.

2. Be able to sell yourself. It's a small world in our modern tech age, and from an internet designer's

perspective, it's additionally a jungle. Net designers face tough competition which can be compared with the gold miners during the California gold rush. However, the fittest and best prepared can survive. So as to form yourself and your business to stand out from the competition, you want to exhibit a clear understanding of who you are and what your skills entail. Designers are typically a square measure breed and are sometimes humble in nature.

- However, once you have achieved some success through your skills, you will have earned your right to elbow the competition and mark your presence. There exists many ways to promote your business, including, word of mouth, social media and simply handing our business cards. You will soon discover which one or combination works better for your particular business model. The last thing you want to do is sit back in your favorite chair and wait for the customers to find you. This spells doom for any new business.

3. Set up before you style. While several designers approach comes with a "wait for inspiration to happen" quite angle, however the very fact is that simply a little little bit of coming up with will facilitate that inspiration return plenty a lot of quickly. As such, it's necessary to set up and analysis well before going into the net coming up with method.

- Researching concerning the client's company.
- Asking the shopper what he desires and expects from the net.
- Pondering upon what his competitors do and therefore the connected business trends.

4. Make a sketch of the web site in your mind so place it on the paper (if possible). though coming

up with could be a feverish and fewer fascinating method (and numerous designers square measure inclined to skip it), pre-design coming up with saves some time, cash and resources the simplest. you'll be able to scan a lot of concerning "design planning" here.

5. Evaluate your own work and obtain feedback. The cycle of an internet style project ends at analysis and analysis of your designed work. having the ability to just accept and implement feedback effectively is a crucial attribute of the artistic professionals. Like all different same factors, having an honest eye in citing mistakes in your own work could be a quality that success-oriented net designers ought to possess. the net designers ought to act as a devil's advocate and decide the success of their web site being within the target audience's shoes. what is more, taking a while to own others check your work for mistakes can go a protracted ways in which further.

6. Be an internet designer, not a graphic designer. It is a general thought that graphic designers, because of their special effects skills, may be net designers and the other way around. whereas this may be true in theory, there square measure only a few professionals that bridge the gap between print-based comes and web-based comes on a daily basis.

- The reality is that net coming up with could be an utterly separate field of coming up with, having its own flare and experience. These square measure 2 totally different mediums and then the target market and objectives of a websites square measure entirely different from a chunk of graphic style. there's forever the likelihood that a graphic designers advances to the extent of an internet designer once he learns bound technical skills, however it's necessary to not assume that a rock star graphic designer can instantly achieve success once coming up with for the net. For the success of your net business, you ought to commit yourself to the sector of net coming up with and specialize yourself in it.

7. Update yourself with new technology. The world of technology changes virtually on a daily basis, and to stay pace with it, an internet designer has to be technologically in tune with the changes within the business. Slice out a phase of your work-day or week and dedicate it to learning new things in your field. resolve what's new, what's trending, and what's falling to the edge. If you don't need to check your competitors subtract your business by showing to be newer and freshman than you, hang to the current tip.

8. Don't neglect the net style "soft skills." If we have a tendency to divide the success factors of an internet designer, net coming up with soft skills is also one in all the foremost necessary ones. As mentioned earlier, the sector of net coming up with keeps change at a quick pace. each different day there's a replacement technique being introduced. notwithstanding you aren't the one programming these new tricks, a flourishing designer has to learn and perceive the way to apply these techniques well.

- Apart from different core style skills, it's necessary to own full grasp on subjects like, the foremost trendy hypertext mark-up language committal to writing, top quality CSS for best cross browser compatibility, good basic computer program optimization practices,

JavaScript UI techniques, and to create a foundational web site therein you'll be able to add a lot of pages or content with the passage of your time. Having even simply a general understanding of those multiple skill-sets will definitely land you an honest job or higher purchasers.

9. Gain expertise. Experience counts, typically even over your qualifications or skills. Likewise, an internet designer's success depends plenty on your expertise within the field. whether or not it's your leader or your potential shopper, folks have an interest in knowing what proportion previous expertise you've got, that firms have you ever worked with, and what comes you've got worked on. From your perspective, having a broad expertise within the field can assist you to quickly establish style solutions as they're conferred to you in conferences.

- If you're still in school, don't simply await school to finish so as to begin operating, it's well worth the time beyond regulation to begin performing on net comes immediately. The a lot of expertise you get underneath your belt, the faster you'll move up within the world of net designers.

10. Be organized. Being organized is vital for each person to achieve success. Likewise, within the case of net coming up with, your work will get extremely untidy occasionally, and this might lead you to several issues. therefore initiate with organizing your laptop by classifying texts, pictures,

graphics, videos and even sound files in separate folders and label them fittingly. Maintaining a things-to-do list might also facilitate the net designers keep themselves organized, amplify their time well and end the duty easier than expected.

11. Have business sense. Web designers, either freelance or salaried workers, ought to have business mentality once approaching any project. style within the universe is all concerning acquirement, creating worth assessments, and equalisation prices. A flourishing net styler doesn't solely design the websites for his or her purchasers, they produce business solutions for them further. If you're sensible at understanding an organization's promoting desires and might get into the minds of the potential guests, you'll actually have a position over your competitors. However, if you discover managing the business facet of style a trifle tough to try to to, it's price trying into operating with a bigger studio which will war the foremost responsibilities for you.

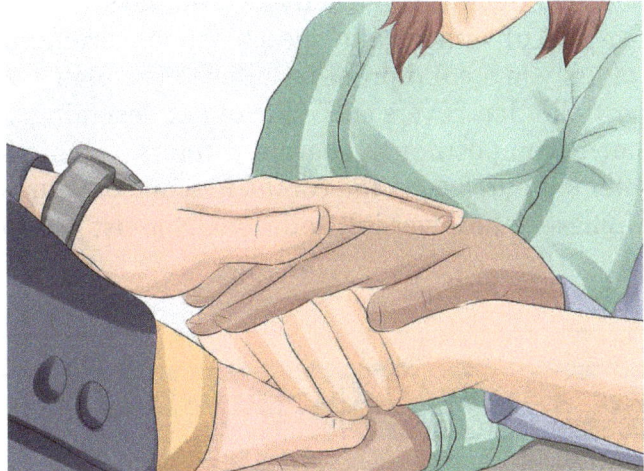

12. Be a team player. Web coming up with isn't a single show. whether or not you're employed in a very huge style studio or with a little shopper, team work is inevitable. whereas an internet designer's work doesn't need an over sized team of execs (in several cases it will desire you're operating all alone), it's necessary to grasp simply however typically your ability to figure with others and delegate tasks can get play over the course of a project. Being an honest team player suggests that

understanding your role within the larger theme of things, and being useful to others – because the recent spoken language goes: 2 heads square measure forever higher than one. Learn to effectively collaborate with others, and watch your work improve.

13. Keep an updated portfolio. Maintaining an honest portfolio is crucial to any designer's success however net designer's face a singular problem: your work has to keep current! whereas an advert designer will in all probability flee with keeping comes from the 1980's in their portfolios as a result of the styles square measure still relevant, take into account however awful your web-design portfolio would be if you unbroken comes from the 1990's.

- The portfolio is that the best medium for net designers to showcase their skills and aesthetics, however a lot of significantly, it shows potential purchasers that you just square measure current, relevant, and active within the style world of immediately, not five years past. instead of without aim speech act concerning the websites you've got done, portfolio offers you a solid proof to indicate the planet what you're capable of. You'll desire a portfolio that covers each side of net designing... together with layouts, content management, composition, typography, colors, techniques and style rationales. Showing your potential purchasers the complete scope of your work can assist you not solely to urge purchasers, however it'll additionally assist you to justify charging more cash as well.

How to become a Web Developer

Web development is a field that is expanding with the introduction of new technologies, such as apps on smartphones and tablets. The demand for people who are familiar with creating new apps and programs is very high. Becoming a web developer is a good strategy for people who are tech savvy, but it will take some work and learning. If you are looking to build a career as a web developer, you will need to learn a set of skills involving programming languages, graphic editing, and marketing.

Part 1

Understanding what is Required to become a Web Developer

1. Know what employers are looking for. Most companies wishing to hire a web developer will advertise for a person who has several qualifications.

- Many employers will want a web developer to hold a Bachelors degree in computer science.
- Computer science degrees prepare an individual by teaching them the skills needed for web development: programming, web design, database management, networking, and mathematics.
- In lieu of getting a degree, many web developers hold professional certifications. You can obtain these from community colleges, continuing education services, and several technology companies.
- For example, Microsoft offers a web development training course that requires you to pass an exam and hold 2-3 years of work experience.
- While having a degree or certification is most desirable, there are many freelance web developers in the market who are building successful business.

2. Understand what computer skills you need to become a web developer. Being able to design a basic website is the bare minimum you will need to be able to do.

- You need to know how the web works and how to program.
- There are many different programming languages that a good web developer should have knowledge of. You will need to know how to code in different programming languages and when to use them.

- New programming languages and interfaces are appearing everyday. You need to keep up with the trends in technology to move forward in this field.

- You will need to know some basic aspects of design: color theory, grid blocking, fonts etc.

- While your job isn't primarily to design graphics, you should know how to make a website or app look attractive and be user friendly at the same time.

3. Understand that web development is a very demanding career. You will need to have the interpersonal skills to relate to clients as well as to handle stress and a busy work environment.

- Interpersonal skills are a very important aspect of the field of web development. You will be interfacing with clients, co-workers and companies on a daily basis.

- Knowing how to handle a person who is impatient or who doesn't understand technology is essential.

- You may be dealing with difficult clients or people who need some extra help in learning how to use the technology you are developing.

- You will also need stress management and time management skills. Being a web developer is very demanding.

- You may be working on several projects at a time and have hard deadlines.

Part 2

Learning about Programming Languages

1. Understand the purpose and function of programming languages and platforms. Without these, the web and other programs wouldn't function properly.

- Programming languages and platforms are what developers use to create applications, scripts, or other sets of instructions for computers to follow.

- There are dozens of different programming languages.

- Each language uses a different platform or program to write scripts, programs, and instructions.

2. Become familiar with HTML. This is one of the simplest and most commonly used programming languages for websites.

- Most people can learn the basics of HTML in an afternoon using one of the many online tutorials available.

- HTML is a language that consists of multiple short codes are typed into a text document. It has its own grammar and syntax just like any language.

- HTML stands for HyperText Markup Language.

- Hypertext is the method by which you move around the internet. You click on a link, which is hypertext that directs you from one page to another.

- When you write in HTML, you will use a series of tags. These tags tell the text what to do: be italicized, link to another page, be a bulleted point etc.

- When you write HTML in a text file, it is then saved as an html file. This file is then opened by a browser, like Google Chrome or Firefox.

- Your browser reads the file and translates your code into visual form. That's the website you see.

- To utilize HTML, you can use a simple text editor or a powerful HTML editing tool like HTML Kit.

- Other programming languages work similarly, but use different syntax and tags. Other languages are available for more complicated types of webpages.

3. Learn about Java. This is a very commonly used programming language for web developers.

- The main goal of Java is to allow web developers to write a script or set of instructions for an application.

- This language allows application writers to "write once, run anywhere".

- Some popular websites that use this language are Netflix, Edmunds and Zappos.

- Some of the most popular tools for writing and coding in Java are JSON and CORE.

4. Develop skills using NET/ C#. This is essential if you work on Microsoft based systems.

- This programming language was created for Microsoft platforms.

- Popular websites that use this as a development tool are ExactTarget, Comcast, and XBOX.

- Development tools that will help you write in NET/C# are Flippy, SQL Helper, Imagehandler, and CodeSmith.

- Other tools that can check your code and help to run your apps more smoothly are FxCop, Regulator, NUnit, and NDoc.

5. Think about learning PHP. This is another language that is especially suited for web development.

- It is the most commonly used scripting language.
- This language allows web developers to write quickly. This language is more flexible in its code than others.
- Some websites utilize PHP as their programming language.
- Some of the top tools for using PHP are Slim.PHP, Secureimage, and Webgrind.
- Other tools for PHP include, but aren't limited to, Scavenger, PHP DOX, and PHP_Debug. Multiple testers, debuggers, and documenters are available for use with PHP.

6. Consider developing skills in writing C++ code. This language is mostly used for systems programming.

- This programming language is easy to use and has flexibility in its code.
- Popular websites that use C++ are JPMorgan Chase, DIRECTTV, and Sony.
- There are multiple tools that can help you code in C++, such as Doxygen, Graphviz, and Mscgen.
- Eclipse is another popular tool for using C++.

7. Learn how to code in Python. This is a very popular coding language used by many popular websites.

- Python is a programming language known for its ease of use that allows developers to quickly create code and integrate systems.

- This language has programming syntax that is easy to read and follow. This reduces the cost of program maintenance.

- Some of the websites that you probably use everyday are Python based, such as Google and Youtube.

- Some of the tools you can try for working with Python are Komodo Edit IDE, PyCharm IDE, and Eclipse with PyDev.

Part 3

Learning about Graphic Design

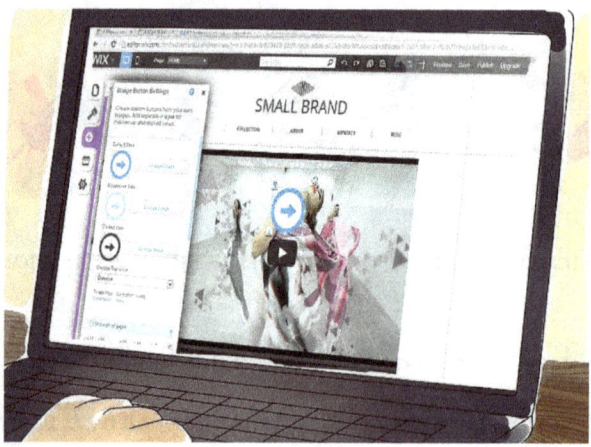

1. Understand the basics of graphics on a webpage. Most web developers don't do their own graphic design, but its important to know the basics.

- You should know how to crop a graphic, resize it, change color scheme, and add text.

- There are many different graphic and photo editing apps and programs for you to use.

- Each has their own interface and methods.

- While most web developers at larger companies don't do the graphic design for apps and pages, its important to have a good general sense of basic graphic editing.

- Many web developers will end up doing some basic graphic editing, especially at smaller firms or if they are self-employed.

2. Download free graphic editing software. This will allow you to practice and get oriented with simple graphic editing.

- Free editing software suites such as GIMP and Inkscape are available for download.

- There are number of online tutorial for GIMP and Inkscape.

- These free editing software packages allow you to do the basics of graphic and photo editing.

- With GIMP and Inkscape you can crop and resize a photo or graphic, add shapes and text, remove red-eye and change the colors of your graphic.

3. Practice adding images to a website. Create a simple website based on a topic you are interested in.

- Use your HTML coding skills to place simple images and graphics onto the website.
- Use GIMP or Inkscape to edit the images.
- Check the website to see how changes in your images affect the way the site looks.
- You will have to practice and play with options to find out the ways you prefer to edit images.
- Once you have a client, you should be able to edit images and graphics according to their needs.

Part 4

Advertising your skills

1. Plan several websites. This is something that you can show potential clients to demonstrate your skills.

- You should make several different types of websites: one for displaying images such as artwork or photos and videos, one for a business and another for a blog, hobby, or interest.
- These types of websites are what you will commonly encounter as a web developer.
- Create a mock business page including the type of business it is, what products and services are sold, images of potential work, a products and services page, and contact page.
- Make your own personal website, including what types of programming you are familiar with, your rates, and links to any websites you have worked on or created.
- This will allow clients to see your work.
- Build a blog site where users can use an interface to add content.
- Work with various languages so your potential clients can see what you can work with.

2. Make business cards. Hand them out at events.

- Make sure you have a link to a personal or business website for your freelance web development.
- Provide contact information on your card.
- Provide links to websites you have worked on so potential clients can see your work.

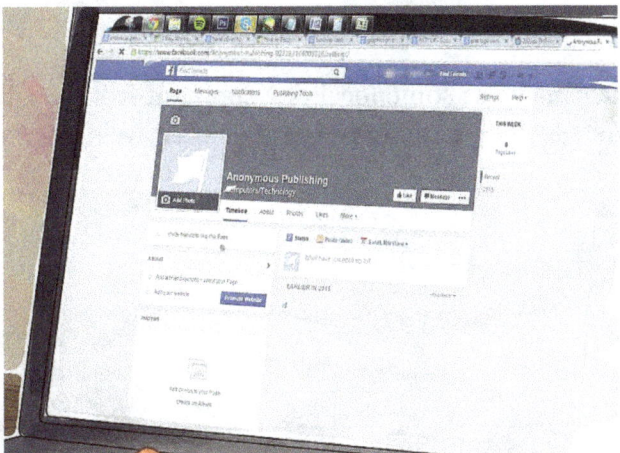

3. Beef up your social media presence. Create a page about your business and what kinds of web development you specialize in.

- Just like a business website, this is a very important step in getting business for yourself.
- Try making a Facebook page for your business, and include what types of programming you can do, your rates for services, and your contact information.
- Create a Twitter account and give updates and links to sites you are working on.
- Make sure you have a Google + page or blog about what you are working on and doing with web development.
- Use LinkedIn to communicate with other industry professionals.

4. Advertise online and in newspapers. Once you are comfortable with doing a wide range of web development services, you should advertise widely.

- Make an ad on Craigslist under the Services page for your area.
- Make sure to include links to sites you have worked on and some contact information.
- Try taking an ad out in local newspapers and magazines.
- This might get your business some local development from local social groups, charities, and business owners looking to build or improve their websites.

Part 5

Getting a Job as a Web Developer

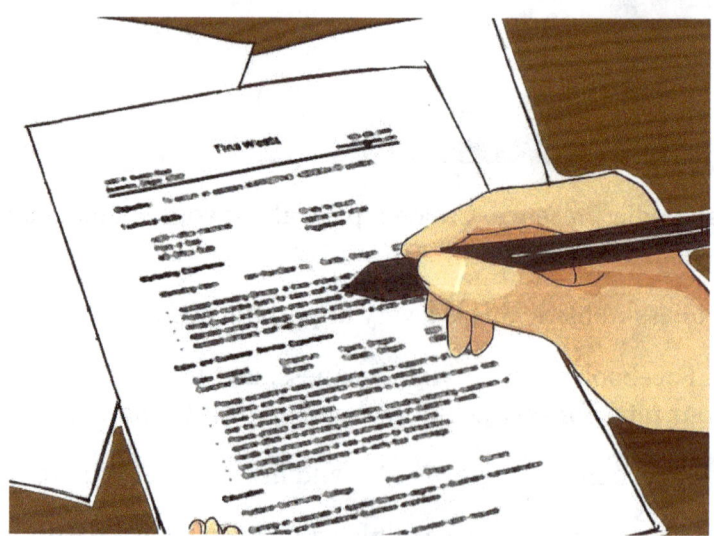

1. Prepare and update your curriculum vitae or resume. Include any experience, even voluntary, that you have designing and programming for websites or apps.

- It is important that you are honest when developing your CV. Don't include false experience or exaggerate.

- Steer clear of industry jargon and buzzwords. Present clearly what your experience is without using words such as "synergy" or "creative".

- Include testimonials of your work and links to code or websites you have developed.

- Have a friend or colleague review your CV before you apply to jobs.

- Put your CV online after it has been completed or updated. Try using sites like LinkedIn or Career 2.0.

- Ask any industry connections you have to look at your CV to see if they know of any opportunities.

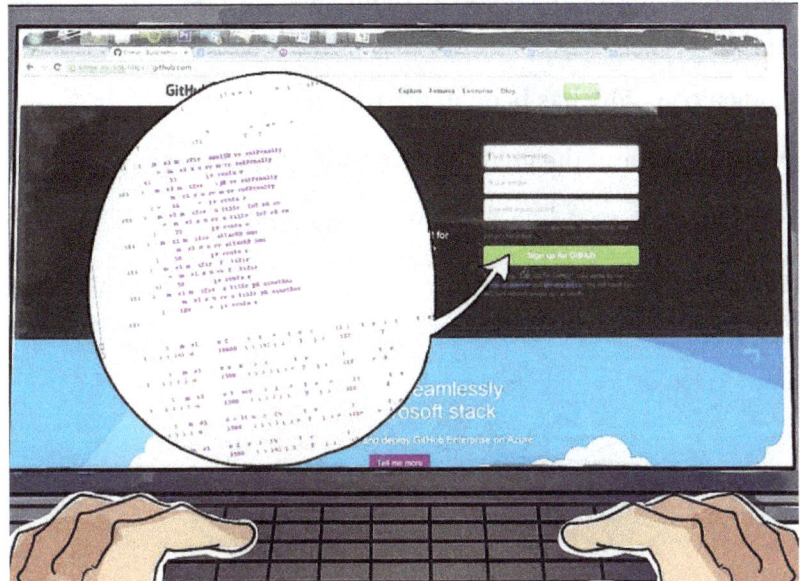

2. Put some of the code you have written online. An online presence for a web developer is vital to a successful career.

- Put out a side project onto collaborative sites like GitHub.

- Contribute to open sourced projects on GitHub and similar websites.

- A prospective employer who sees that a candidate works with others on a web project in their spare time will be an attractive potential employee.

- Put your highest quality code on your online profiles.

- Once you have written some code or contributed to a project, you can put this on your CV.

- You could also start a blog about projects you are working on or trends in web development. Put a link to this on you CV. Potential employers will often look to see if a candidate is keeping up to date on trends and projects in the field.

3. Research tech companies. Especially if you are contacted by a recruiter or have applied to a specific job, it is important to know the ins and outs of a company.

- Know how long a company has been in operation.
- Make sure you understand the goals and mission of the company.
- Become familiar with the companies products or services.
- A potential employer won't want to interview someone who clearly does not know what his company does or how they operate.

4. Spend time on technical tests. Many companies will want you to take a technical competency test before or after an interview.

- Take this seriously, even if the task seems trivial.
- Companies will want to see if you can code in a particular language or develop a specific type of website.
- Put as much effort into the exam as you can. You will want to make sure you don't have any errors in your code and that it compiles correctly.

- Use an online test to deploy your code for the test. This will show a potential employer that you know how to deploy code you have written.

5. Go to any interviews prepared. Do some of your own research about the company climate.

- You should try to deduce what the company dress code is, the hours required, and if you will need to travel.

- Arrive 15 minutes early for an interview. This will show you are punctual and have time management skills.

- Prepare several questions of your own to ask an interviewer. You should ask questions about the work environment, company culture, what types of projects you will be expected to work on etc.

- Going to an interview with questions about the job is a good indicator to an employer that you have thought carefully about the interview and the job.

- Avoid common interview pitfalls. Don't ask about salary or badmouth past employers and colleagues. Don't exaggerate your experience when asked about projects you have worked on.

How to Outsource your Web Development Project Effectively

Web development industry have transformed magically globally. It becomes a global business, now most of organization moving on outsourcing their project rather than hiring their own developer. The main advantage of outsourcing your web development project is you will have access to the availability of cheaper labor whilst not comprising on the quality of output. By outsourcing you will have access to expertise, high concentration and core focus which ultimately help reduce overhead cost as well as risk.

Steps

1. Research your business need. The first step while outsourcing your project, is to analyze and research your business need. What type of web development project you need. It may vary from business to business. It helps to choose best partner company.

2. Outline the step by step plan. Drawing on a prior document regarding how you want the project to be done, not only helps to examine the work but also support recruiting company to go thoroughly as per your need. It's always vital to make a roadmap of your web development project.

3. Explore Additional Alternatives. It is always vital to analyze SWOT for the business organization.

The main reason behind outsourcing your web development project is reduction of cost and overhead. Try to come to different alternatives before placing your project with any companies. For example: If you want to develop your ecommerce site on a CMS, which CMS will be best for you.

4. Choose the best offshore IT Company. You want to outsource your web development project because you want quality work while paying a cheaper price at the same time. Recruiting custom web developer and expertise always tends to have a higher cost.

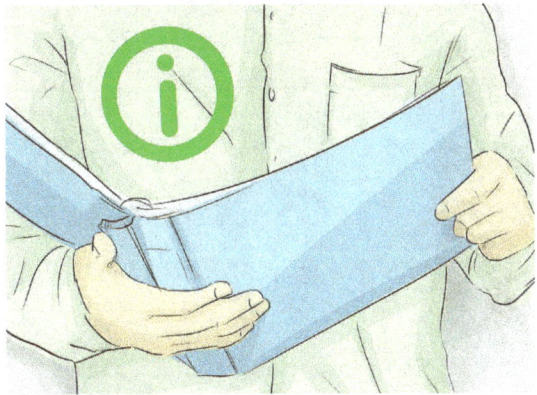

5. Examine portfolio and work expertise. While choosing the company which is going to be your outsource partner, first analyze their portfolio critically. You need to be sure that they can fulfill your need. It is always best to choose that company who've worked on the similar portfolio before.

6. Analyze Time, Cost and Quality. After analyzing the expertise, you need to check whether they

can accomplish your task before your deadline or not. Generally outsourcing your project to the country like Nepal, India will help you to reduce your cost without compromising the quality assurance.

7. Request a demo or assign small task. Before heading to outsource your project, you need to be sure about your partnering IT Company. Assigning small but tricky tasks may help you to judge their expertise. Some company also offer demos for free.

8. Contact the company you want to partner with. Requesting and proposing your work proposal only through email or online submission isn't sufficient for effective outsourcing. Contact them directly through phones and Skype them regularly. Stay in contact as much as possible; however let them finish their responsibilities freely.

9. Examine your final web development project. After receiving your final product, examine

them thoroughly. Observe their work critically and let them know the shortcoming and drawbacks.

10. Stay in Regular contact. Web development is not one time work; you may need to update your application as per your need to cope with external changes. Partnering another offshore company to update your site isn't a wise idea, so regularly communicate your partner company and make them long term friends by fulfilling the commitment of paying and reimbursement.

Permissions

All chapters in this book are published with permission under the Creative Commons Attribution Share Alike License or equivalent. Every chapter published in this book has been scrutinized by our experts. Their significance has been extensively debated. The topics covered herein carry significant information for a comprehensive understanding. They may even be implemented as practical applications or may be referred to as a beginning point for further studies.

We would like to thank the editorial team for lending their expertise to make the book truly unique. They have played a crucial role in the development of this book. Without their invaluable contributions this book wouldn't have been possible. They have made vital efforts to compile up to date information on the varied aspects of this subject to make this book a valuable addition to the collection of many professionals and students.

This book was conceptualized with the vision of imparting up-to-date and integrated information in this field. To ensure the same, a matchless editorial board was set up. Every individual on the board went through rigorous rounds of assessment to prove their worth. After which they invested a large part of their time researching and compiling the most relevant data for our readers.

The editorial board has been involved in producing this book since its inception. They have spent rigorous hours researching and exploring the diverse topics which have resulted in the successful publishing of this book. They have passed on their knowledge of decades through this book. To expedite this challenging task, the publisher supported the team at every step. A small team of assistant editors was also appointed to further simplify the editing procedure and attain best results for the readers.

Apart from the editorial board, the designing team has also invested a significant amount of their time in understanding the subject and creating the most relevant covers. They scrutinized every image to scout for the most suitable representation of the subject and create an appropriate cover for the book.

The publishing team has been an ardent support to the editorial, designing and production team. Their endless efforts to recruit the best for this project, has resulted in the accomplishment of this book. They are a veteran in the field of academics and their pool of knowledge is as vast as their experience in printing. Their expertise and guidance has proved useful at every step. Their uncompromising quality standards have made this book an exceptional effort. Their encouragement from time to time has been an inspiration for everyone.

The publisher and the editorial board hope that this book will prove to be a valuable piece of knowledge for students, practitioners and scholars across the globe.

Index

A
Adobe Creative Cloud, 12
Adobe Dreamweaver, 8, 12, 2031, 49
Adobe Muse, 4
Ajax, 18-19, 200
Asp, 4, 13, 19, 200
Asp.net, 200

B
B2b, 1
Berkeleydb, 12
Blank Document, 94, 128

C
Captcha, 13, 148
Client Liaison, 11
Client Referral Incentive Program, 207
Cms, 12, 17, 112, 200, 229
Codecademy, 7, 102
Coding Language, 2, 4, 27, 220
Content Blocks, 2, 59
Copyediting, 13
Css3, 3

D
Doctype, 3, 28, 95, 155, 165-168
Domain Name, 40, 48, 72, 89119, 182, 186, 190
Dropbox, 12

E
Ease of Access, 2
Element Content, 95, 100
Errors In Code, 3

F
Fireworks, 126, 198
Front-end, 1

G
Gedit, 93
Glassfish, 12
Google Adsense, 92, 183

Google Keywords, 183
Graphic Designers, 5, 210
Gray Box Method, 59

H
Head Tags, 95, 100

I
Information Architecture, 513, 193
Interactive Design, 2
Internet Copywriter, 5
Internet Marketing, 5, 178, 181
Intuitive, 2, 68, 112, 176
Ip Addresses, 148

J
Javascript, 9, 15-16, 18-19, 5084-85, 101-102, 145, 155, 161164-165, 179, 187, 198-199212
Jekyll, 4
Joomla!, 12
Jquery, 9, 18, 85, 198-199

L
Linux, 12, 82, 93, 141
Logout Script, 154

M
Markup Tags, 94-95
Metadata, 101
Microsoft Expression Web, 8
Microsoft Visual Studio, 12
Mobile Browsing, 70
Model-view-controller (MVC), 15
Mongodb, 4
Mozilla Firefox 3.5, 3

N
Navigation Areas, 2
Nosql, 4

O
Online Advertising, 205
Online Communities, 205
Opera 10, 3

P
Page Layout, 2-3
Page Pixel Width, 2
Pagerank, 178-179, 181
Pay Per Click (PPC), 41, 181
Perl, 4, 10, 12-13, 50
Php, 4, 10, 12-13, 19, 50140-146, 149-150, 153-157160-161, 164-169, 198-200219
Pop-ups, 71
Portfolio, 11, 200-201, 214, 229
Processing Pages, 153
Pull-based Architecture, 15
Purchasing System, 177
Push-based Architecture, 15

R
Rdbms, 16
Relational Database, 4
Responsive Design, 50, 71, 77
Responsive Web Design, 3, 84
Rich Text, 93
Rss Feeds, 5
Ruby, 10, 13, 15-19, 50, 82-83

S
Safari 3.1, 3
Search Engine Optimization (SEO), 175, 178, 205
Seo Writers, 5
Server Port Hardening, 13
Shopping Cart System, 177
Social Media Share, 189
Spamming, 13, 178, 188
Sql Injection, 13, 146
Static Website, 4, 49

T
Tag Soup, 3
Testimonials, 192, 201-202, 225
Tls Certificates, 13
Top Level Domain, 182, 186
Typography, 3, 5, 214

U
User Experience (UX), 5, 200
User Interface Design, 2, 68
User Testing, 5
User-friendly, 2, 193

V
Visual Design, 5

W
W3c Standards, 1
Wamp Server, 172-173
Web Application Framework15
Web Caching, 17
Web Development, 1, 11-1315, 18, 83, 107, 181, 214-216, 219, 223-225, 227-231
Web Engineering, 1, 11
Web Navigation, 1
Wire Framing Program, 60
World Wide Web Consortium3
Wysiwyg, 1, 12, 49

X
Xss, 145, 147, 167

Z
Zend Framework, 16

CPSIA information can be obtained
at www.ICGtesting.com
Printed in the USA
BVHW062120290822
645775BV00003B/148